The Train-Watcher's Guide to North American Railroads

COMPILED BY GEORGE H. DRURY

385

Editor: Bob Hayden   Copy Editor: Marcia Stern   Art Director: Lawrence Luser   Staff Artist: Bill Scholz

On the cover: An eastbound Burlington Northern coal train leaves Crawford, Nebraska, in September 1981. TRAINS Magazine photo by J. David Ingles.

KALMBACH k BOOKS

INTRODUCTION

Back in olden days you found out about railroads first by reading all the railroad books in the public library (there were three, one by Lucius Beebe) and then by hanging around the depot, the latter at some cost in parental disapproval and underdone homework. It was a bright day when the agent in the ticket office gave you a system timetable. In it were schedules and equipment lists for the passenger trains of the railroad, perhaps an ad for the road's freight service, and a map. On the map, which usually occupied the center spread, the railroad's own lines were straight and thick. Friendly connections were narrower, and competing roads, even the four-track main line of the New York Central, were squiggly hairlines.

Then came a day when the agent gave you an old copy of *The Official Guide of the Railways* — a pulp paper monthly, 7 inches by 10 and a couple of inches thick. After perusing it for a few minutes you knew how Keats felt, standing silent on that peak in Darien, looking into his copy of Chapman's Homer.

The *Guide* contained timetables for every railroad in North and Central America and maps for most of them — the same maps that were in the railroads' timetables, but you could average the straight and crooked lines. The *Guide* showed you where each railroad went and which connected with which. It gave substance to the freight cars you saw at trackside and on hobby shop shelves. You could pinpoint those decrepit short lines Beebe admired. You could read yourself to sleep at night planning trips. It was great stuff.

Now it's different. The depot has been torn down, the agent works out of a van, and kids hang around shopping malls. The *Guide* is a pair of books, a passenger edition with timetables for Amtrak, VIA, National of Mexico, and a few suburban lines, and a freight edition that's mostly piggyback schedules and lists of officials.

The *Guide* wasn't a complete reader's companion — it couldn't tell you how many freight cars Santa Fe owned, or where Union Pacific's major classification yards were, or what the initials "DWP" stood for. Some of those questions were answered in the *Handbook of American Railroads* by Robert G. Lewis, published by Simmons-Boardman in 1951 and 1956, but now long out of date and even longer out of print. The more recent *American Short Line Railway Guide* by Edward A. Lewis was an excellent reference to the smaller railroads; it too is now out of print. Today's railroad enthusiast needs some sort of unofficial guide, a combination field guide, modeler's bluebook, reader's companion, and friendly station agent — in other words, a good quick source of short answers and a pointer to longer ones. This book should satisfy that need.

Railroads included: Included in this book are all the Class 1 railroads (currently those with annual operating revenue greater than $50 million — the figure has increased over the years), railroads more than 50 miles long, those with more than 1000 freight cars in interchange service, and commuter operating authorities. A few roads in the book meet none of these criteria; I included them because they are interesting in one way or another. For this book the definition of railroad has been left loose enough to include operating companies such as VIA Rail Canada that own cars and locomotives but no track, but I have excluded "invisible railroads" — those that are leased to or operated by other railroads, either singly or jointly, and have no rolling stock of their own.

I have not included museum and tourist railroads nor have I included full descriptions of rail transit operations — subways, streetcars, light rail vehicles — because these operations are usually not part of the national freight railroad network. Tourist railroads are well documented in the *Steam Passenger Services Directory*, and a list of North American rail transit systems appears on pages 210-213.

Organization: This book is organized alphabetically by railroad name. Until 1974 *The Official Guide* was arranged geographically, east to west with odd exceptions, followed by Canada, Mexico, and the electric railroads, with some of the "families" — the former Jay Gould roads, the Harriman lines, the Hill roads — grouped together. Such an organization assumes the reader knows the facts he's seeking. The index on pages 216-219 also lists nicknames and recently merged railroads.

Systems and subsidiaries: A few railroads created organization problems. For example, is Baltimore & Ohio a separate railroad or part of the Chessie System? Its diesels are lettered "Chessie System" in big letters and "B&O" in small ones. I followed the lead of *The Official Guide*, which refers readers seeking B&O, Chesapeake & Ohio, and Western Maryland to Chessie System. Chessie-owned Chicago South Shore & South Bend is listed separately. Southern Railway has two subsidiaries, Alabama Great Southern and Cincinnati, New Orleans & Texas Pacific, that are all-but-invisible Class 1 railroads, and Southern itself is half of Norfolk Southern. Most of Canadian National's U. S. lines are owned by Grand Trunk Corporation but they have separate listings in the *Guide*. However, Grand Trunk Western's subsidiary Detroit, Toledo & Ironton is listed with its parent as a component of the GT Rail System. Copying Canadian Pacific, which calls its rail operation CP Rail, Canadian National now refers to itself as CN Rail. The *Guide* alphabetizes them as if they were spelled out; I have done the same.

The railroad scene is not a static one. In the past 15 years rail passenger service has become almost exclusively a government business. The formation of Conrail in 1976 was the end of several of the oldest railroads in the U. S. (and one of the newest, Penn Central), but it was also the beginning of a large number of short lines, as Conrail sold many of its branch and secondary lines. Guilford Transportation Industries has united three small railroads (Maine Central, Boston & Maine, and Delaware & Hudson) to form a new railroad system in the Northeast. While this book was in preparation the Western Pacific became simply a division of Union Pacific, and the Ann Arbor was split up among three operators. It will be several more years before the dust settles and the smoke clears over the wreckage of the Rock Island, which ceased running in 1980. Things keep changing, and if present trends continue, we will have a very few large railroad systems, a lot of short lines, and very little in the way of medium-size roads. Canada has long had just two major railroads, and in the U. S. almost all the railroading east of the Mississippi River and south of a line between Chicago and Washington is done by either CSX Corporation or Norfolk Southern. The western half of the country is dominated by four railroad systems: Santa Fe, Burlington Northern, Union Pacific-Missouri Pacific, and Southern Pacific-Cotton Belt. The best any book can do is document the situation at a particular time.

Information sources: For each railroad the information items and their sources are:

- Company name (using an ampersand for "and," whether or not the railroad does) — *Official Guide*
- Mailing address of general offices — *Official Guide*
- Brief history and description — drawn from several sources: *Moody's Transportation Manual*, books, and articles in TRAINS Magazine and other periodicals. Here I chose to stick to the basics of where and when the railroad began and how it became what it is rather than detail each corporate change. For definitions of such terms as "receivership" and "reorganization" see the glossary on pages 214-215.
- Reporting marks, the initials with which each railroad marks its freight cars. These may include initials of predecessor railroads and initials used on cars assigned to special services. — *The Official Railway Equipment Register*.
- Miles of road operated — in some cases this is ambiguous or hard to determine. The Boston & Maine, for example, operates freight trains over its own rails, has freight operating rights on Amtrak and Massachusetts

Kalmbach Publishing Co.: George H. Drury.

Baltimore & Ohio? Chessie System? What do we call it? Hood units at Cincinnati illustrate the dilemma.

Tom Nelligan.

Once Waterbury, Connecticut, was a one-railroad town — New York, New Haven & Hartford. Now things have changed: SPV-2000 No. 999 is owned by the Connecticut Department of Transportation but it is painted and lettered for Amtrak. Here it is operating as a Metro-North Commuter Railroad train to Bridgeport on track owned by the Connecticut DOT. Freight service to Waterbury is now the province of Boston & Maine, which bought the tracks north and east of Waterbury from Conrail and has freight operating rights south of there on state-owned track.

Bay Transportation Authority tracks, and has trackage rights on some Central Vermont lines; in addition B&M operates commuter trains for MBTA with MBTA equipment on MBTA rails and Amtrak trains on B&M and CV tracks. The figure cited is taken from *The Official Railway Equipment Register* or *The Pocket List of Railroad Officials*. In many cases it is a figure furnished by the railroad itself.

- Number of locomotives — *The Pocket List of Railroad Officials.*
- Number of freight cars in revenue interchange service (that is, omitting cabooses, maintenance of way equipment, and other items not found off home rails) — *The Official Railway Equipment Register.*
- Radio frequencies — *Compendium of American Railroad Radio Frequencies.* Unless the entry is noted otherwise, the frequencies given are channel 1, channel 2, and yard/other.

Tom Nelligan.

- Principal commodities carried — annual reports of the railroads and *Moody's Transportation*, but omitted if no item was predominant.
- Location and name of major yards and shops (for large railroads) — various sources. Short lines usually have a small shop near their headquarters and nothing that could be considered a major yard.
- Junctions with other railroads (for small railroads) — *The Official Railway Equipment Register*, January 1983. I have omitted junctions not used for interchange and connections made through another railroad.
- Passenger routes, lines of the railroad you can ride as a paying passenger — *The Official Railway Guide, North American Travel Edition.*
- Recommended reading — in my opinion the best book for general information on the railroad. I have tried to cite books that are in print. Often on public library shelves you'll find older books, such as the corporate histories that many railroads commissioned in the 1940s and 1950s.
- Historical and technical society — the criterion for inclusion is receipt of some publication from the group within the past year. MODEL RAILROADER carries a current list of these groups in its February issue; the list also appears annually in TRAINS.
- Map — the purpose of the map is to cast the railroad in its geographic setting, not show every line in full detail. The maps are not drawn to a uniform scale. Maps for two or more railroads have been combined where appropriate. For a few small railroads the map is omitted, and the descriptive paragraph should suffice. A copy of the current Rand McNally *Handy Railroad Atlas* is indispensable. Railroad lines are shown on some highway maps, in particular those published by the American Automobile Association and some state highway departments.
- Date — the individual railroad entries were submitted to the railroads for review and correction; I have taken their word as the best authority. The date shown is that of the railroad's response.

For further information: Since a book the size of this one can't begin to tell everything, turn to:
- *The Official Railway Guide — North American Freight Service Edition* (bimonthly)
- *The Official Railway Guide — North American Travel Edition* (8 issues a year with schedules of North American passenger trains except most commuter services and Mexican branchline mixed trains)

- *The Official Railway Equipment Register* (quarterly list of all the freight cars in North America)
- *The Pocket List of Railroad Officials* (quarterly)

The preceding four are all published by the National Railway Publication Company, 424 W. 33rd Street, New York, NY 10001.
- *The Railroad — What It Is, What It Does*, by John H. Armstrong, published by Simmons-Boardman Publishing Corporation, 1809 Capitol Avenue, Omaha, NE 68102.
- *Diesel Locomotive Rosters: United States, Canada, Mexico*, by Charles W. McDonald, published by Kalmbach Publishing Co., 1027 N. Seventh Street, Milwaukee, WI 53233.
- *Handy Railroad Atlas of the United States* (revised every few years), published by Rand McNally & Co. (railroad maps for each state).
- *1928 Handy Railroad Atlas of the United States*, published by Kalmbach Publishing Co., 1027 N. Seventh Street, Milwaukee, WI 53233.
- *Railway Passenger Car Annual*, by W. David Randall, published by RPC Publications, P. O. Box 296, Godfrey, IL 62035 (lists the passenger cars of the railroads, commuter authorities, and transit systems of the U. S. and Canada).
- *Compendium of American Railroad Radio Frequencies*, compiled by Gary L. Sturm and Mark J. Landgraf, published by Mark J. Landgraf, 3 Coralberry Circle, Albany, NY 12203.
- *Steam Passenger Services Directory*, published annually by Empire State Railway Museum, P. O. Box 666, Middletown, NY 10940 (lists the tourist railroads and railroad museums).
- TRAINS Magazine, published by Kalmbach Publishing Co., 1027 N. Seventh Street, Milwaukee, WI 53233.

Acknowledgments: There are more than 140 persons working for railroads in the U. S., Canada, and Mexico who reviewed copy and made corrections and additions — their willingness to cooperate in the project deserves more appreciation than there is room here to convey.

GEORGE H. DRURY

Milwaukee, Wisconsin
November 1983

Aberdeen & Rockfish GP18 300 is returning from Fayetteville to the road's headquarters at Aberdeen. The unit is blue and gray with orange trim.

ABERDEEN & ROCKFISH RAILROAD

The Aberdeen & Rockfish was incorporated in 1892. The first section of the line opened that year, and the remainder was put in operation in 1911 and 1913. The line runs from Aberdeen to Fayetteville, North Carolina.

Address of general offices: P. O. Box 917, Aberdeen, NC 28315
Miles of road operated: 47
Reporting marks: AR
Number of locomotives: 3
Number of freight cars: 224
Principal commodities carried: Chemicals, feeds, grains, animal by-products, building supplies, fertilizer solution
Shops: Aberdeen, N. C.
Junctions with other railroads:
Cape Fear: Skibo, N. C.
Laurinburg & Southern: Raeford, N. C.
Seaboard System: Aberdeen, N. C.; Fayetteville, N. C.
Southern: Fayetteville, N. C.
Radio frequencies: 160.530, 161.280
Recommended reading: RAILROADS YOU CAN MODEL, by Mike Schafer, published in 1976 by Kalmbach Publishing Co., 1027 North Seventh Street, Milwaukee, WI 53233 (ISBN 0-89024-526-6)
Date: January 1983

J. W. Swanberg.

ALASKA RAILROAD

The Alaska Railroad is descended from two short lines: the Alaska Northern, reorganized in 1909 from the Alaska Central, a standard gauge line built inland from Seward; and the Tanana Valley, a narrow gauge line connecting Fairbanks to the head of navigation on the Tanana River. There was pressure to build a tidewater-to-interior railroad to unlock the treasure chest which Alaska was considered at the time, but the lack of population in the territory made it clear that such a line would have to be built by the government. In 1912 President Taft asked Congress for such a measure; Congress provided it later that year as a rider on a bill granting Alaska self-government. The Alaska Central and the Tanana Valley were taken over by the Alaska Engineering Commission, which then built a railroad connecting the two, no small task. The line was renamed the Alaska Railroad in 1923, the year of its completion. The last spike was driven by President Harding.

The railroad is owned by the U. S. Department of Transportation; negotiations are under way to sell it to the State of Alaska.

Continued on next page.

Train 2, the *Denali Express*, prepares to depart Anchorage for Fairbanks. The consist includes cars purchased from Union Pacific, Southern, and Amtrak. The building beside the rear of the train houses the road's general offices.

Address of general offices: Pouch 7-2111, Anchorage, AK 99510
Miles of road operated: 526
Reporting marks: ARR
Number of locomotives: 57
Number of freight cars: 1251
Principal commodities carried: Sand and gravel, coal, petroleum, manufactured goods
Shops: Anchorage, Alaska
Junctions with other railroads:
Alaska Hydro-Train (rail barges from Seattle): Whittier, Alaska
Canadian National Aqua Train (rail barges from Prince Rupert, B. C.): Whittier, Alaska
Radio frequencies: 164.625, 165.3375 (train to dispatcher), 165.2625
Passenger routes: Anchorage-Fairbanks, Anchorage-Whittier
Recommended reading:
Railroad in the Clouds, by William H. Wilson, published in 1977 by Pruett Publishing Co., 2928 Pearl, Boulder, CO 80301 (ISBN 0-87108-510-0)
The Alaska Railroad, by Edwin M. Fitch, published in 1967 by Praeger Publishers, 111 Fourth Avenue, New York, NY 10003
Date: December 1982

ALGOMA CENTRAL RAILWAY

The Algoma Central was chartered in 1899 to build into the Ontario wilderness north of Sault Ste. Marie to bring out pulpwood and iron ore. In 1901 the ambitions of its founder added "& Hudson Bay" to the corporate title. It was 1912 before the road reached Hawk Junction; construction north to Hearst took another two years. The name reverted to simply Algoma Central in 1965.

In recent years the railroad has developed an excursion train business carrying tourists north from Sault Ste. Marie to the Agawa River canyon, where the railroad has developed a park. The company has shipping, trucking, real estate, and land and forest subsidiaries.
Address of general offices: P. O. Box 7000, Sault Ste. Marie, ON, Canada P6A 5P6
Miles of road operated: 322
Reporting marks: AC, ACIS
Number of locomotives: 34
Number of freight cars: 1223
Number of passenger cars: 42
Principal commodities carried: Iron ore, forest products
Shops: Sault Ste. Marie, Ont.
Junctions with other railroads:
Canadian National: Hearst, Ont.; Oba, Ont.
CP Rail: Franz, Ont.; Sault Ste. Marie, Ont.
Soo Line: Sault Ste. Marie, Ont.
Radio frequencies: 160.530 (road), 160.650 (yard)
Passenger routes: Sault Ste. Marie-Hearst, Ont.
Recommended reading: *Algoma Central Railway*, by O. S. Nock, published in 1975 by A & C Black Limited, London (ISBN 0-7136-1571-0)
Date: January 1983

MODEL RAILROADER: Jim Hediger.

A trio of Algoma Central GP38-2s waits at the head of a 21-car excursion train at Canyon, Ontario, deep in the Agawa River gorge. The gray, maroon, and yellow livery of the diesels is like that used by the former Erie Lackawanna; the passenger cars, purchased secondhand from several railroads, wear a silver and maroon paint scheme reminiscent of Canadian Pacific's *Canadian* of 1955.

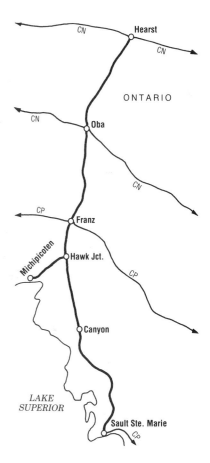

ALTON & SOUTHERN RAILWAY

The Alton & Southern was incorporated in 1913 and was controlled for many years by the Aluminum Corporation of America (Alcoa). In 1966 Missouri Pacific petitioned the ICC for permission to buy the A&S, offering to match a previous bid by the St. Louis Southwestern (Cotton Belt). The ICC recommended joint ownership by MP, SSW, and Chicago & North Western; MP and C&NW purchased the road in 1968. In 1973 SSW purchased C&NW's 50 percent interest in the road. The A&S is a belt line serving East St. Louis, Illinois, and connects with all the railroads entering the area. Its Gateway Yard is used by several other roads.

Address of general offices: 1000 S. 22nd Street, East St. Louis, IL 62207

Miles of road operated: 32

Reporting marks: ALS

Number of locomotives: 20

Major yards: Gateway Yard

Shops: East St. Louis, Ill.

Connects with:
Burlington Northern
Chessie System
Chicago & North Western
Conrail
Illinois Central Gulf
Manufacturers Railway
Missouri-Kansas-Texas
Missouri Pacific
Norfolk & Western
St. Louis Southwestern
Seaboard System
Southern Railway
Terminal Railroad Association of St. Louis
all within the St. Louis-East St. Louis Switching Districts

Radio frequencies: 160.770, 160.355

J. David Ingles.

An Alton & Southern transfer run headed by a pair of blue-and-yellow SW1500s leaves the east end of the MacArthur Bridge.

AMTRAK
(National Railroad Passenger Corporation)

In the decade after World War Two, the railroads invested heavily in their passenger business, streamlining and dieselizing their trains and accelerating their schedules. They offered all kinds of enticements to the passenger: Vista-Domes, private-room sleepers, and food and lounge service of every description. However, the passenger business declined and the railroads' passenger deficits increased. Chief among the many reasons were the prosperity that put a new car in every garage and construction of the federally financed Interstate highway system.

In the late 1960s it was clear that there was still some need for rail passenger service and also that the railroads were no longer willing to provide that service at a loss. A government corporation was formed to take over rail passenger business. Railroads had the opportunity to join and discontinue their passenger trains or not join and continue running them. Most joined.

On May 1, 1971, the National Railroad Passenger Corporation — using the name Amtrak — took over supervision of the operation of most remaining intercity passenger trains in the U. S. At first the railroads continued to operate the trains for Amtrak's account as they had on their own in the past; gradually Amtrak hired the on-board service people, station staff, and so on.

Shortly after it began operation Amtrak purchased secondhand passenger cars and locomotives from the railroads, but in succeeding years the corporation began to purchase new locomotives and cars and to completely rebuild the best of its old equipment. One major achievement has

John R. Armstrong.

Amfleet coaches are used in all parts of the country on short-haul trains, such as the _Ann Rutledge_ and the _Inter-American_, shown meeting at Springfield, Illinois. (The Chicago-Laredo _Inter-American_ has since been replaced by the Chicago-San Antonio _Eagle_.)

been to replace steam for car heating and generators and batteries on each car for lighting and air conditioning with electric systems powered from the locomotive. A more important achievement has been reversal of the long decline in passenger train ridership.

Amtrak's routes and operations are established by Congress, and the corporation is subsidized by the federal government. In addition, states can request and subsidize the operation of trains, so-called "403-b" trains. In 1983 Amtrak took over operation of the twice-daily Baltimore-Washington commuter trains that Conrail had been operating for the Maryland Department of Transportation.

Continued on next page.

Amtrak's trains are for the most part operated over the track of other railroads, but Amtrak owns much of its own right of way in the Northeast Corridor — lines that were part of the New Haven and Pennsylvania railroads between Boston and Washington, Springfield and New Haven, and Philadelphia and Harrisburg. State agencies own the right of way and track from Boston to the Rhode Island state line and from New Haven to New Rochelle, N. Y. Several other railroads operate freight service through trackage rights on various portions of this route. Amtrak also owns the former New York Central line between Kalamazoo, Mich., and Porter, Ind.

Address of general offices: 400 N. Capitol Street, N. W., Washington, DC 20001

Miles of road operated: 23,400

Reporting marks: AMTK

Number of locomotives: 295

Number of freight cars: 840 (for maintenance-of-way service)

Number of passenger cars: 2128

Number of self-propelled passenger cars:

RDC: 11

Rohr Turboliner: 35 (powered and unpowered cars)

Metroliner: 61

Principal shops: Beech Grove, Ind.; Wilmington, Del.

Radio frequencies: 160.800 (road — Northeast Corridor)

Passenger routes: (train names in italics, operating railroads and junctions in parentheses)

Boston-Washington (AMTK)

Boston-Albany-Chicago: *Lake Shore Limited* (CR)

Springfield-New Haven (AMTK)

New York-Newport News: *Colonial, Tidewater* (AMTK-Washington-RF&P-Richmond-C&O)

New York-Miami/St. Petersburg: *Silver Star, Silver Meteor* (AMTK-Washington-RF&P-Richmond-SBD)

New York-Savannah: *Palmetto* (AMTK-Washington-RF&P-Richmond-SBD)

Tampa-Miami: *Silver Palm* (SBD)

New York-Atlanta-New Orleans: *Crescent* (AMTK-Washington-SOU)

New York-Cincinnati-Chicago: *Cardinal* (AMTK-Washington-C&O)

New York-Philadelphia-Pittsburgh-Chicago: *Broadway Limited* (AMTK-Harrisburg-CR)

Philadelphia-Pittsburgh: *Pennsylvanian* (AMTK-Harrisburg-CR)

Valparaiso, Ind.-Chicago: *Calumet, Indiana Connection* (CR)

New York-Buffalo-Chicago: *Lake Shore Limited* (CR)

New York-Albany-Syracuse-Niagara Falls: Empire Service (CR)

New York-Buffalo-Toronto: *Maple Leaf* (CR-Niagara Falls-VIA)

New York-Montreal: *Adirondack* (CR-Schenectady-D&H-Rouses Point-NJ)

Washington-Chicago: *Capitol Limited* (B&O-Pittsburgh-CR)

Washington-Martinsburg, W. Va.: *Blue Ridge* (B&O)

Washington-New York-Montreal: *Montrealer* (AMTK-Springfield-B&M-White River Jct.-CV-East Alburgh, Vt.-CN)

Chicago-Toronto: *International Limited* (CR-Battle Creek-GTW-Port Huron-VIA)

Chicago-Detroit-Toledo: *Lake Cities* (CR)

Chicago-Detroit: *Wolverine, Twilight Limited* (CR)

Chicago-Indianapolis: *Hoosier State* (SBD-Crawfordsville, Ind.-CR)

Chicago-New Orleans: *City of New Orleans* (ICG)

Chicago-Carbondale, Ill.: *Shawnee* (ICG)

Chicago-Decatur: *Illini* (ICG-Tolono-NW)

Chicago-St. Louis-San Antonio: *Eagle* (ICG-St. Louis-MP-Fort Worth-AT&SF-Temple-MKT-Taylor-MP-San Antonio)

Chicago-St. Louis: *State House, Ann Rutledge* (ICG)

Chicago-Los Angeles: *Southwest Limited* (AT&SF)

Chicago-West Quincy, Mo.: *Illinois Zephyr* (BN)

Chicago-Oakland: *California Zephyr* (BN-Denver-D&RGW-Salt Lake City-UP-Ogden-SP)

St. Louis-Kansas City: *Ann Rutledge, Kansas City Mule, Missouri Mule* (MP)

Salt Lake City-Los Angeles: *Desert Wind* (UP-Barstow-AT&SF)

Ogden-Seattle: *Pioneer* (UP-Portland-BN)

Chicago-Milwaukee-Seattle/Portland: *Empire Builder* (MILW-St. Paul-BN)

Chicago-Milwaukee: *Nicollet, Radisson, Marquette, LaSalle*

St. Paul-Duluth: *North Star* (BN)
Los Angeles-New Orleans: *Sunset* (SP)
Los Angeles-San Diego: *San Diegans* (AT&SF)
Los Angeles-Oakland-Sacramento-Seattle: *Coast Starlight* (SP-Portland-BN)
Los Angeles-Sacramento: *Spirit of California* (SP)
Portland-Seattle: *Mount Rainier* (BN)
Oakland-Bakersfield: *San Joaquins* (SP-Port Chicago-AT&SF)

Recommended reading:
JOURNEY TO AMTRAK, by Harold A. Edmonson, published in 1972 by Kalmbach Publishing Co., 1027 North Seventh St., Milwaukee, WI 53233
Zephyrs, Chiefs & Other Orphans, by Fred W. Frailey, published in 1977 by RPC Publications, P. O. Box 296, Godfrey, IL 62035

William D. Middleton.

Double-deck Superliners provide luxury accommodations on most long-distance trains west of Chicago. The Seattle-Los Angeles *Coast Starlight*, shown north of San Luis Obispo, Calif., is one of Amtrak's best-patronized trains; its route is among Amtrak's most scenic.

J. W. Swanberg.

Rohr-built Turboliners operate between New York and Niagara Falls. The Syracuse-to-New York *Salt City Express* is pictured here running along the bank of the Harlem River in The Bronx. The train is just minutes from the end of its run in New York's Grand Central Terminal.

APALACHICOLA NORTHERN RAILROAD

The Apalachicola Northern was incorporated in 1903. It entered brief receiverships in 1907 and 1914 and was purchased by the St. Joe Paper Co., its present owner, in 1936. Recently AN has begun operating unit coal trains from Port St. Joe, deepest natural harbor on the Gulf of Mexico, to the Seaboard System connection at Chattahoochee for forwarding to a power plant near Palatka, Florida.

Address of general offices: P. O. Box 250, Port St. Joe, FL 32456
Miles of road operated: 96
Reporting marks: AN
Number of locomotives: 11
Number of freight cars: 1069
Principal commodities carried: Pulpwood, lumber, paper products, coal
Shops: Port St. Joe, Fla.
Junctions with other railroads:
   Seaboard System: Chattahoochee, Fla.
Radio frequencies: 160.380 (road), 160.500 (yard)
Date: December 1982

Three SW1500s idle outside Apalachicola Northern's enginehouse at Port St. Joe, Fla. Later they will haul the daily freight train north to the Seaboard System interchange at Chattahoochee. AN owns three SW9s, Nos. 709-711, and eight SW1500s, Nos. 712-719.

John C. Illman

14

ARKANSAS & LOUISIANA MISSOURI RAILWAY

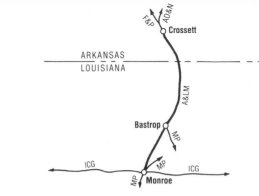

The Arkansas & Louisiana Missouri was incorporated in 1920 to take over the Arkansas & Louisiana Midland Railway, which was successor to the Arkansas, Louisiana & Gulf (chartered in 1906; entered receivership 1913). The A&LM runs from Crossett, Arkansas, to Monroe, Louisiana. All the capital stock of the railroad is owned by Olinkraft, Inc., a division of Olin Mathieson.

Address of general offices: P. O. Box 1653, Monroe, LA 71201

Miles of road operated: 54

Reporting marks: ALM

Number of locomotives: 4

Number of freight cars: 374

Principal commodities carried: Pulpwood, paper products, fertilizer

Shops: Monroe, La.

Junctions with other railroads:

Ashley, Drew & Northern: Crossett, Ark.

Fordyce & Princeton: Crossett, Ark.

Illinois Central Gulf: Monroe, La.

Missouri Pacific:

   Bastrop, La.

   Crossett, Ark.

   Monroe, La.

Radio frequencies: 160.980, 160.440

Deep in the woods at Rawls, Ark., A&LM's daily southbound freight from Crossett to Monroe moves along behind SW9 No. 14. The diesel is especially well equipped for sound, with a standard horn pointing toward the hood and a Hancock air whistle toward the cab end of the unit.

R. T. Sharp.

15

ASHLEY, DREW & NORTHERN RAILWAY

In 1905 the Crossett Railway was chartered to serve the Crossett Lumber Co. of Crossett, Ark. In 1912 the 10-mile line was sold to the Crossett, Monticello & Northern, which planned to extend the line north to a junction with the St. Louis, Iron Mountain & Southern (now Missouri Pacific) at Monticello. The line got partway there, ran out of money, and was resold to a new company, the Ashley, Drew & Northern, which reached Monticello in 1913. The railroad was leased to the Arkansas, Louisiana & Gulf in 1914 and regained its independence in 1920. The Georgia Pacific Corporation purchased the AD&N and the Crossett Lumber Co. in 1963. Georgia Pacific also owns the Fordyce & Princeton; the two railroads serve the largest interrelated mill complex in the world — 12 plants making paper, building products, and chemicals derived from the southern pine tree.

Address of general offices: P. O. Box 757, Crossett, AR 71635
Miles of road operated: 41
Reporting marks: ADN
Number of locomotives: 6
Number of freight cars: 2056
Principal commodities carried: Pulpwood, paper products
Junctions with other railroads:
Arkansas & Louisiana Missouri: Crossett, Ark.
Fordyce & Princeton: Crossett, Ark.; Whitlow Jct., Ark.
Missouri Pacific: Monticello, Ark.
Radio frequencies: 160.770, 161.535
Recommended reading: *Short Line Railroads of Arkansas*, by Clifton E. Hull, published in 1969 by the University of Oklahoma Press, Norman, OK
Date: January 1983

Much of Ashley, Drew & Northern's traffic comes from mills and factories at Crossett. Here a switcher shuffles cars at the flakeboard plant. AD&N's locomotives are numbered to indicate horsepower — No. 1205 is a 1200-h.p. switcher — and roster sequence — it was the road's fifth diesel.

Terry A. Holley.

ATCHISON, TOPEKA & SANTA FE RAILWAY

The Santa Fe was chartered in 1859 to join the two Kansas cities of its title with Santa Fe, New Mexico. In its early years the railroad opened Kansas to settlement, and a large portion of its revenue came from wheat grown there and from cattle driven north from Texas to Wichita and Dodge City. Rather than turn south at Dodge City toward Santa Fe, the railroad chose to head southwest over Raton Pass because of coal deposits near Trinidad and Raton. The Denver & Rio Grande was also aiming at Raton Pass, but the Santa Fe crews rose early one morning in 1878 and occupied the pass. At the same time the two railroads had a series of skirmishes over occupancy of the Royal Gorge west of Canon City, Colo.; the Rio Grande won that right of way.

The Santa Fe reached Albuquerque in 1880 (Santa Fe became the terminal of a short branch line from Lamy, N. Mex.) and connected with the Southern Pacific line from Los Angeles at Deming, N. Mex., in 1881. The railroad then built southwest from Benson, Ariz., to Nogales to connect with the Sonora Railway, with which it was affiliated, that had been built northward from Guaymas to the U. S. border at Nogales.

The Santa Fe still wanted to reach California on its own rails, and California eagerly sought the railroad in order to break Southern Pacific's monopoly in the state. In 1879 the Santa Fe signed an agreement with the Frisco and the Atlantic & Pacific to build the A&P line west from Al-buquerque along the 35th parallel. In 1883 that line reached Needles, Calif., where it connected with a Southern Pacific line from Mojave.

The Santa Fe then began a period of expansion: a line from Barstow, Calif., to San Diego in 1885; to Los Angeles in 1887; control of the Gulf, Colorado & Santa Fe (Galveston to Fort Worth) in 1886 and a line between Wichita and Fort Worth in 1887; lines from Kansas City to Chicago, southwest from Kansas to Amarillo, Tex., and from Pueblo to Denver paralleling the Denver & Rio Grande in 1888; and purchase of the St. Louis-San Francisco and the Colorado Midland in 1890.

The depression of 1893 had the same effect on the Santa Fe that it had on many other railroads: financial problems and subsequent reorganization — in 1895, at which time the Frisco and the Colorado Midland were sold and the losses written off. However, Santa Fe retained control of the Atlantic & Pacific, and in 1897 the railroad traded the Sonora Railway to Southern Pacific for the SP line between Mojave and Barstow, giving the Santa Fe a line of its own from Chicago to the Pacific. (The Sonora Railway became the Southern Pacific of Mexico and later the Ferrocarril del Pacifico — see page 150.)

Subsequent expansion of the Santa Fe encompassed lines from Amarillo to Pecos (1899); from Ash Fork, Ariz., to Phoenix (1901); the Belen Cutoff from the Pecos Valley line at Texico to Isleta, south of Albuquerque, bypassing the grades of Raton Pass (1907); and the Coleman Cutoff, from Texico to Coleman, Tex., near Brownwood (1912). In 1907 Santa Fe and Southern Pacific jointly formed the Northwestern Pacific, which took over several short railroads and built new lines connecting them to form a route from San Francisco north to Eureka. In 1928 Santa Fe sold its half to Southern Pacific; that same year the railroad purchased the U. S. portion of the Kansas City, Mexico & Orient (the Mexican portion of the line is now the Chihuahua-Pacific — see page 62). More recent construction has included an entrance to Dallas from the north and relocation of the main line across northern Arizona.

Because of its long stretches of main line through areas without water, Santa Fe was one of the first purchasers of diesel locomotives for road freight service. The road was known for its passenger service, notably the *Super Chief* (Chicago-Los Angeles), and for the eating houses and dining cars that were operated by Fred Harvey.

Continued on next page.

Address of general offices: 80 E. Jackson Boulevard, Chicago, IL 60604
Miles of road operated: 12,056
Reporting marks: ATSF, SFLC, SFRB, SFRC, SFRE
Number of locomotives: 1997
Number of freight cars: 62,018
Major yards: Barstow, Calif.; Chicago (Corwith); Kansas City, Kans. (Argentine)
Principal shops: Barstow, Calif.; Cleburne, Texas; Kansas City, Kans. (Argentine); San Bernardino, Calif.; Topeka, Kans.
Radio frequencies: 160.650, 161.370 (yard)

Passenger routes:
Amtrak — Chicago-Los Angeles (*Southwest Limited*), Barstow-Los Angeles (*Desert Wind*), Los Angeles-San Diego (*San Diegans*), Fort Worth-Temple, Tex. (*Eagle*), Port Chicago, Calif.-Bakersfield (*San Joaquins*)
Historical and technical society: Santa Fe Modelers Association, P. O. Box 284, Comer, GA 30629
Recommended reading:
History of the Atchison, Topeka and Santa Fe Railway, by Keith L. Bryant, Jr., published in 1974 by Macmillan Publishing Co., New York (ISBN 0-02-517920-9)
Route of the Warbonnets, written and published in 1977 by Joe McMillan, 3208 Halsey Drive, Woodridge, IL 60515
Date: January 1983

Chris Raught.

Not so well known as Santa Fe's crossing of the Colorado River at Topock, Ariz., is the bridge over the same river a few miles south. GP30 2776 and four GP35s bring a westbound freight over the bridge from Parker, Ariz., into Earp, Calif., on Labor Day 1982.

Tim Zukas.

Seven high-horsepower six-motor diesels bring the 77 cars of a westbound freight train through Ludlow, Calif., in the Mojave Desert between Needles and Barstow.

18

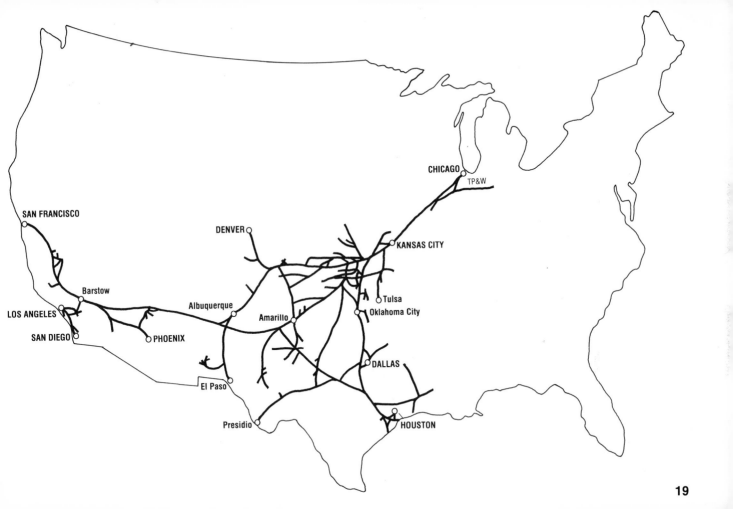

CHICAGO
TP&W
SAN FRANCISCO
DENVER
KANSAS CITY
Barstow
Tulsa
Albuquerque
Oklahoma City
LOS ANGELES
Amarillo
SAN DIEGO
PHOENIX
DALLAS
El Paso
Presidio
HOUSTON

ATLANTA & ST. ANDREWS BAY RAILWAY

The Atlanta & St. Andrews Bay was incorporated in 1906 and completed in 1908. It was conceived as a logging line but its name reflected a more grandiose notion, that of a railroad linking Atlanta to the Gulf of Mexico. The railroad did reach the shores of St. Andrews Bay at Panama City, Fla., but penetrated no further north than Dothan, Ala. The line was owned for a while by the United Fruit Co., which intended to make Panama City the nation's banana port, and in 1931 it was sold to International Paper Co. The railroad is now owned by Southwest Forest Industries.

Address of general offices: P. O. Box 729, Dothan, AL 36302
Miles of road operated: 89
Reporting marks: ASAB
Number of locomotives: 13

Number of freight cars: 806
Principal commodities carried: Pulpwood, paper products, chemicals, grain
Junctions with other railroads:
Southern: Dothan, Ala.
Hartford & Slocomb: Dothan, Ala.
Seaboard System:
　Cottondale, Fla.
　Graceville, Fla.
　Dothan, Ala.
Radio frequencies: 160.770 (road), 160.815 (maintenance of way)
Map: See Apalachicola Northern, page 14
Date: January 1983

Robert E. Gabbey.

Three green and yellow diesels, a GP38-2, an SD40, and an SD9, lead a Bay Line freight north through the pinewoods of the Florida panhandle in 1976. The railroad parallels U. S. highway 231 for much of its length.

ATLANTIC & WESTERN RAILWAY

The Atlantic & Western was incorporated in 1927 to take over the line of the Atlantic & Western Railroad, which ran between Sanford and Lillington, North Carolina, 26 miles. In 1962 the line was abandoned between Lillington and Jonesboro, its present terminus. In 1967 most of the road's stock was purchased by the Atlantic & Western Corp., and in 1970 the railroad was merged into the parent company. The railroad is noteworthy for its large fleet of freight cars — were they all to return to their home road, they would fill its track several times over.

Address of general offices: P. O. Box 1208, Sanford, NC 27330
Miles of road operated: 3

Reporting marks: ATW
Number of locomotives: 2
Number of freight cars: 1606
Principal commodities carried: Scrap iron, sand and gravel, mineral wool, furniture
Junctions with other railroads:
Seaboard System: Jonesboro, N. C.; Sanford, N. C.
Southern: Sanford, N. C.
Radio frequencies: 160.275
Date: January 1983

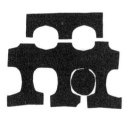

Mike Small.

Red-and-yellow GE 70-tonner No. 100, half of Atlantic & Western's locomotive fleet, carefully crosses U. S. 421 in Jonesboro, N. C.

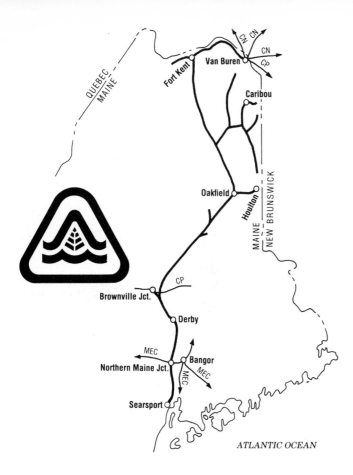

Ronald N. Johnson.

Bangor & Aroostook kept a fleet of first-generation diesels running into the 1980s. Here a GP7, two F3s, and two BL2s power a southbound freight carrying pulpwood and wood chips at Island Falls.

BANGOR & AROOSTOOK RAILROAD

The Bangor & Aroostook was incorporated in 1891 to build north from Brownville, Maine, to Caribou, Ashland, and Fort Fairfield. Shortly thereafter it purchased several smaller railroads to form a system giving the northern half of Maine an outlet to tidewater at Searsport and a rail connection to the rest of the U. S. By 1910 the road had attained full growth. In 1922 the first line abandonment took place, and since then a number of branches and duplicate lines have been trimmed.

BAR discontinued rail passenger service in 1961 but continues to operate buses between Bangor and Aroostook County points. In the 1950s the railroad achieved recognition out of proportion to its size and remoteness: for a fleet of red, white, and blue boxcars blazoned "State of Maine Products," for purchasing sufficient diesels to cover peak traffic and then leasing them during most of the year to the Pennsylvania Railroad, and for working a similar arrangement with Pacific Fruit Express to keep its fleet of potato-carrying refrigerator cars moving and thus earning money.

More than 99 percent of the outstanding stock is owned by the Amoskeag Co.

Address of general offices: Northern Maine Junction Park, R.R. 2, Bangor, ME 04401
Miles of road operated: 494
Reporting marks: BAR
Number of locomotives: 45
Number of freight cars: 3590
Principal commodities carried: Forest products

Shops: Derby, Maine
Junctions with other railroads:
Canadian National: St. Leonard, New Brunswick
Canadian Pacific: Brownville Jct., Maine; St. Leonard, New Brunswick
Maine Central: Northern Maine Jct., Maine
Radio frequencies: 160.440, 160.530
Passenger routes: Bangor-Caribou, Maine (bus)
Historical and technical society: Railroad Historical Society of Maine, Box 8057, Portland, ME 04104
Date: January 1983

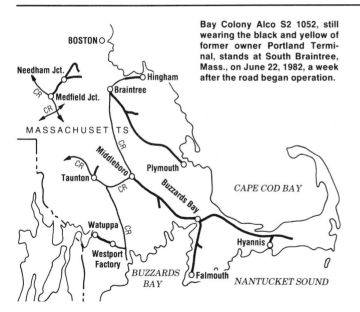

Bay Colony Alco S2 1052, still wearing the black and yellow of former owner Portland Terminal, stands at South Braintree, Mass., on June 22, 1982, a week after the road began operation.

Tom Nelligan.

BAY COLONY RAILROAD

Bay Colony Railroad Corporation was formed in 1982 to operate freight service on several state-owned ex-Conrail, ex-New Haven branch lines south and west of Boston. At present two of the road's five locomotives are assigned to service east of Middleboro and two others work the lines from Braintree to Plymouth and from East Braintree to Hingham. Bay Colony

Continued on next page.

uses a Whiting Trackmobile owned by Springfield Terminal Railway to serve its Needham, Dean St. (Taunton), and Watuppa lines. This vehicle moves daily between the lines on a flatbed trailer. Bay Colony's lines include one notable feat of engineering, the vertical lift bridge over the Cape Cod Canal at Buzzards Bay.

Address of general offices: 420 Bedford Street, Lexington, MA 02173
Miles of road operated: 124
Reporting marks: BCLR
Number of locomotives: 5

Number of freight cars: 47
Principal commodities carried: Building materials, LP gas, food products, packaging products, salt, grain, coal
Junctions with other railroads: Conrail: Braintree, Medfield Jct., Middleboro, Weir Jct. (Taunton), and Westport Factory, Mass.
Radio frequencies: 161.355, 160.305
Passenger routes: Falmouth-Hyannis (Cape Cod & Hyannis Railroad — crews and locomotives furnished by Bay Colony)
Date: February 1983

BELT RAILWAY OF CHICAGO

The Belt Railway of Chicago was built between 1880 and 1882 as the Belt Division of the Chicago & Western Indiana, a terminal road owned by the predecessors of the Chicago & Eastern Illinois, Monon, Erie, Wabash, and Grand Trunk Western railroads. The purpose of the belt line was to provide connections between line haul railroads away from the congestion of downtown Chicago. The railroad was reincorporated in 1882 as the Belt Railway Company of Chicago, and control passed from the C&WI to its five owners.

The BRC was to have a large yard that could serve as a freight car clearinghouse in Chicago (hence the name of the yard, Clearing Yard). Originally a circular design was proposed by A. B. Stickney of the Chi-

KALMBACH BOOKS: Harold A. Edmonson.

Belt Railway of Chicago uses its 6 Alco C424s in coal train and transfer service. The units are gray and black with yellow trim.

cago Great Western, but only a small portion of that was built and of more or less conventional layout. Even so, when Clearing Yard opened in 1902 it was the largest freight yard in the world and one of the first three hump yards in the U. S. (The other two were the Pennsylvania's East Altoona, Pa., Yard and New York Central's DeWitt Yard at Syracuse, N. Y.)

In 1911 the Lowrey Agreement resulted in flat rate switching charges for Chicago, and in 1912 the Belt Operating Agreement brought several more railroads into the ownership and operation of the BRC: Atchison, Topeka & Santa Fe; Chesapeake & Ohio; Chicago, Burlington & Quincy; Illinois Central; Pennsylvania; Rock Island; and Soo Line. Pere Marquette became an owner in 1923. Clearing Yard was extensively rebuilt in 1912, and in 1938 retarders were added, eliminating the men who were needed to brake each car as it rolled down the hump.

BRC is currently owned by Atchison, Topeka & Santa Fe; Burlington Northern; Chesapeake & Ohio; Grand Trunk Western; Illinois Central Gulf; Missouri Pacific; Norfolk & Western; Rock Island; and Soo Line — one thirteenth each — and Seaboard System and Conrail — two thirteenths each. It connects with all line-haul roads serving Chicago.

Address of general offices: 6900 S. Central Avenue, Chicago, IL 60638
Miles of road operated: 48
Reporting marks: BRC
Number of locomotives: 41
Major yards: Chicago (Clearing Yard)
Principal shops: Clearing Yard
Connects with:
Atchison, Topeka & Santa Fe
Burlington Northern
Chessie System
Chicago & Illinois Western
Chicago & North Western
Chicago & Western Indiana
Chicago, Milwaukee, St. Paul & Pacific
Chicago Short Line
Chicago South Shore & South Bend
Chicago, West Pullman & Southern
Conrail
Elgin, Joliet & Eastern
Grand Trunk Western
Illinois Central Gulf
Indiana Harbor Belt
Manufacturers' Junction
Missouri Pacific
Norfolk & Western
Seaboard System
Soo Line
all within the Chicago Switching District
Radio frequencies: 160.500, 160.380 (yard/other)
Date: January 1983

BESSEMER & LAKE ERIE RAILROAD

The Bessemer & Lake Erie began life around 1865 as the Bear Creek Railroad, which was built to serve the coalfields southeast of Greenville, Pa. Renamed Shenango & Allegheny in 1867 and reorganized as the Pittsburgh, Shenango & Lake Erie in 1888, the road was extended north to Lake Erie, reaching Erie in 1891 and Conneaut, Ohio, in 1892.

In 1896 the railroad joined in a three-way agreement with the Union Railroad and the Carnegie Steel Co. to build a line from Butler to East Pittsburgh. Carnegie already controlled the iron mines in Minnesota, the railroads from the Mesabi Range to the docks on Lake Superior, and the Union Railroad, a terminal railroad serving the steel mills in Pittsburgh.

Continued on next page.

Southbound iron ore meets northbound coal on Bessemer's well maintained double track.

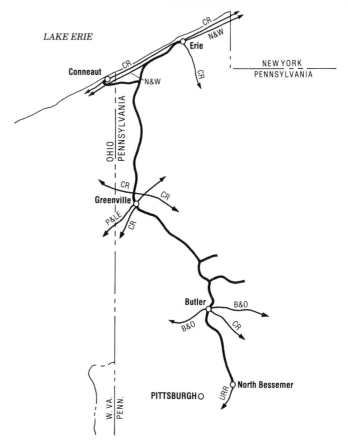

By financing the construction of the line from Butler to the connection with the Union Railroad, Carnegie gained control over all the transportation companies involved in bringing ore to the mills. In 1897 the railroad was renamed the Pittsburg, Bessemer & Lake Erie, and in 1900 Carnegie Steel chartered the Bessemer & Lake Erie, which then leased the PB&LE. In 1901 the United States Steel Corporation was formed.

The Bessemer embarked on a series of projects to improve its line, and by the mid-1950s it had relocated or reduced the grade of approximately half the route between Pittsburgh and Conneaut. The topography of the area through which the Bessemer runs is hilly and lacks convenient watercourses to follow. The B&LE is noted for its bridges; two of the largest are a 1724-foot-long viaduct near Osgood, Pa., and the 2327-foot bridge over the Allegheny River northeast of Pittsburgh, adjacent to the Pennsylvania Turnpike (I-76) bridge.

B&LE purchased the Western Allegheny from the Pennsylvania Railroad at the end of 1967 and operates it as a separate division. B&LE also operates over trackage of the Unity Railways Co., a 3.9-mile line between Unity Jct. and Renton, Pa. Bessemer & Lake Erie is owned by U. S. Steel; other major roads in the family are Duluth, Missabe & Iron Range; Elgin, Joliet & Eastern; and Union Railroad.

Address of general offices: P. O. Box 68, Monroeville, PA 15146

Miles of road operated: 205

Reporting marks: BLE

Number of locomotives: 62

Number of freight cars: 7222

Principal commodities carried: Iron ore, coal, coke, limestone

Major yards: Albion, Pa.; Conneaut, Ohio

Principal shops: Greenville, Pa.

Junctions with other railroads:

Chessie System: Butler, Pa.

Conrail:

  Butler, Pa.

  Erie, Pa.

  Osgood, Pa.

  Shenango, Pa.

Norfolk & Western: Erie, Pa.; Wallace Jct., Pa.

Pittsburgh & Lake Erie: Shenango, Pa.

Union: North Bessemer, Pa.

Unity Railways: Unity Jct., Pa.

Radio frequencies: 160.830, 161.310 (yard/other)

Recommended reading: *The Bessemer and Lake Erie Railroad*, by Roy C. Beaver, published in 1969 by Golden West Books, P. O. Box 8136, San Marino, CA 91108 (ISBN 87095-033-9)

Date: January 1983

BIRMINGHAM SOUTHERN RAILROAD

The Birmingham Southern was incorporated in 1899. Its original line was built from Birmingham to what is now Pratt City, Alabama, in 1878 and extended to Ensley in 1887. It carried coal from the Pratt Fields to blast furnaces at Ensley and Birmingham and steel products from Ensley to Birmingham for interchange with other railroads. Shortly after its organization the line was purchased by the Louisville & Nashville and the Southern Railway and operated as a joint facility of those companies. It was subsequently acquired by Tennessee Coal, Iron & Railroad Co., which became a part of United States Steel Corporation in 1906.

Continued on next page.

In 1966 Birmingham Southern acquired Federal Barge Line Railroad, running 18 miles from Birmingham to Port Birmingham on the Warrior River. The road performs general terminal service in the Birmingham area and also freight and switching service for its owner, U. S. Steel.

Address of general offices: P. O. Box 579, Fairfield, AL 35064
Miles of road operated: 91
Reporting marks: BS
Number of locomotives: 22
Number of freight cars: 796
Principal commodities carried: Steel products and raw materials, slag, coal
Junctions with other railroads:
Burlington Northern
Illinois Central Gulf
Seaboard System
Southern: all at Bessemer, Birmingham, and Ensley, Ala.
Radio frequencies: 160.290, 160.890
Date: January 1983

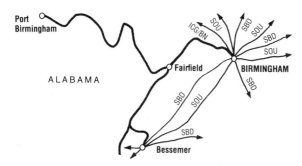

A quartet of Birmingham Southern SW1001s works the mineral transfer facilities on the Warrior River at Port Birmingham, northwest of Birmingham, Ala., where iron ore is transloaded from barges to ore cars for shipment to U. S. Steel's Fairfield works.

G. W. Reed.

28

BOSTON & MAINE CORPORATION

The Boston & Maine's original purpose was to connect Boston, Massachusetts, with Portland, Maine. Its first section of line opened in 1833. Through the 19th century the railroad grew by absorbing neighboring and competing railroads, chief among them the Boston & Lowell (opened in 1835), the Eastern, and the Fitchburg. At its zenith the B&M reached as far north as Sherbrooke, Quebec. Its present extent is not much less, except for lines north of Wells River, Vermont, which were sold to Canadian Pacific. However, the dense network of branch lines that covered northern New England has largely been abandoned.

The Boston & Maine declared bankruptcy in 1970 but chose to pursue its own reorganization plans rather than join Conrail in 1976. Part of the reorganization was the sale of most lines in eastern Massachusetts and B&M's fleet of Budd Rail Diesel Cars, the world's largest, to the Massachusetts Bay Transportation Authority (page 118) in 1976. B&M continued to operate commuter service on those lines for MBTA and later assumed operation of commuter service on former New Haven and New York Central lines south and west of Boston. In 1982 B&M purchased several former New Haven lines in Massachusetts and Connecticut from Conrail.

B&M's two principal freight routes are from Mechanicville, New York, north of Albany, through the 4.7-mile Hoosac Tunnel in northwestern Massachusetts to Portland, Maine, and the Connecticut River line from Springfield, Mass., to Berlin, New Hampshire. The railroad was purchased in 1982 by Timothy Mellon's Guilford Transportation Industries, which also owns Maine Central and Delaware & Hudson.

Continued on next page.

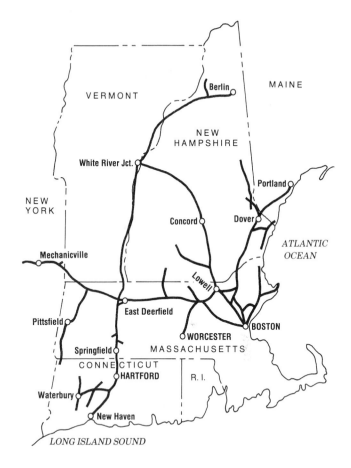

Address of general offices: Iron Horse Park, North Billerica, MA 01862

Miles of road operated: 1393

Reporting marks: BM

Number of locomotives: 160

Number of freight cars: 3127

Radio frequencies: 161.520 (train to dispatcher), 161.160 (dispatcher to train), 161.400 (yard), 161.310 (commuter)

Principal commodities carried: Paper, food products, fuels, building materials

Major yards: Mechanicville, N. Y.; East Deerfield, Mass.

Shops: North Billerica, Mass.

Passenger routes:

Amtrak — Springfield, Mass.-White River Jct., Vt. (*Montrealer*)

Massachusetts Bay Transportation Authority — Boston to Gardner, Lowell, Haverhill, Ipswich, and Rockport, Mass.

Historical & technical society: Boston & Maine Railroad Historical Society, P. O. Box 2362, Harwood Station, Littleton, MA 01460

Recommended reading: *Route of the Minute Man*, by Tom Nelligan and Scott Hartley, published in 1980 by Quadrant Press, 19 W. 44th St., New York, NY 10036 (ISBN 0-915276-26-7)

Date: September 1982

Three blue GP40-2s, Boston & Maine's newest locomotives, lead freight train NE-2 (Mechanicville, N. Y.-Portland, Maine) along the Hoosic River at Pownal Center, Vt., in 1978.

Jack Armstrong.

BRITISH COLUMBIA HYDRO & POWER AUTHORITY

British Columbia Hydro & Power Authority, owned by the province of British Columbia, is the successor to the British Columbia Electric Railway. BCER, incorporated in 1897, was a street and interurban railway that served the Vancouver area and stretched 76 miles east to Chilliwack. Rail passenger operations ended in 1958. British Columbia Hydro supplies electric power to most of the province and distributes gas in the lower mainland and in Victoria.

Address of general offices: 260 12th Street, New Westminster, BC, Canada V3M 4H3
Miles of road operated: 104
Reporting marks: BCH
Number of locomotives: 22
Number of freight cars: 231
Principal commodities carried: Automobiles, forest products, food products
Shops: New Westminster, B. C.
Junctions with other railroads:
Burlington Northern: Huntingdon, B. C.; New Westminster, B. C.
Canadian National: Chilliwack, B. C.; New Westminster B. C.

T. O. Repp.

A British Columbia Hydro freight crests short but steep Kennedy Hill in Surrey, B. C. The lineside poles testify that the line was once an electric interurban railway. BCH's lone SD38AC leads two of its three SD38-2s.

Canadian Pacific:
  Abbotsford, B. C.
  Huntingdon, B. C.
  New Westminster, B. C.
  Vancouver, B. C.
Radio frequencies: 160.275, 160.515 (maintenance of way), 160.545 (yard), 160.695 (yard)
Map: See British Columbia Railway, page 32
Date: January 1983

BCR.

Two M630s and an M420B, the latter a model unique to British Columbia Railway, lift a freight up the 2.2 percent grade out of the Fraser River Canyon at Pavilion, B. C., a few miles north of Lillooet.

BRITISH COLUMBIA RAILWAY

The British Columbia Railway began its existence in 1912 as the Pacific Great Eastern. It constructed a 12-mile line from North Vancouver westward to Horseshoe Bay and took over a bankrupt line that had built a few miles north from Squamish, which was 28 miles west of Horseshoe Bay along the shore of Howe Sound. In 1918 the government of the province of British Columbia acquired the remaining capital stock of the railway. The PGE reached Quesnel in 1921 but got no farther until 1952, when the line was pushed north to a junction with the Canadian National at Prince George. It was PGE's first rail connection with another railroad.

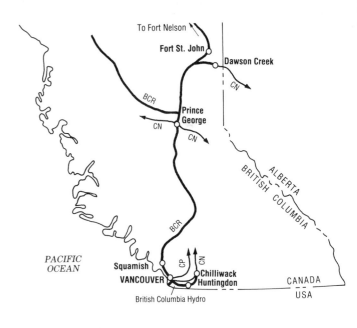

The railroad abandoned its initial line in 1928 but replaced it in 1956 and constructed a line between Horseshoe Bay and Squamish, finally completing a route between North Vancouver and Prince George. The railroad built extensions north from Prince George to Dawson Creek and Fort Nelson in 1958 and 1971, respectively. The name was changed to British Columbia Railway in 1972.

Construction of an extension to Dease Lake in northwestern British Columbia was halted in 1977. Construction of the 80-mile Tumbler Ridge Branch began in 1981. This branch, scheduled for completion in late 1983, will serve a large coalfield and will be electrified to preclude the need for extensive ventilation in its tunnels.

Address of general offices: P. O. Box 8770, Vancouver, BC, Canada V6B 4X6

Miles of road operated: 1261

Reporting marks: BCIT, BCOL, PGE, PGER

Number of locomotives: 126

Number of freight cars: 9793

Number of passenger cars: 6 (self-propelled)

Principal commodities carried: Forest products, coal

Principal shops: North Vancouver, B. C.; Prince George, B. C.; Squamish, B. C.

Junctions with other railroads:

Canadian National
 Dawson Creek, B. C.
 North Vancouver, B. C.
 Prince George, B. C.

Canadian Pacific: North Vancouver, B. C.

Radio frequencies: 159.570 (road), 161.370 (dispatcher), 161.235 (yard)

Passenger routes: North Vancouver-Prince George (*Cariboo Dayliner*); North Vancouver-Squamish (summer steam train pulled by former Canadian Pacific Royal Hudson No. 2860)

Date: January 1983

BURLINGTON NORTHERN

Burlington Northern was created in 1970 by the merger of four railroads: Northern Pacific; Great Northern; Chicago, Burlington & Quincy; and Spokane, Portland & Seattle.

Northern Pacific: The Northern Pacific was a land-grant railroad completed in 1883 from Duluth, Minnesota, west through Billings, Montana, and Spokane, Washington, to Tacoma. NP acquired access to St. Paul and later extended its line south from Tacoma to Portland, Oregon.

Great Northern: James J. Hill built the Great Northern west from

St. Paul, reaching Puget Sound at Seattle in 1893. The route was north of Northern Pacific's and included a system of branches north toward the Canadian border in Minnesota and North Dakota plus lines to Superior, Wisconsin, Winnipeg, Manitoba, and Butte, Montana. In 1931 Great Northern completed its Inside Gateway route south from the Columbia River to a junction with the Western Pacific at Bieber, California, using a combination of Spokane, Portland & Seattle's Oregon Trunk Railway, trackage rights over Southern Pacific, and new construction.

Spokane, Portland & Seattle: Hill planned the Spokane, Portland & Seattle to give Great Northern access to Portland. The road was financed jointly by Great Northern and Northern Pacific; its route was southwest from Spokane to Pasco, Wash., and then along the north bank of the Columbia River to Vancouver, Wash., across the Columbia River from Portland. The last spike was driven in 1908. SP&S subsidiary Oregon Electric connected Portland to Eugene, Oreg., and the Oregon Trunk, owned jointly with Union Pacific, followed the Deschutes River south from the Columbia at Wishram, Wash., to Bend, Oreg.

Continued on next page.

Chicago, Burlington & Quincy: The Chicago, Burlington & Quincy, chartered in 1849, was one of the Midwest's oldest railroads. Its principal routes were Chicago-Denver (completed in 1882), Chicago-St. Paul (1886), Omaha-Alliance-Billings, and Billings-Denver-Fort Worth-Houston, the last including the lines of CB&Q subsidiary Colorado & Southern and C&S subsidiary Fort Worth & Denver. In 1934 the Burlington purchased the nation's first diesel-powered streamlined train, the *Zephyr*. Other *Zephyrs* followed — among them the *Twin*, *Denver*, *Texas*, and *California Zephyrs* — forming one of the best-known streamliner families. The Burlington constructed the first Vista-Dome car in its shops in 1945.

Great Northern's and Northern Pacific's general offices were on opposite sides of a large building in St. Paul; each owned almost 49 percent of Burlington's stock after 1901 and each owned 50 percent of SP&S. The Burlington Northern merger was a long time coming (and one of its early handicaps was the proposed name, Great Northern Pacific & Burlington Lines).

St. Louis-San Francisco: In 1980 the St. Louis-San Francisco (Frisco) was merged into BN. Frisco's history dates from 1853, when ground was broken for the South-West Branch of the Pacific Railroad of Missouri at Franklin (now Pacific), Missouri. The line was aimed at Springfield — and eventually the Pacific Ocean. The railroad reached Springfield in 1870 and merged with the Atlantic & Pacific, which was chartered to build west along the 35th parallel. The western portion of the A&P eventually became the Santa Fe's main line, and the St. Louis-San Francisco, successor to the South-West Branch, became an X-shaped regional system, with lines from St. Louis to Fort Worth and Quanah, Texas, and from Kansas City and Wichita to Birmingham, Alabama, and Pensacola, Florida.

At the end of 1981 BN absorbed the Colorado & Southern, which had been a CB&Q subsidiary, and transferred C&S's Denver-Texline route to the Fort Worth & Denver, a C&S subsidiary. On January 1, 1983, FW&D was also merged into BN.

BN's former Great Northern line includes the two longest railroad tunnels in North America, the Cascade Tunnel, 7.79 miles, between Scenic and Berne, Wash., and the 7.75-mile-long Flathead Tunnel, east of Libby,

Paul D. Schneider.

Burlington Northern operates an intense commuter service for Chicago's Regional Transportation Authority on its 38-mile 3-track line between Chicago and Aurora. Here an inbound train with a cab-coach leading meets an outbound at Halsted Street.

Mont. The Crooked River Bridge, north of Redmond, Oreg., on the Oregon Trunk line, is second highest (320 feet) in the U. S.

Address of general offices: 176 East Fifth Street, St. Paul, MN 55101

Miles of road operated: 27,361

Reporting marks: BN, BNFE, BRE, CBQ, CS, FWD, GN, NP, RBBN, RBBQ, RBCS, RBW, SLSF, SPS, USLF, WFB, WFE, WHI

Number of locomotives: 3294

Number of freight cars: 108,607

Text continued on page 36.

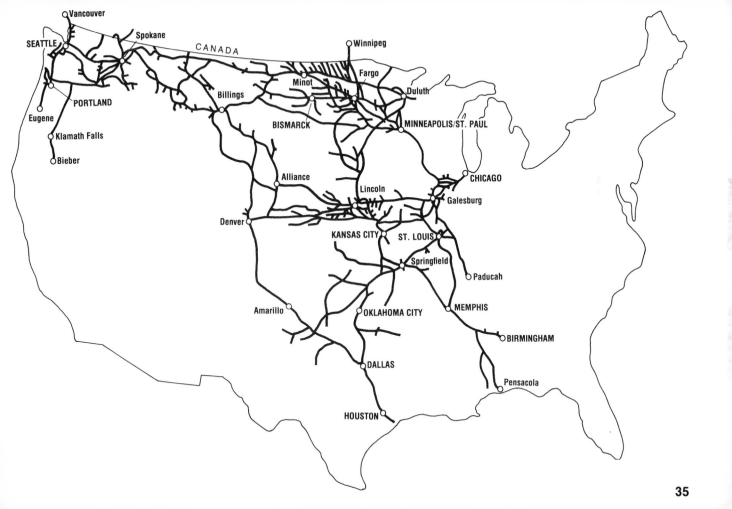

Principal commodities carried: Coal, grain, forest products
Major yards: Chicago (Cicero); Galesburg, Ill.; Kansas City, Mo.; Lincoln, Nebr.; Minneapolis (Northtown); Pasco, Wash.; Seattle; Springfield, Mo.
Principal shops: Alliance, Nebr.; Havelock, Nebr.; Havre, Mont.; Livingston, Mont.; St. Cloud, Minn.; Springfield, Mo.; West Burlington, Iowa
Radio frequencies: 161.100, 161.160 (yard — eastern; channel 2, ex-SLSF lines), 161.250 (yard — western)
Passenger routes:
Amtrak — Chicago-Denver (*California Zephyr*), Chicago-W. Quincy, Mo. (*Illinois Zephyr*), St. Paul-Seattle and Spokane-Portland (*Empire Builder*), St. Paul-Duluth (*North Star*), and Seattle-Portland (*Coast Starlight*, *Pioneer*, and *Mt. Rainier*)
Regional Transportation Authority — Chicago-Aurora, Ill.
Historical and technical societies:
Burlington Route Historical Society, Box 196, Bensenville, IL 60106
Frisco Modelers Information Group, 2541 W. Allen Drive, Springfield, MO 65807
Great Northern Railway Historical Society, 6161 Willow Lake Drive, Hudson, OH 44236
Recommended reading: *Burlington Northern Annuals*, published by Motive Power Services, P. O. Box 17111, Denver, CO 80217
Date: September 1982

Howard Patrick

Burlington Northern is the top coal hauler in the U. S., largely because of the development of coalfields in eastern Wyoming. At Ashby, Nebr., an eastbound coal train meets a westbound freight.

BUTTE, ANACONDA & PACIFIC RAILWAY

The Butte, Anaconda & Pacific was incorporated in 1892 to connect copper mines at Butte, Montana, with a smelter at Anaconda. The mines, the smelter, and the railroad were all owned by Marcus Daly. The railroad was opened in 1893.

By 1911 the Anaconda Copper Mining Co., Daly's company, had acquired considerable experience using electric motors to drain and ventilate its mines. The BA&P electrified its line to take advantage of the economies that would result from electric operation. The railroad chose

General Electric's 2400-volt D. C. system; electric locomotives started hauling trains in 1913.

Except for the addition of two locomotives in 1957 to the original fleet of 28, electric operation continued without major change until 1967, when the installation of a new ore concentrator at Butte changed the railroad's traffic patterns. The seven GP7s and GP9s that had been working the non-electrified trackage took over all of BA&P's operation. In 1972 BA&P acquired an SW1200 from the Tooele Valley, a short line in Utah also owned by Anaconda. In 1980 the road sold the switcher and bought two GP38-2s.

The closing of Anaconda's smelter in Anaconda again changed the road's traffic patterns — indeed, eliminated most of them — and BA&P's operations changed from daily to "as required."

Address of general offices: P. O. Box 1421, Anaconda, MT 59711
Miles of road operated: 43
Reporting marks: BAP
Number of locomotives: 9
Number of freight cars: 411
Principal commodities carried: Copper ore

Junctions with other railroads:
Burlington Northern:
 Butte, Mont.
 Rocker, Mont.
 Silver Bow, Mont.
Union Pacific: Silver Bow, Mont.
Radio frequencies: 160.320, 160.380
Recommended reading: "Montana Copper Carrier," a chapter of WHEN THE STEAM RAILROADS ELECTRIFIED, by William D. Middleton, published in 1974 by Kalmbach Publishing Co., 1027 North Seventh Street, Milwaukee, WI 53233 (ISBN 0-89024-028-0)
Date: February 1983

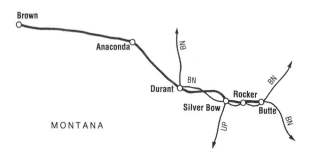

Two GP9s bring a train of modern ore cars along the Northern Pacific (now Burlington Northern) main line near Durant in the early 1960s.

Donald Sims.

37

CADILLAC & LAKE CITY RAILWAY

The Cadillac & Lake City operated a former Pennsylvania Railroad branch from Missaukee Jct., Michigan, north of Cadillac, to Lake City and Falmouth. Until 1971 it operated both steam-powered passenger trains as a tourist railroad and diesel-powered freight trains. In the 1970s the road gradually withered. The railroad's Michigan track remains in place, unused.

On July 1, 1980, the company began operation of Rock Island's Duban Switching Operations in Denver. On July 1, 1981, C&LC began operations between Limon and Stratton, Colorado, on the former Rock Island main line, and a month later extended that operation east to Goodland, Kansas. A week later C&LC began serving Rock Island's Colorado Springs Switching District, succeeding the Denver & Rio Grande Western, which had been providing service since the Rock Island shut down. On February 21, 1983, the Rock Island trustees sold the Colorado Springs trackage to the Rio Grande. On March 9, 1983, C&LC Denver operations shrank to a connection between Union Pacific at Sandown Jct. and the Duban area, as most of the Rock's Denver trackage was sold to the Colorado & Eastern Railway.

Address of general offices: 121 E. Pikes Peak Ave., Suite 335, Colorado Springs, CO 80903
Miles of road operated: 112
Reporting marks: CLK
Number of locomotives: 4

David M. Johnston.

F7A 716, formerly on Burlington Northern's roster, sits east of the station at Limon, Colo., facing toward Colorado Springs. The crossing that was removed from the Union Pacific track has been replaced since this photo was taken.

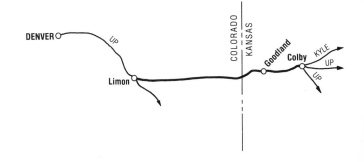

Number of freight cars: 2
Principal commodities carried: Wheat, fertilizer, farm implements, scrap paper, chemicals
Junctions with other railroads:
Burlington Northern: Denver
Denver & Rio Grande Western: Colorado Springs; Denver
Kyle Railroad: Goodland, Kans.

Michigan Northern: Missaukee Jct., Mich.
Union Pacific:
Colby, Kans.
Denver, Colo.
Limon, Colo.
Radio frequencies: 160.965
Date: March 1983

CWR.

CALIFORNIA WESTERN RAILROAD

In the early 1880s Charles R. Johnson organized the Fort Bragg Lumber Co. to cut, mill, and market redwood lumber from the north coast of California. In 1885 he incorporated the Fort Bragg Railroad; its purpose was to bring the logs out of the forest to the mill at Fort Bragg. Names changed: In 1893 the Union Lumber Co. was incorporated as an expansion of the Fort Bragg Lumber Co. and the railroad became the California-Western Railroad and Navigation Co. More construction pushed the railroad east to a connection with the Northwestern Pacific at Willits in 1911. For a while the CW and NWP even provided through Pullman service to Sausalito, NWP's terminal on San Francisco Bay.

In 1925 the California Western received a Mack railbus which was nicknamed "Skunk." One explanation of the nickname is that the exhaust of the gasoline engine smelled different from that of the steam train it replaced. By the 1950s tourists had discovered the Skunk and the railroad was in the excursion business, eventually with a fleet of four rail motor cars, two steam locomotives, and a number of coaches. The railroad continues to haul forest products for its owner, Union Lumber Co.

Address of general offices: Foot of Laurel Street, Fort Bragg, CA 95437

Continued on next page.

In summer conventional diesel-hauled trains carry tourists through the redwoods, but during fall, winter, and spring passengers ride in California Western's bright yellow "Skunk" railcars. Number M300 is an ACF Motorailer that served the Aberdeen & Rockfish and the Salt Lake, Garfield & Western before coming to the CW.

Miles of road operated: 40
Reporting marks: CWR
Number of locomotives: 6 (4 diesel, 2 steam)
Number of passenger cars: 11
Principal commodities carried: Forest products
Junctions with other railroads: Northwestern Pacific (Southern Pacific): Willits, Calif.
Radio frequencies: 160.650
Passenger routes: Willits-Fort Bragg
Recommended reading: *Redwoods, Iron Horses, and the Pacific,* by Spencer Crump, published in 1971 by Trans-Anglo Books, Costa Mesa, CA (ISBN 0-87046-021-8)

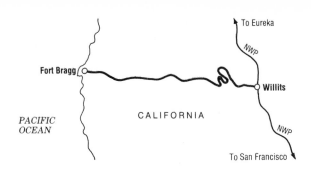

CALTRAIN

CALTRANS (State of California Department of Transportation)

On July 1, 1980, Caltrans signed an agreement with Southern Pacific to finance the commute trains SP operated between San Francisco and San Jose. In October 1981 Caltrans revised the schedules, adding trains to accommodate reverse commuting (southbound in the morning and northbound in the evening) and renumbered those trains, the last trains on the railroad to display train numbers on their engine number boards (as much an Espee characteristic as calling the service "commute," not "commuter").

A year later Caltrans inaugurated a pair of Oxnard-Los Angeles commuter trains, also operated by SP. The Oxnard trains began operating with Amfleet coaches, then used bilevel cars leased from Chicago's Re-

Steve Sloan.

Southern Pacific GP9 3187 and three bilevel commuter coaches were repainted in Caltrans colors — blue, silver, and red — for display at an Amtrak Family Days celebration at San Jose in May 1982.

gional Transportation Authority, and still later, bilevel cars borrowed from the San Francisco-San Jose service. The Oxnard service was temporarily suspended in early 1983 while the participants discussed payment terms.

Caltrans also finances the operation of several Amtrak trains and buses that connect with Amtrak trains.

Address of general offices: P. O. Box 1499, Sacramento, CA 95807
Miles of road operated: 113
Number of locomotives: leased from Southern Pacific
Number of passenger cars: leased from Southern Pacific
Passenger routes: San Francisco-San Jose; Oxnard-Los Angeles
Radio frequencies: 161.550 (Southern Pacific)
Date: March 1983

CAMBRIA & INDIANA RAILROAD

The Cambria & Indiana was begun as a logging railroad from Rexis to Stiles, Pennsylvania. It was later incorporated in 1904 as the Blacklick & Yellow Creek Railroad, and its cargo changed from logs to coal. In 1911 the railroad received its present name, taken from the names of the two Pennsylvania counties in which it operates. That same year it was extended north from Stiles to Manver and east to Colver to serve several more coal mines being developed by the owners of the railroad. In 1916 a branch was constructed to Nanty Glo, again to reach coal mines. A flood in 1977 washed out a bridge on the branch from Elkdale to Rexis; it has not been replaced.

One of the two owners sold his 40 percent interest in the road to a New York Central coal mining subsidiary in 1922; in 1950 Bethlehem Steel Corp. acquired the other 60 percent and now owns all the capital stock of the line.

Address of general offices: 1275 Daly Avenue, Bethlehem, PA 18015
Miles of road operated: 57
Reporting marks: CI
Number of locomotives: 18
Number of freight cars: 956

Ronald N. Johnson

Five EMD switchers, four of them yellow and black and the fifth (No. 36) specially painted to commemorate the nation's bicentennial, lead a coal train out of Revloc, Pa., along the bank of Blacklick Creek.

Principal commodities carried: Coal
Junctions with other railroads: Conrail: Manver, Pa.; Nanty Glo, Pa.
Radio frequencies: 160.490
Map: See Pittsburgh & Shawmut, page 151
Date: February 1983

CANADIAN NATIONAL RAILWAYS (CN RAIL)

Canadian National Railways was organized in 1922 to operate a number of railroads that had come under control of the Canadian government because of financial difficulties. A brief history of each of the principal components of CN follows.

Grand Trunk Pacific was incorporated in 1903 to build a railroad from Winnipeg, Manitoba, west to the Pacific at Prince Rupert, British Columbia. Construction costs of the GTP far exceeded the estimates. The Grand Trunk Railway had guaranteed the GTP's bonds; GT's failure was a consequence of GTP's revenue being insufficient to cover costs.

The National Transcontinental Railway was built from Moncton, New Brunswick, to Winnipeg via Edmundston, N. B., Quebec and Senneterre, Quebec; and Cochrane and Nakina, Ontario, through an area with almost no population. The railroad was built by the Canadian government for eventual operation by the Grand Trunk Pacific, but GT refused to accept the line. It was operated from 1915 to 1923 by Canadian Government Railways, a predecessor of Canadian National.

Canadian Northern was begun in 1899 as a line from Winnipeg to Vancouver via Saskatoon and Edmonton, well north of the route of the Canadian Pacific. Canadian Northern and Grand Trunk Pacific built duplicate lines from Edmonton west to Yellowhead Pass in the Rockies; Canadian Northern and Canadian Pacific occupied opposite banks of the Fraser River for many miles in British Columbia. Canadian Northern reached Vancouver in 1915.

Canadian Northern also built southeast from Winnipeg through the northernmost portion of Minnesota to Lake Superior at Port Arthur, Ontario (now Thunder Bay). The Canadian Northern system included lines from Montreal and Toronto through Capreol, Ont., to Port Arthur; the

John C. Illman

A CN freight powered by a pair of wide-nose SD40-2s accelerates west out of Blue River, B. C., along the upper reaches of the North Thompson River.

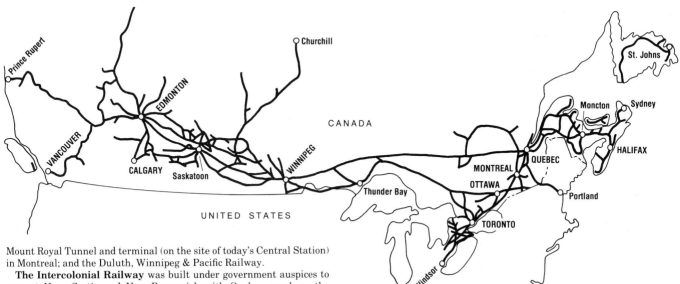

Mount Royal Tunnel and terminal (on the site of today's Central Station) in Montreal; and the Duluth, Winnipeg & Pacific Railway.

The Intercolonial Railway was built under government auspices to connect Nova Scotia and New Brunswick with Quebec, much as the Canadian Pacific was built as a condition of British Columbia's entering the confederation. The Intercolonial's main line is CN's present route from Halifax through Truro, N. S., Moncton and Campbellton, N. B., and Riviere du Loup, Que., to Montreal.

The Grand Trunk Railway was originally conceived to connect Montreal and Toronto. To that was added in 1853 a line from Montreal to the nearest seaport, Portland, Maine. Construction and acquisition at the west end of the line put Grand Trunk across the St. Clair River by ferry and through Michigan and Indiana into Chicago in 1880. Grand Trunk's tunnel under the St. Clair between Sarnia, Ont., and Port Huron, Mich., was completed in 1886. Grand Trunk was amalgamated into Canadian National in 1923.

Thus in 1923 Canadian National had two lines across the continent from Moncton, N. B., to the Pacific at Vancouver and Prince Rupert, B. C., and a dense network of lines in Quebec and Ontario and on the prairies between Winnipeg and the Rockies. In 1923 Canadian National built a 30-mile cutoff from Longlac to Nakina in northern Ontario, forming a connection between the former Canadian Northern and National Transcontinental lines and shortening the rail distance between Toronto and Winnipeg. CN has pushed lines into the subarctic area north of the prairies to tap mineral deposits. Notable among these is the Great Slave Lake Railway.

Continued on next page.

Other railroads in the CN system are the 3′6″-gauge Newfoundland Railway, which became part of CN in 1949 when Newfoundland joined the confederation, and the Northern Alberta, which was incorporated in 1929 to take over several lines owned and operated by the province of Alberta. NAR was jointly owned by CN and Canadian Pacific until CP sold its half to CN in 1980.

Canadian National also runs hotels, truck and express companies, ferries in the Maritime Provinces, and a communications system. Recently the company's divisions have been given generic titles such as CN Hotels, CN Marine, and CN Rail, just like privately owned competitor Canadian Pacific. CN divested itself of its interest in Air Canada in 1978.

CN owns the Grand Trunk Corporation, which in turn owns several U. S. railroads: Grand Trunk Western; Central Vermont; Duluth, Winnipeg & Pacific; Detroit, Toledo & Ironton; and Detroit & Toledo Shore Line. The portion of the Winnipeg-Thunder Bay line in Minnesota and the line from Island Pond, Vermont, to Portland, Maine, are considered part of CN proper, not Grand Trunk Corporation.

Address of general offices: P. O. Box 1800, Montreal, PQ H3C 3N4
Miles of road operated: 22,518
Reporting marks: CN, CNA, CNF, CNIS, NAR
Number of locomotives: 1782 standard gauge, 51 narrow gauge
Number of freight cars: 79,461 standard gauge, 1227 narrow gauge (CNF)
Principal commodities carried: Grain, lumber, coal, potash
Major yards: Edmonton, Moncton, Montreal (Taschereau), Toronto, Winnipeg

Principal shops: Montreal (Pointe St. Charles), Winnipeg (Transcona)
Radio frequencies: 161.415, 161.205, 160.935 (dispatcher to train)
Passenger routes:
Terra Transport (a CN division operating services in Newfoundland) — St. Johns-Argentia, St. Johns-Carbonear, Bishops Falls-Corner Brook, Clarenville-Bonavista (mixed trains; the company has petitioned for discontinuance)
VIA Rail Canada — Sydney-Truro, N. S.; Moncton-Saint John, N. B.; Halifax-Montreal; Matapedia-Gaspe, Que.; Quebec-Montreal; Montreal-Hervey-Chicoutimi, Que.; Hervey, Que.-Cochrane, Ont.-Kapuskasing, Ont.; Montreal-Ottawa; Ottawa-Smiths Falls, Ont.; Montreal-Toronto; Toronto-North Bay; Toronto-Stratford-London, Ont.; Toronto-Brantford-London-Windsor; London-Sarnia, Ont.; Toronto-Hamilton-Niagara Falls; Toronto-Parry Sound, Ont.; Capreol, Ont.-Winnipeg-Portage la Prairie, Man.; Hearst-Nakina, Ont.; Thunder Bay-Sioux Lookout, Ont. (mixed); Regina, Sask.-Saskatoon-Edmonton-Jasper, Alta.-Prince Rupert, B. C.; Winnipeg-Thompson-Churchill, Man.; The Pas-Lynn Lake, Man. (mixed)
Montreal Urban Community Transportation Commission — Montreal-Deux Montagnes, Que. (electrified)
GO Transit — Pickering-Toronto-Hamilton; Toronto-Bradford; Toronto-Stouffville; Toronto-Georgetown
Amtrak — Montreal-E. Alburgh, Vt. (*Montrealer*)
Recommended reading: *Canadian National Railways*, by G. R. Stevens, O. B. E., published in 1962 by Clarke, Irwin & Co., Ltd., Toronto and Vancouver

CANADIAN PACIFIC (CP RAIL)

The history of Canadian Pacific is intimately tied to Canadian politics. When British Columbia joined the confederation in 1871, the Canadian government promised that a railroad would link the province to the rest of the country within 10 years. The barriers to such a railroad were formidable: the wilderness of northern Ontario, the emptiness of the prairies, the Rocky Mountains, and, of course, financing. Canada's principal rail-

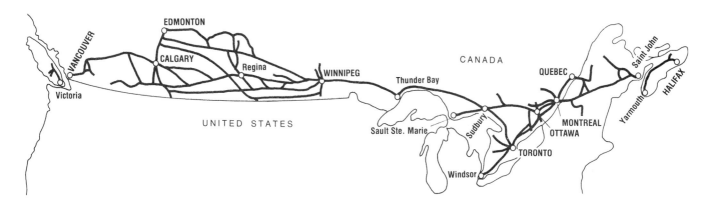

road, the Grand Trunk, was not interested in the project, so in 1881 the Canadian Pacific Railway was incorporated to build a railroad from Callander, Ontario, near North Bay, to the Pacific at what is now Vancouver. The line was completed in 1885. Construction along the north shore of Lake Superior was very difficult, and the crossing of the Rockies at Kicking Horse Pass was accomplished only by resorting to 4.5 percent grades as an interim solution and later a pair of spiral tunnels.

Early in its existence CP absorbed the Canada Central to gain access to Ottawa and Montreal. In 1884 CP leased the Ontario & Quebec, gaining a line from Perth, Ont., to Toronto. In 1887 that line was extended east to Montreal and west to Windsor, opposite Detroit. By 1890 the road had extended east from Montreal across Maine to Saint John, N. B., creating a transcontinental line.

The discovery in 1887 of silver in southeastern British Columbia, an area that geographically and socially was much closer to the U. S. (and to James J. Hill's Great Northern) than to Canada sparked an outbreak of railroad fever. CP built a line into the Kootenay region from Medicine Hat, Alberta, across Crows Nest Pass. The line, which ran across, rather than with, the topography, was expensive to build and operate. The

Canadian government provided a cash grant for its construction in exchange for a permanent reduction in grain rates — the Crows Nest Pass Agreement of 1897. In 1916 CP's Kettle Valley subsidiary completed the line through to a connection with the main line at Hope, British Columbia, creating a secondary main line across the southern tier of British Columbia and part of Alberta. Much of the western portion of the Kettle Valley line was abandoned in recent years.

In 1968 Canadian Pacific, which by then also included ships, hotels, and an airline, revised its corporate image. The railway emerged as CP Rail. CP Rail has three subsidiary railroads, Dominion Atlantic (Halifax-Yarmouth, N. S.), Quebec Central (Quebec-Newport, Vermont), and Esquimault & Nanaimo (Victoria-Courtenay, B. C., on Vancouver Island). The three have been leased since 1912. Though they maintain individual corporate identities, they are operated as a part of CP Rail. CP Rail also controls the Soo Line and owns the Toronto, Hamilton & Buffalo.

Address of general offices: P. O. Box 6042, Station A, Montreal, PQ H3C 3E4

Miles of road operated: 15,316

Continued on next page.

Greg McDonnell.

Heading up a westbound freight near Cambridge, Ont., is one of CP's (and Canada's) two GP30s.

Reporting marks: CP, CPAA, CPI, DA, EN, QC
Number of locomotives: 1252
Number of freight cars: 58,260
Principal commodities carried: Coal, grain, potash
Major yards: Calgary, Montreal, Toronto, Vancouver, Winnipeg
Principal shops: Calgary (Ogden), Montreal (Angus), Winnipeg (Weston)
Radio frequencies: 161.475, 161.115 (yard)
Passenger routes:
Montreal Urban Community Transportation Commission — Montreal-Rigaud, Que.

GO Transit — Toronto-Milton, Ont.
VIA Rail Canada — Halifax-Yarmouth, N. S., Parry Sound, Ont.-Sudbury, Ont.-Winnipeg, Man.; Portage la Prairie, Man.-Calgary, Alta.-Vancouver, B. C.; Saint John-Fredericton, N. B.; Montreal-Quebec; Ottawa-Sudbury, Ont.; Smiths Falls-Brockville, Ont.; Calgary-South Edmonton, Alta.; Victoria-Courtenay, B. C.
Recommended reading: *Canadian Pacific Diesel Locomotives*, by Murray W. Dean and David B. Hanna, published in 1981 by Railfare Enterprises Limited, Box 33, West Hill, ON, Canada M1E 4R4 (ISBN 0-919130-32-1)
Date: February 1983

CARTIER RAILWAY (La Compagnie de Chemin de Fer Cartier)

The Quebec Cartier Mining Co., a subsidiary of U. S. Steel, was formed in 1957 to mine iron ore in eastern Quebec and transport it south to the St. Lawrence River. Construction of the Cartier Railway began in 1958, and by the end of 1960 the line was completed from Port Cartier, 40 miles west of Sept Iles, 193 miles north to Lac Jeannine, near Gagnon. In the early 1970s the line was extended north from a junction at milepost 174 to a mine and concentrator at Mount Wright. Trains are operated year round, because a dryer built into the ore concentrator eliminates the problem of ore freezing in the cars.

Address of general offices: Port Cartier, PQ G5B 2H3

Miles of road operated: 281
Reporting marks: QCM
Number of locomotives: 54
Number of freight cars: 1400
Principal commodities carried: Iron ore
Shops: Port Cartier, Que.
Junctions with other railroads: None
Radio frequencies: 161.130, 160.800
Map: See Quebec North Shore & Labrador, page 158
Date: March 1983

Two six-motor 3600-h.p. units, No. 82 built by Montreal and No. 77 by Alco, lead empty ore gondolas north out of Port Cartier, Que., in June 1981.

Greg McDonnell.

CENTRAL CALIFORNIA TRACTION CO.

Central California Traction Co. was incorporated in 1905. It encompassed streetcar lines in Stockton and Sacramento and a third-rail-powered interurban line between Stockton and Sacramento with a short branch to Lodi. In 1928 joint and equal control of the company was acquired by Santa Fe, Southern Pacific, and Western Pacific. Passenger service was discontinued in 1933, except for the streetcar lines in Sacramento, which lasted until 1946. Freight service was dieselized in 1946. CCT's line between Stockton and Sacramento lies a few miles east of the Southern Pacific route between those cities. The railroad serves the rich area east of the San Joaquin-Sacramento delta.

Address of general offices: 526 Mission Street, San Francisco, CA 94105

Miles of road operated: 50

Reporting marks: CCT

Number of locomotives: 4

Number of freight cars: 4

Principal commodities carried: Grocery products, canned goods, wine

Major yards: Fruitridge; Lodi; Stockton

Principal shops: Stockton

Junctions with other railroads:

Atchison, Topeka & Santa Fe: Stockton

Sacramento Northern: Sacramento

Southern Pacific: Lodi, Polk, Sacramento, Stockton

Stockton Terminal & Eastern: Stockton

Tidewater Southern: Stockton

Western Pacific: Sacramento, Stockton

Radio frequencies: 160.335, 161.415

Date: March 1983

Dave Stanley.

Central California Traction's two bright-red GP18s, 1795 and 1790, lead a Sacramento-bound local over the Cosumnes River bridge betweeen Wilton and Sheldon.

CENTRAL VERMONT RAILWAY

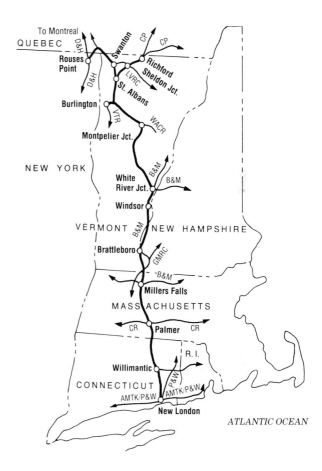

The Vermont Central was opened in 1849 between the Connecticut River at Windsor, Vt., and Lake Champlain at Burlington to tap traffic between Boston and the Great Lakes. By 1871 the company controlled a system reaching from New London, Connecticut, to Ogdensburg, New York, including lines that later became parts of the Rutland and the Boston & Maine. The Vermont Central reached its greatest extent in 1873. At the time of its 1898 reorganization as the Central Vermont with the Grand Trunk as its majority stockholder, it was essentially the CV of today except for a few branches that have since been abandoned. Control passed from Grand Trunk to Canadian National in 1923 and then to the present Grand Trunk Corporation in 1971.

In conjunction with Boston & Maine, CV operates a fast piggyback train named *The Rocket* between St. Albans, Vt., and New Haven, Conn.

Address of general offices: 2 Federal Street, St. Albans, VT 05478
Miles of road operated: 377
Reporting marks: CV, CVC
Number of locomotives: 29
Number of freight cars: 1291
Principal commodities carried: Forest products, agricultural products
Major yards: St. Albans, Vt.
Principal shops: St. Albans, Vt.
Junctions with other railroads:
Boston & Maine:
  Brattleboro, Vt.
  Millers Falls, Mass.
  White River Jct., Vt.
  Windsor, Vt.

Continued on next page.

A Central Vermont freight rolls south between forested hills at Windsor, Vt., behind a quartet of CV and Boston & Maine GP9s.

Canadian National: East Alburgh, Vt.; Rouses Point, N. Y.
Canadian Pacific: Richford, Vt.
Conrail: Palmer, Mass.
Delaware & Hudson: Rouses Point, N. Y.
Lamoille Valley:
   St. Albans, Vt.
   Sheldon Jct., Vt.
   Swanton, Vt.
Providence & Worcester: New London, Conn.; Willimantic, Conn.
Vermont Railway: Burlington, Vt.

Washington County: Montpelier Jct., Vt.
Radio frequencies: 161.415, 161.205 (yard and maintenance of way), 160.935 (yard)
Passenger routes: Amtrak — White River Jct.-East Alburgh, Vt. (*Montrealer*)
Recommended reading: *Central Vermont Railway*, by Edward H. Beaudette, published in 1982 by Carstens Publications, P. O. Box 700, Newton, NJ 07860 (ISBN 911868-44-5)
Date: January 1983

CHATTAHOOCHEE INDUSTRIAL RAILROAD

The Chattahoochee Industrial Railroad was built by the Great Northern Nekoosa Paper Co. to serve a new paper products plant near Cedar Springs, in the southwest corner of Georgia. The railroad began operation in 1963. Other customers of the line are plywood, chemical, and steel tubing plants and several forest-products-related industries.

Don't confuse the CIRR with the Chattahoochee Valley, a 10-mile line at West Point, Ga., about 110 miles north on the Chattahoochee River, which forms much of the boundary between Georgia and Alabama.

Address of general offices: P. O. Box 253, Cedar Springs, GA 31732
Miles of road operated: 15

Number of locomotives: 8
Number of freight cars: 1013
Reporting marks: CIRR
Principal commodities carried: Paper products, coal
Shops: Saffold, Ga.
Junctions with other railroads:
Seaboard System: Saffold, Ga.
Southern: Hilton, Ga.
Radio frequencies: 160.860, 160.620, 161.235 (shops)
Map: see Apalachicola Northern, page 14

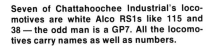

Seven of Chattahoochee Industrial's locomotives are white Alco RS1s like 115 and 38 — the odd man is a GP7. All the locomotives carry names as well as numbers.

John W. Coniglio.

CHESSIE SYSTEM RAILROADS
Baltimore & Ohio Railroad
Chesapeake & Ohio Railway
Western Maryland Railway

The Chessie System was incorporated in 1973 and has little history of its own; its components more than compensate in that regard, as does its B&O Railroad Museum in Baltimore.

The Baltimore & Ohio Railroad was incorporated in 1827 to build a railroad from Baltimore to, at that time, an undetermined point in the west. Motive power was to be horses — the steam locomotive was still in the future. The railroad reached Harpers Ferry in 1834, built a branch to Washington in 1835, and attained an early goal, the Ohio River, at Wheeling, West Virginia, in 1853. By then steam had replaced horses.

The B&O continued west, taking over existing lines through Newark and Willard, Ohio, and building a line from there to Chicago, which it reached in 1874. The railroad was extended east to Philadelphia in 1886. It made an agreement with the Philadelphia & Reading (later to become the Reading) and the Central of New Jersey for a route to New York.

In 1891 B&O completed a route between Cumberland and Willard, the present main line through Pittsburgh and Akron. Subsidiary Baltimore & Ohio Southwestern took over the Ohio & Mississippi in 1893, extending the B&O from Cincinnati to St. Louis. In 1910 the Baltimore & Ohio Chicago Terminal was formed as the successor to the Chicago Terminal Transfer Railroad.

Other acquisitions included a large interest in the Reading, acquired in 1901 (and the Reading was a major stockholder of the Central of New Jersey); a one-sixth interest in the Richmond-Washington Line (Richmond, Fredericksburg & Potomac) that same year; the Cincinnati, Hamilton & Dayton in 1917, creating a Cincinnati-Toledo route; control of the Buffalo, Rochester & Pittsburgh in 1929; and acquisition of the Alton Railroad in 1931. B&O sold the Alton to the Gulf, Mobile & Ohio in 1947 and disposed of its Reading interests to private investors in 1973. In the early 1960s control of the Baltimore & Ohio was acquired by the Chesapeake & Ohio.

The Chesapeake & Ohio had its beginnings in the Louisa Railroad, incorporated in 1836 to serve Louisa County, northwest of Richmond, Virginia. The railroad was renamed the Virginia Central in 1850, by which time it had reached Charlottesville. In 1867 the name was changed to Chesapeake & Ohio Railroad. The railroad reached the Ohio River at Huntington, W. Va., in 1873. The present C&O was incorporated in 1878. One component of the railroad traces its ancestry to the James River Canal, which was surveyed by George Washington.

The C&O built eastward to tidewater at Newport News in 1881. In 1910 it acquired the former Chicago, Cincinnati & Louisville line across Indiana, and throughout the 1920s it absorbed a number of short lines serving the coalfields of Kentucky and West Virginia. In the 1930s it became part of the Van Sweringen group of railroads, which also included Nickel Plate, Erie, Pere Marquette, and Hocking Valley. In 1945 a merger of those roads and others was proposed; the result was a merger of C&O and PM in 1947. At that same time under the leadership of Robert R. Young Chesapeake & Ohio became New York Central's largest stockholder, but C&O sold its NYC stock in 1954. Young is remembered for his desire to rebuild C&O's passenger business, manifestations of which included an enormous order for passenger cars from Pullman-Standard (not all were built, and many that were went directly to other roads) and the Budd-built steam-turbine-powered *Chessie* (which never operated in revenue service), named for the cat that had been C&O's trademark since 1933.

J. J. Young Jr.

Western Maryland diesels first traded glossy black paint for red and white and then Chessie System's yellow, vermilion, and blue. WM's station at Gettysburg, Pa., still stands, though it now houses a tourist information center rather than railroad offices.

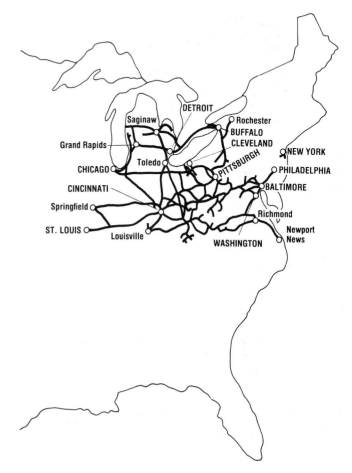

In more recent times, C&O obtained stock control of Baltimore & Ohio in the early 1960s; B&O in turn owned 43 percent of the stock of Western Maryland. C&O acquired control of Chicago South Shore & South Bend in 1966; however, the South Shore retains an identity separate from the Chessie System railroads.

The Western Maryland's oldest ancestor is the Baltimore, Carroll & Frederick, incorporated in 1852 to build from Baltimore to Hagerstown, Md. The road eventually made a connection with the Baltimore & Ohio east of Cumberland and extended lines into nearby portions of Pennsylvania. Just after the turn of the century George Gould acquired WM with

Continued on next page.

Baltimore & Ohio's image included double track, color-position-light signals, and the capitol-dome emblem. This photo shows the Chicago Trailer Jet on Sand Patch grade between Cumberland and Connellsville.

the intent of using it as the eastern end of a transcontinental system that was to include Wabash, Wheeling & Lake Erie, Missouri Pacific, and Denver & Rio Grande. The link between WM and W&LE was to be a Western Maryland extension to Connellsville, Pa., and the Wabash Pittsburgh Terminal, which later became the Pittsburgh & West Virginia. WM reached Cumberland in 1906 and met lines that extended southwest to Elkins and Durbin, W. Va., deep in coal country. WM reached Connellsville in 1912, but by then competing roads had begun to divert traffic, with the result that bankruptcy overtook WM, P&WV, and W&LE. The Pittsburgh & Lake Erie reached Connellsville in 1912, and P&WV got there in 1931.

WM became a coal carrier and a fast freight line, the latter in conjunction with Nickel Plate, Wheeling & Lake Erie, P&WV, Reading, and Central of New Jersey — the "Alphabet Route."

Baltimore & Ohio acquired WM stock in 1927 when John D. Rockefeller sold his holdings in WM and Wheeling & Lake Erie. B&O, Nickel Plate, and New York Central each bought part of the W&LE stock, but the other two roads had no interest in acquiring WM. In 1932 B&O was required to place its WM stock in trust. C&O and B&O acquired control of WM in 1968. The Connellsville Extension, which paralleled B&O's line between Cumberland and Connellsville, has been abandoned, and WM is largely a feeder to other portions of Chessie System.

In November 1980 Chessie System, Inc., merged with Seaboard Coast Line Industries to form CSX Corporation (page 70). CSX's principal holdings are the Chessie System railroads and Seaboard System. In late 1982 Chessie System sought ICC approval to purchase the Newburgh & South Shore, a switching line at Cleveland, from U. S. Steel.

Address of general offices: P. O. Box 6419, Cleveland, OH 44101
Miles of road operated: 11,142
Reporting marks: BO, CO, WM
Number of locomotives: 2080
Number of freight cars: 119,377
Principal commodities carried: Coal, steel, grain, chemicals, automobiles, auto parts
Major yards: Chicago (Barr), Cincinnati (Queensgate), Cumberland, Md., Hampton Roads, Va., Russell, Ky., Toledo (Walbridge)

The Chessie railroads have long been coal haulers, and Chesapeake & Ohio has the greatest association with coal, as exemplified by this lash-up of GE and EMD hood units heading a coal train at Tuckahoe, W. Va.

Gary Dolzall

Principal shops:
Locomotive: Cumberland, Grand Rapids, Mich. (Wyoming), Huntington, W. Va.
Car: Raceland, Ky.
Radio frequencies: 160.230, 160.320, 160.530 (B&O yard), 161.160 (C&O yard)
Passenger routes:
Amtrak — Washington-Pittsburgh (*Capitol Limited*, *Blue Ridge*), Washington-Cincinnati-Chicago (*Cardinal*); Richmond, Va.-Newport News (*Colonial*, *Tidewater*)
Maryland Dept. of Transportation — Washington-Baltimore, Washington-Brunswick, Md.-Martinsburg, W. Va.
Port Authority of Allegheny County — Pittsburgh-Versailles, Pa.
Historical and technical societies:

Baltimore & Ohio Railroad Historical Society, Box 13578, Baltimore, MD 21203
Chesapeake & Ohio Historical Society, 372 Walnut Avenue, Waynesboro, VA 22980
Western Maryland Railway Historical Society, Union Bridge, MD 21791
Recommended reading:
Impossible Challenge, by Herbert H. Harwood Jr., published in 1975 by Barnard, Roberts & Co., Baltimore (ISBN 0-934118-17-5)
Western Maryland Railway, by Roger Cook and Karl Zimmermann, published in 1981 by Howell-North, P. O. Box 3051, La Jolla, CA 92038 (ISBN 0-8310-7139-7)
Chessie's Road, by Charles W. Turner, published in 1956 by Garrett & Massie, Richmond, VA
Date: March 1983

CHICAGO & ILLINOIS MIDLAND RAILWAY

In 1888 the Pawnee Railroad was chartered to build west from Pawnee, Illinois, a few miles south of Springfield, to a connection with the St. Louis & Chicago (now Illinois Central Gulf), a distance of 4 miles. In 1892 the road more than doubled its mileage with an extension west to the Chicago & Alton (now also ICG) at Auburn.

The Illinois Midland Coal Co., owned jointly by Peabody Coal Co. and Samuel Insull's Chicago Edison and Commonwealth Electric companies, had mines in the area. In 1905 the coal company purchased the railroad and organized it as the Central Illinois Railway. Later that year the railroad's name was changed to Chicago & Illinois Midland to avoid confusion with the neighboring Illinois Central. During the teens the railroad was extended east to Taylorville to connect with the Baltimore & Ohio and the Wabash and west to a connection with the Chicago & North Western.

In 1926 the railroad purchased the Springfield-Peoria trackage of the defunct Chicago, Peoria & St. Louis and obtained trackage rights from Illinois Central from Pawnee Jct. (now Cimic) to Springfield. As a result the coal traffic pattern changed: Instead of moving to connecting roads for rail haulage north to Chicago, it now moved to the Illinois River at Havana and then north by barge.

C&IM's steam power was noteworthy on a couple of counts. Passenger trains were handled by a trio of 4-4-0s built in 1927 and 1928 by Baldwin, the last of their wheel arrangement built for a Class 1 railroad. In the 1940s and early 1950s C&IM purchased a number of ex-Wabash and ex-Atlantic Coast Line 2-10-2s to replace smaller locomotives; the road did not dieselize until 1955.

Construction of a mine-mouth generating plant in the 1960s and later the restrictions against burning high-sulfur Illinois coal in generating stations again changed the railroad's traffic pattern. Now much of the traffic is unit coal trains of low-sulfur coal from Wyoming and Montana received from the Burlington Northern and Chicago & North Western at Peoria for delivery to Edison's generating station at Powerton, near Pekin, and to Havana for shipment by barge to generating stations in the Chicago area.

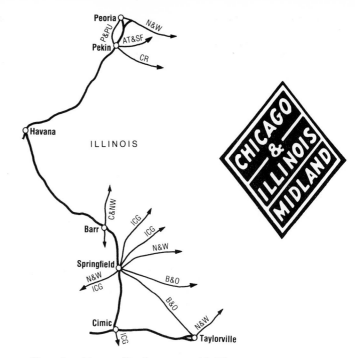

The railroad is owned by Commonwealth Edison, formed in 1907 by the merger of Chicago Edison and Commonwealth Electric.

Address of general offices: P. O. Box 139, Springfield, IL 62705
Miles of road operated: 121
Reporting marks: CIM
Number of locomotives: 20
Number of freight cars: 1198

Principal commodities carried: Coal
Shops: Springfield, Ill.
Junctions with other railroads:
Atchison, Topeka & Santa Fe: Pekin
Baltimore & Ohio: Springfield; Taylorville
Chicago & North Western: Barr
Conrail: Pekin
Illinois Central Gulf: Cimic; Pekin; Springfield
Norfolk & Western: Peoria; Springfield; Taylorville
Peoria & Pekin Union: Peoria; Peoria
Radio frequencies: 160.950, 160.290 (yard)
Recommended reading: *Chicago & Illinois Midland*, by Richard R. Wallin, Paul H. Stringham, and John Szwajkart, published in 1979 by Golden West Books, P. O. Box 8136, San Marino, CA 91108 (ISBN 0-87095-077-0)
Date: February 1983

Three dark-green SD38s lift a unit coal train bound for the car dumper at Havana, Ill., out of the Mackinaw River valley in April 1978.

Wayne Bridges

CHICAGO & NORTH WESTERN TRANSPORTATION COMPANY

The railroad capital of the United States, Chicago, saw its first locomotive in 1848: the *Pioneer* of the Galena & Chicago Union Railroad. The G&CU, chartered in 1836, lay dormant for 12 years before construction began. By 1850, though, its rails reached west to Elgin and in 1853 to Freeport, where it connected with the Illinois Central line under construction from Cairo at the southern tip of Illinois to Galena in the northwest corner of the state. The Galena & Chicago Union then built westward from what is now West Chicago, reaching Fulton, Illinois, on the Mississippi River, in 1855.

In 1855 the Chicago, St. Paul & Fond du Lac was organized to extend an existing road northwest from Cary, Ill., through Madison and La Crosse, Wisconsin, to St. Paul, Minnesota, and north through Fond du Lac, Wisconsin, to the iron and copper country south of Lake Superior.

The road was reorganized in 1859 as the Chicago & North Western Railway. In 1864 it was consolidated with the Galena & Chicago Union. In 1866 the C&NW leased the Chicago & Milwaukee, which linked the two cities of its name.

The C&NW continued to acquire other railroads, notable among them the Chicago, St. Paul, Minneapolis & Omaha (the "Omaha Road"), which retained a separate corporate existence until 1972. By the early part of the twentieth century C&NW rails reached west to Rapid City, South Dakota, and Lander, Wyoming, north to Duluth, Minn., and south almost to St. Louis. The road became Union Pacific's preferred eastern connection and handled UP's fleet of *City* streamliners between Chicago and Omaha until 1955, when they were transferred to the Milwaukee Road.

In the late 1950s and 1960s C&NW merged with several smaller rail-

Continued on next page.

57

Two distinctive Chicago & North Western characteristics appear in this photo: left-hand operation on double track and an odd type of semaphore signal (being replaced here with color-light signals).

J. David Ingles.

roads: Litchfield & Madison in 1958, giving C&NW a route into St. Louis; Minneapolis & St. Louis in 1960; Chicago Great Western in 1968; and Des Moines & Central Iowa (which owned the Fort Dodge, Des Moines & Southern) in 1968. In 1972 C&NW joined with Missouri Pacific to purchase the Alton & Southern from Alcoa, but in 1973 C&NW sold its half to St. Louis Southwestern.

The Chicago & North Western Transportation Company was incorporated in 1970 as the North Western Employees Transportation Co. In 1972 it took its present name and purchased the transportation assets of the Chicago & North Western Railway.

Address of general offices: 1 North Western Center, Chicago, IL 60606

Miles of road operated: 8243

Reporting marks: CGW, CMO, CNW, FDDM, LM, MSTL

Number of locomotives: 1040

Number of freight cars: 36,086

Principal commodities carried: Grain, coal, food products

Major yards: Chicago (Proviso)

Principal shops: Chicago; Clinton, Iowa; Oelwein, Iowa

Radio frequencies: 160.890, 160.455 (yard), 161.040 (commuter)

Passenger routes: Regional Transportation Authority — Chicago-Kenosha, Wis.; Chicago-Harvard, Ill.; Chicago-McHenry, Ill.; Chicago-Geneva, Ill.

Historical and technical society: Chicago & North Western Historical Society, 17004 Locust Drive, Hazel Crest, IL 60429

Recommended reading:

The 400 Story, by Jim Scribbins, published in 1982 by PTJ Publishing Inc., P. O. Box 397, Park Forest, IL 60466 (ISBN 0-937658-07-3)

Prairie Rails, by Robert Olmsted, published in 1979 by McMillan Publications, 3208 Halsey Drive, Woodbridge, IL 60515 (ISBN 0-934228-02-7)

CHICAGO, MILWAUKEE, ST. PAUL & PACIFIC RAILROAD

The Milwaukee & Mississippi Rail Road was chartered in 1847. It laid its first rails in 1850, and in 1851 it reached from Milwaukee 20 miles west to Waukesha, Wisconsin. The road reached Prairie du Chien on the Mississippi River in 1857. In 1863 the LaCrosse & Milwaukee (completed in 1858 between the cities of its name) was reorganized as the Milwaukee & St. Paul, and in 1867 it purchased the Milwaukee & Prairie du Chien, successor to the Milwaukee & Mississippi. By then these predecessors of the Milwaukee Road had covered much of southern Wisconsin with rail lines.

In 1874 the railroad's name was changed to Chicago, Milwaukee & St. Paul. At that time it extended from Chicago north and northwest well into Minnesota and embarked on a period of expansion. The road reached Council Bluffs, Iowa, across the Missouri River from Omaha, in 1882, and reached Kansas City in 1887. By then the map of the railroad included four east-west lines across northern Iowa and southern Minnesota.

In 1901 the railroad decided it needed an outlet to the Pacific. Its western connections were controlled by Harriman and Hill, both of whom also controlled competitive lines parallel to the Milwaukee Road. In 1902 a proposal was made to build west to the Pacific at Eureka, California, but in 1905 the decision was made to head for Seattle instead. Construction began in 1906, and in 1909 the Pacific Coast Extension was completed — through the territory served by the Northern Pacific and indeed often within sight of the NP. The cost of construction was more than four times the estimate, and on top of that the Milwaukee Road then electrified 656 miles of the new line, from Harlowton, Montana, to Avery, Idaho, and from Othello, Washington, to Tacoma and Seattle.

In 1921 the Milwaukee Road leased the Chicago, Terre Haute & Southeastern to gain access to the coalfields of southern Indiana, and in 1922 it acquired the Chicago, Milwaukee & Gary to gain access to the CTH&SE. Both acquisitions were heavily in debt, and bankruptcy for their parent soon followed.

The Milwaukee Road emerged from reorganization in 1928, entered receivership in 1935, was again reorganized in 1945, and yet again entered reorganization proceedings in 1977. Throughout this period the Milwaukee Road projected an image of resourcefulness — or quick footwork. It built almost all the passenger cars for the fleet of *Hiawathas* in the Milwaukee shops. After 1955 it served as the Omaha-Chicago route of Union Pacific's *City* streamliners. It scheduled fast freights between Chicago and the Pacific Northwest. It dealt with its aging electrified plant in several ways — purchase of locomotives intended for Russia, multiple unit operation of diesels and electrics, and eventual dismantling.

The major result of the 1977 reorganization was the amputation of everything west of Miles City, Mont., to concentrate on a "Milwaukee II" system serving Chicago, Kansas City, Minneapolis and St. Paul, Duluth

Continued on next page.

Since 1978 Milwaukee Road has operated a fleet of fast piggyback trains over its double-track main line between Chicago and the Twin Cities — they are called *Sprints*.

MILW

(on BN rails from St. Paul), and Louisville (by trackage rights over the former Monon line of the Seaboard System). At present it is anticipated that Grand Trunk Corporation will purchase the railroad.

Address of general offices: 516 W. Jackson Boulevard, Chicago, IL 60606

Miles of road operated: 3200

Reporting marks: MILW

Number of locomotives: 324

Number of freight cars: 10,500

Principal commodities carried: Agricultural products, wood and lumber, coal

Major yards: Bensenville, Ill., Milwaukee, Wis., St. Paul, Minn.

Principal shops: Milwaukee, Wis.

Radio frequencies: 160.770

Passenger routes:

Amtrak — Chicago-Milwaukee-St. Paul (*Empire Builder, LaSalle, Nicollet, Marquette, Radisson*)

Regional Transportation Authority (through RTA's subsidiary Northeast Illinois Railroad Corp.) — Chicago-Elgin, Ill.; Chicago-Fox Lake, Ill.

Historical and technical society: Milwaukee Road Railfans Association, 7504 W. Ruby Avenue, Milwaukee, WI 53218

Recommended reading:

THE HIAWATHA STORY, by Jim Scribbins, published in 1970 by Kalmbach Publishing Co., 1027 North Seventh Street, Milwaukee, WI 53233

Milwaukee Rails, by Robert P. Olmsted, published in 1980 by McMillan Publications, 3208 Halsey Drive, Woodridge, IL 60517 (ISBN 0-934228-04-3)

Date: April 1983

CHICAGO SOUTH SHORE & SOUTH BEND RAILROAD

Late in 1901 the Chicago & Indiana Air Line Railway was incorporated. Nearly two years later it opened a 3.4-mile streetcar line between East Chicago and Indiana Harbor, Indiana. In 1904 the name of the company was changed to Chicago, Lake Shore & South Bend. The pace of construction accelerated, and in 1908 the entire line was in service from Hammond to South Bend, 76 miles. The line was electrified at 6600 volts AC, unusual for an interurban, and the grades and curves of the line were more typical of a heavy steam railroad than of a light electric railway. A year later the line was extended west across the state line to a connection with Illinois Central at Kensington, Illinois.

Samuel Insull acquired control of the company in 1925, reorganized it as the Chicago South Shore & South Bend, and undertook a reconstruction that changed it from an interurban to a heavy electric railroad. The modernization included steel cars, change of power system to 1500 volts DC, and operation through to Chicago over IC's newly electrified suburban line.

Insull's control ended in 1932 and the company entered bankruptcy. New management continued to improve the road, though, and moved it further into the steam-road category — interurbans were dying off faster than they had been born a few decades before — with interline passenger ticketing, off-line freight solicitation, rebuilt passenger cars, and in 1956 a bypass around the city streets of East Chicago on a right of way shared with the Indiana Toll Road.

Chesapeake & Ohio acquired control of the South Shore in 1967. Electric freight operation ended in 1981, but passenger service continued under the wires, and the arrival in 1982 of new cars purchased by the Northern Indiana Commuter Transportation District permitted the retirement

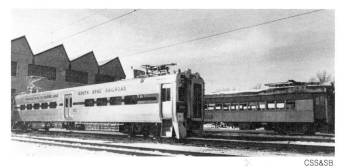

CSS&SB.

New and old passenger cars pose at South Shore's Michigan City shops. In the foreground is one of 36 new cars acquired in 1982. The shell was built in Japan by Sumitomo Corporation, and the electrical equipment is by General Electric. Car No. 13, beyond, was built by Pullman in 1926 and lengthened and modernized in 1946 by the railroad.

of the Insull-era cars, which had begun to show their age in the early 1960s.

Address of general offices: Carroll Avenue, Michigan City, IN 46360
Miles of road operated: 76
Reporting marks: CSS

Continued on next page.

Number of locomotives: 10
Number of freight cars: 28
Number of passenger cars: 73
Shops: Michigan City
Junctions with other railroads:
Belt Railway of Chicago: Chicago
Chessie System: East Chicago, Gary, Chicago, Michigan City
Conrail: Gary, Michigan City, South Bend, Terre Coupee
Elgin, Joliet & Eastern: Gary
Illinois Central Gulf: Kensington

Indiana Harbor Belt: Chicago
Norfolk & Western: Gary, Michigan City
Seaboard System: Chicago
Radio frequencies: 161.355, 161.010, 161.025 (on ICG)
Passenger routes: Chicago (Randolph St.)-South Bend (Chicago-Kensington on ICG)
Recommended reading: *South Shore — The Last Interurban*, by William D. Middleton, published in 1970 by Golden West Books, P. O. Box 8136, San Marino, CA 91108
Date: March 1983

CHIHUAHUA PACIFIC RAILWAY
(Ferrocarril de Chihuahua al Pacifico)

The ancestor of the Chihuahua Pacific was the Kansas City, Mexico & Orient, organized in 1900 by Arthur Stilwell, who had built the Kansas City Southern. Stilwell's goal was to build a line from Kansas City to Topolobampo, Sinaloa, Mexico, on the Gulf of California — Pacific tidewater that was nearer Kansas City than San Francisco Bay. The U. S. portion of the road — Wichita, Kansas, to Alpine, Texas — became part of the Santa Fe in 1928.

At that time the Mexican portion of the line was in two separate pieces. The major part extended from Ojinaga, Chihuahua, on the U. S. border (there was as yet no rail connection on the U. S. side) through the city of Chihuahua to Creel and included the former Northwestern of Mexico line from Ciudad Juarez, opposite El Paso, Texas, to La Junta, Chihuahua. The smaller part extended inland from Topolobampo to El Fuerte. Separating the two portions of the line was some of the roughest and wildest landscape in North America, Mexico's Sierra Madre. The Mexican line was organized as the Chihuahua Pacific, and in 1940 it was acquired by the Mexican government. Construction resumed in 1952 and the two parts of the line were joined in 1961.

Address of general offices: P. O. Box 46, Chihuahua, Chih., Mexico
Miles of road operated: 942

Joe McMillan.

Three Ch-P trains meet at Divisadero Barrancas at the rim of the Copper Canyon: a westbound pair of Fiat railcars (autovias), the eastbound Vista Train behind GP28 803, and an eastbound freight occupying the siding ahead of the Vista Train.

Reporting marks: CHP
Number of locomotives: 57
Number of freight cars: 1459
Number of passenger cars: 48
Shops: La Junta, Chih.
Junctions with other railroads:
Atchison, Topeka & Santa Fe: Ciudad Juarez, Chih.; Ojinaga, Chih.
Mexican Pacific: Los Mochis, Sin.
Missouri Pacific: El Paso, Tex.
National Railways of Mexico:
 Ciudad Juarez, Chih.

Morse, Chih.
 Tabalaopa, Chih.
Pacific (Ferrocarril del Pacifico): Sufragio, Sin.
Southern Pacific: El Paso, Tex.
Passenger routes: Chihuahua, Chih.-Los Mochis, Sin.; Ciudad Juarez, Chih.-La Junta, Chih.
Map: See National Railways of Mexico, page 132
Recommended reading: *Destination Topolobampo*, by John Leeds Kerr, published in 1968 by Golden West Books, P. O. Box 8136, San Marino, CA 91108

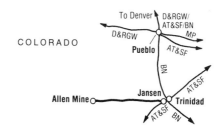

COLORADO & WYOMING RAILWAY

At the turn of the century the Colorado Fuel & Iron Co. of Pueblo was expanding and needed a new source of iron ore. Ore was found at Sunrise, Wyoming, on the North Platte River almost due north of Cheyenne. The steel company incorporated the Colorado & Wyoming Railway in 1899 to build and operate a railroad from Pueblo to Sunrise and also from Pueblo to the headwaters of the Purgatoire River in the mountains west of Trinidad, Colorado. The railroad quickly constructed a line from Hartville Junction, on the Colorado & Southern north of Wheatland, 14.5 miles to Hartville and Sunrise.

At the same time construction began on the Southern Division, beginning from a junction with the Santa Fe 2 miles west of Trinidad. That line was opened to coal mines at Primero and Segundo in 1901. As other

mines and coke ovens were established, the railroad was extended to Tercio, Cuatro, Quinto, and Sexto.

The road's Middle Division was formed in 1902 when C&W took over switching duties at parent CF&I's Minnequa Works in Pueblo from Santa Fe, Denver & Rio Grande, and Colorado & Southern.

In 1915 the Chicago, Burlington & Quincy built westward along the North Platte River to a connection with the Colorado & Southern at Wendover, Wyo., 3 miles north of Hartville Junction and crossing C&W's Northern Division at Guernsey. In 1916 C&W abandoned its line between Guernsey and Hartville Junction in favor of an interchange with CB&Q and C&S at Guernsey.

There have been two major changes in recent years. In 1975 construc-

Continued on next page

tion of the Trinidad Dam caused relocation of the Southern Division between Jansen and Madrid. The closing of the iron mine at Sunrise caused the shutdown of the Northern Division in 1980, leaving C&W with only two separate divisions, not three. The road is owned by CF&I Steel, successor to Colorado Fuel & Iron.

Address of general offices: P. O. Box 316, Pueblo, CO 81002
Miles of road operated: 110
Reporting marks: CW
Number of locomotives: 18
Number of freight cars: 168
Principal commodities carried: Coal
Junctions with other railroads:
Atchison, Topeka & Santa Fe
Burlington Northern
Denver & Rio Grande Western: all at Jansen and Minnequa, Colo.
Radio frequencies: 161.250
Recommended reading: *Mountain to Mill*, by William H. McKenzie, published in 1982 by MAC Publishing, P. O. Box 7037, Colorado Springs, CO 80933 (ISBN 0-936206-16-0)

Barry E. Silver.

Colorado & Wyoming's two orange-and-white GP38-2s prepare to depart from Jansen, on the outskirts of Trinidad, Colo., with a train of empty hopper cars for the Allen Mine.

COLUMBUS & GREENVILLE RAILWAY

The narrow gauge Greenville, Columbus & Birmingham was chartered in 1878 to build a railroad across Mississippi. It was soon allied with the Georgia Pacific Railway (no relation to the present-day wood products company) and was standard-gauged in 1889. The Georgia Pacific eventually became part of the Southern Railway System, but it was necessary for the line in Mississippi to remain a separate entity because of a state law requiring that railroads operating in the state be incorporated there.

In 1920 Southern cast off its Mississippi stepchild as the Columbus & Greenville Railroad. It quickly became a bankrupt operation. It was purchased by A. T. Stovall, reorganized as the Columbus & Greenville Railway, and operated at a profit into the 1960s. The road then asked to be included in the merger of Illinois Central and Gulf, Mobile & Ohio — it intersected IC at 6 points and GM&O at 3. In September 1972 the road

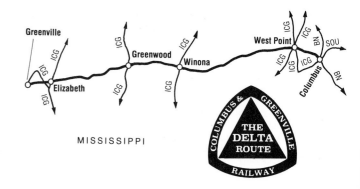

A westbound freight prepares to leave Columbus behind a pair of ex-Florida East Coast GP7s.

became part of Illinois Central Gulf. Floods in 1973 closed part of the line. Shipper groups petitioned and the state public service commission ordered ICG to restore service. ICG suggested that local interests buy the railroad and return it to independent status. That happened in 1975, and since then the new management has been rebuilding the line.

Address of general offices: P. O. Box 6000, Columbus, MS 39701

Miles of road operated: 168

Reporting marks: CAGY

Number of locomotives: 17

Number of freight cars: 1425

Principal commodities carried: Steel, agricultural products, furniture, pulpwood, coal, food products

Shops: Columbus

Junctions with other railroads:

Burlington Northern: Columbus

Illinois Central Gulf:

Columbus

Elizabeth

Greenville

West Point

Winona

Southern: Columbus

Radio frequencies: 160.230 (switching), 160.245 (road)

Recommended reading: *Delta Route*, by Louis R. Saillard, published in 1981 by the Columbus & Greenville Railway, P. O. Box 6000, Columbus, MS 39701

Date: March 1983

CONRAIL (Consolidated Rail Corporation)

Shortly after Penn Central went bankrupt in 1970, Congress created the United States Railway Association to plan a reorganization of Penn Central and act as its banker. The result was Consolidated Rail Corporation (Conrail), which began operation on April 1, 1976. It took over the railroad properties and operations of six bankrupt eastern railroads — Central of New Jersey, Erie Lackawanna, Lehigh & Hudson River, Lehigh Valley, Penn Central, and Reading — and Pennsylvania-Reading Seashore Lines. Penn Central was the product of the merger in 1968 of the two rival giants of eastern railroading, Pennsylvania and New York Central, with the later addition of the New Haven. Its collapse, hastened by the depressed steel and automobile industries which provided much of Penn Central's traffic, was the precipitating factor in the formation of Conrail. The other railroads included all the "anthracite railroads," those traditionally associated with mining and carrying anthracite coal. Their financial problems had been aggravated by damage from hurricanes that had hit New York and Pennsylvania in 1972.

Conrail started out with $2.1 billion from the U. S. government, which purchased Conrail debentures and preferred stock. Early in its existence Conrail sold the Northeast Corridor lines (Boston-Washington, Springfield-New Haven, and Philadelphia-Harrisburg) to Amtrak; abandoned, sold to short lines, or agreed to operate with state subsidy another 6000 route miles; and gradually shed its commuter operations to other railroads or operating authorities (except for the Cleveland-Youngstown train, which was discontinued). Conrail embarked on an intense program of rebuilding roadbed and track, repairing old locomotives and cars, and purchasing new ones.

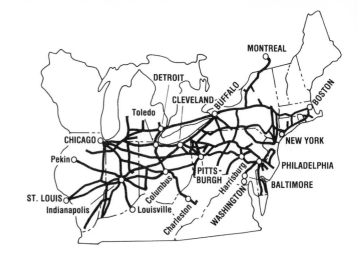

Like Chessie System, Conrail has only a few years of its own history, but the history of its predecessors is extensive.

Central Railroad of New Jersey was opened in 1852 between Elizabeth and Phillipsburg, New Jersey. In 1864 the line was extended a few miles east to Jersey City, and in 1871 the railroad leased the Lehigh & Susquehanna, expanding into Pennsylvania. CNJ also had a line into southern New Jersey, the route of the Jersey City-Atlantic City *Blue Comet*, a deluxe coach train operated from 1929 to 1941. In the 1940s CNJ's lines in Pennsylvania (the leased Lehigh & Susquehanna) were reorganized for a while as the Central Railroad of Pennsylvania in an attempt to avoid taxation by New Jersey. In 1961 CNJ purchased about 40 miles of the defunct Lehigh & New England. CNJ was controlled by the Reading Company, with which it formed a Jersey City-Philadelphia passenger route also used until 1958 by Baltimore & Ohio.

Erie Lackawanna was created in 1960 by the merger of the Erie and the Delaware, Lackawanna & Western. The Erie — built originally with a track gauge of 6 feet — was completed from Piermont, N. Y., on the Hudson, to Dunkirk, on Lake Erie, in 1851. It was later extended to Jersey City, Buffalo, and Chicago. The Erie always seemed to be the subject of one financial manipulation or another; eventually it achieved some stability as a New York-Chicago route, primarily for freight.

The Delaware, Lackawanna & Western was built from Scranton, Pa., to the Delaware River in 1856 and made a connection with the Central of New Jersey in 1857 for a route to New York. In 1868 it leased the Morris & Essex to gain its own route to the Hudson. In 1882 the Lackawanna reached Buffalo, its western terminus. In the early part of the twentieth century the railroad embarked on a number of engineering projects: line relocations, massive concrete viaducts, and a general upgrading of the property. In 1930 DL&W electrified its suburban service out of its ferry terminal at Hoboken, N. J. The original physical plant of that electrification is only now being replaced.

The Lackawanna advertised that it used clean-burning anthracite for fuel. The road's symbol was Phoebe Snow, a young woman whose gown, to quote one of the many verses, "stayed white from morn 'til night upon the Road of Anthracite."

Lehigh & Hudson River was incorporated in 1882. Its line from Easton, Pa., to Maybrook, N. Y., was a bridge route: It connected the New Haven's route from New Haven to Maybrook with the Pennsylvania at Phillipsburg, N. J., and the Central of New Jersey and the Lehigh Valley at Easton. Inclusion of the New Haven in Penn Central in 1968 altered traffic patterns, drying up much of L&HR's business, and destruction of part of New Haven's bridge over the Hudson at Poughkeepsie bridge by fire in 1974 rendered L&HR even more redundant. L&HR was owned by Central of New Jersey, Erie Lackawanna, Lehigh Valley, Pennsylvania, and Reading.

Lehigh Valley's earliest ancestor was the Delaware, Lehigh, Schuylkill, & Susquehanna, incorporated in 1846 to haul anthracite from Mauch Chunk, Pa., to Easton. In 1853 the company took Lehigh Valley as its name. It opened the line in 1855. By construction and by acquisition of other railroads LV made a connection with the Erie at Waverly, Pa., in

Leigh F. Savoye.

Typical of Conrail operations is this piggyback train speeding west along the Mohawk River at Palatine Bridge, N. Y. Note that the former New York Central main line has been slimmed from four tracks to two mains plus a siding. The carefully aligned welded rail is a result of Conrail's massive upgrading program.

1869. In 1876 the road reached Buffalo by financing the addition to Erie's broad gauge track of a third rail for standard gauge trains. LV reached Buffalo with its own line in 1892. The eastern end of the railroad was pushed east to Perth Amboy in 1875 and to Newark and a terminal on New York Harbor in 1891.

LV discontinued the last of its passenger trains in 1961, one of the first major roads to do so. In 1962 the ICC authorized the Pennsylvania Rail-

Continued on next page.

road to acquire control of Lehigh Valley. Through subsidiaries the Pennsy had held a substantial interest in LV since the late 1920s. By 1965 PRR had acquired 97 percent of LV's stock.

Penn Central was formed in 1968 by the merger of Pennsylvania and New York Central. Later that year PC absorbed the New York, New Haven & Hartford. PC was scarcely two years old when it declared bankruptcy in June 1970. As for PC's antecedents:

New York Central started with the Mohawk & Hudson, which was opened between Albany & Schenectady in 1831. In 1853 it was merged with nine other railroads to form the New York Central, which connected Albany with Buffalo. The Hudson River Railroad was opened in 1851 from New York to Albany; in 1869 it was merged with NYC to form the New York Central & Hudson River. In 1914 the New York Central title returned as the name of the merger of the NYC&HR and the Lake Shore & Michigan Southern. By then the New York Central System was virtually complete: New York and Boston through Albany and Buffalo to Chicago via both Cleveland and Detroit, with other lines to such diverse points as St. Louis, Cincinnati, Charleston, West Virginia, Montreal, and Ottawa. Among NYC's subsidiaries were Boston & Albany; Michigan Central; Big Four (Cleveland, Cincinnati, Chicago & St. Louis); West Shore; Peoria & Eastern; and Toledo & Ohio Central. In addition NYC owned large interests in Pittsburgh & Lake Erie; Indiana Harbor Belt; and Toronto, Hamilton & Buffalo.

By following the Hudson and Mohawk rivers NYC's main line avoided the mountains that other eastern lines had to battle — hence the road's slogan, "The Water Level Route." NYC's New York-Chicago *20th Century Limited* was generally acknowledged to be the country's finest passenger train. The road's Grand Central Terminal in New York was — and is — a notable feat of railroad engineering.

New York, New Haven & Hartford was incorporated in 1872 as a consolidation of the New York & New Haven and the Hartford & New Haven. It leased and purchased other lines and soon expanded to cover all of southeastern Massachusetts, Rhode Island, and Connecticut. The New Haven was an early experimenter with electrification — it owned a number of traction lines — and between 1905 and 1914 it electrified its four-track main line between New York and New Haven.

The New Haven entered bankruptcy in 1935 and emerged from reorganization in 1947 only to go bankrupt again in 1961. There were several causes of its financial problems: flamboyant and shady management, construction of parallel superhighways that allowed trucks to siphon off much of the freight traffic, revenues that were derived almost as much from passenger service as from freight traffic, and flood damage from hurricanes.

The Pennsylvania Railroad was incorporated in 1846. It was opened from Harrisburg to Altoona in 1850 and on to Pittsburgh in 1852. It extended east and west by acquiring other railroads. West of Buffalo and Pittsburgh it went most of the places that New York Central did; its principal eastern lines were New York-Philadelphia-Washington, Philadelphia-Harrisburg-Pittsburgh, and Baltimore-Harrisburg-Buffalo, with branches, secondary lines, and freight bypasses blanketing the region.

Pennsy was for many years the largest U. S. railroad in terms of tonnage and revenue, and its slogan was "The Standard Railroad of the World." A number of traits were distinctive to PRR: steam locomotives with Belpaire boilers (simply put, a flat-topped firebox), a random numbering scheme for steam locomotives, and position-light signals, whose aspects were made up of vertical, horizontal, and diagonal rows of amber lights.

Recognizing the advantage that rival New York Central had with a terminal in Manhattan, Pennsy responded with Pennsylvania Station, opened in 1910. Included in the project were tunnels under the Hudson and East rivers, massive yards on Long Island, and, a few years later, construction of the Hell Gate Bridge to afford a connection with the New Haven. Another piece of engineering that was almost a Pennsylvania trademark was Horseshoe Curve west of Altoona. Although one of the four tracks has been removed recently and traffic is far less than it once was, it remains an impressive sight. PRR electrified most of its mainline trackage east of Harrisburg in the late 1920s and 1930s.

Either directly or through subsidiaries Pennsy controlled a number of other railroads: Norfolk & Western; Wabash; Detroit, Toledo & Ironton; Long Island; Toledo, Peoria & Western (owned jointly with Santa Fe); and Lehigh Valley.

Pennsylvania-Reading Seashore Lines was formed in 1933 to con-

Ernest L. Novak.

A pair of brand new General Electric B23-7s leads a freight across the Maumee River bridge at Toledo, Ohio.

solidate the operations of Pennsylvania's West Jersey & Seashore and Reading's Atlantic City Railroad in southern New Jersey between Camden, across the Delaware River from Philadelphia, and the seashore resort cities.

The Reading Company began as the Philadelphia & Reading Railroad, chartered in 1833 and opened from Philadelphia through Reading to Pottsville, Pa., in 1842. An affiliated company, the Philadelphia & Reading Coal & Iron Co., began to buy much of the anthracite land in the

area. In a reorganization in 1896 the Reading Company, a holding company, acquired the railroad and the coal and iron company and in 1901 control of the Central Railroad of New Jersey. In 1923 the company merged a large number of wholly owned subsidiaries and became an operating company.

Reading's passenger business was almost totally suburban, and its freight business was also largely short-haul. Reading had considerable anthracite traffic, and its route west from Allentown through Reading and Harrisburg carried much freight that bypassed Philadelphia, Baltimore, and Washington.

Address of general offices: 6 Penn Center Plaza, Philadelphia, PA 19104

Miles of road operated: 15,602

Reporting marks: BA, BCK, CNJ, CR, CRI, DLW, EL, ERIE, LHR, LNE, LV, NB, NH, NYC, PAE, PE, PC, PCA, PCB, PRR, RDG, RR, TOC

Number of locomotives: 3903

Number of freight cars: 106,234

Principal commodities carried: Coal, grain, intermodal traffic

Major yards: Albany, N. Y. (Selkirk); Columbus, Ohio (Buckeye); Elkhart, Ind.; Harrisburg, Pa. (Enola); Indianapolis (Avon); Pittsburgh (Conway); Syracuse, N. Y. (DeWitt)

Principal shops: Altoona, Pa.; Meadville, Pa.; Hollidaysburg, Pa.; Reading, Pa.

Radio frequencies: 160.800, 161.070

Passenger routes:

Amtrak — New York (Grand Central)-Albany-Buffalo-Chicago (*Lake Shore*, *Maple Leaf*, *Adirondack*, Empire Service), Harrisburg-Pittsburgh-Valparaiso, Ind.-Chicago (*Broadway Limited*, *Pennsylvanian*, *Calumet*, *Indiana Connection*), Boston-Albany (*Lake Shore*), Toledo-Detroit-Chicago (*Lake Cities*, *Wolverine*, *St. Clair*)

Commuter — None of these services are now operated by Conrail, and some operate on rails owned by Amtrak. They are grouped here by predecessor railroad for clarity. See also the pages for the various commuter authorities.

New Haven — New York (Grand Central)-New Haven, Bridgeport-Waterbury, Norwalk-Danbury, Stamford-New Canaan

Continued on next page.

New York Central — New York (Grand Central) to Dover Plains and Poughkeepsie, N. Y.

Erie Lackawanna — Hoboken to Dover, Gladstone, Montclair, and Netcong, N. J., and Port Jervis and Spring Valley, N. Y.

Central of New Jersey — Newark-Phillipsburg, N. J.

Pennsylvania Railroad — New York (Penn Station) to Bay Head and Trenton, N. J.; Princeton Jct.-Princeton, N. J.; Philadelphia (Suburban Station) to Trenton, N. J., and Chestnut Hill, Manayunk, Marcus Hook, Paoli, and West Chester, Pa.; Baltimore-Washington

Reading — Philadelphia (Reading Terminal) to Chestnut Hill, Doylestown, Newtown, Norristown, Warminster, and Yardley, Pa.

Historical and technical societies (for predecessor railroads):

Anthracite Railroads Historical Society (CNJ, DL&W, L&HR, L&NE, LV, RDG), P. O. Box 119, Bridgeport, PA 19405

Erie Lackawanna Historical Society (also covers Erie and Lackawanna), 22 Duquesne Court, New Castle, DE 19720

New Haven Railroad Historical & Technical Association, 9 Shady Lane, Oxford, MA 01540

New York Central System Historical Society, P. O. Box 10027, Cleveland, OH 44110

Pennsylvania Railroad Technical & Historical Society, P. O. Box 389, Upper Darby, PA 19082

Reading Company Technical & Historical Society, P. O. Box 356, Birdsboro, PA 19508

CSX CORPORATION

On November 1, 1980, Chessie System, Inc. (Baltimore & Ohio, Chesapeake & Ohio, Western Maryland) and Seaboard Coast Line Industries, Inc. (Seaboard Coast Line, Louisville & Nashville) were merged into the new CSX Corporation. The two components maintain their separate identities. The SCL railroads are now known as Seaboard System Railroad, after a short period of being called "Family Lines."

CSX's lines reach out to New Orleans, St. Louis, Bay View, Mich., Rochester, N. Y., Philadelphia, and Homestead, Fla. The heaviest concentrations are along the eastern seaboard south of Norfolk, Va., and in West Virginia and southern Ohio.

Robert E. Gabbey

The two major railroad properties owned by CSX are Chessie System, whose three railroads are represented in this photo taken at Bliss, N. Y., and the newly named Seaboard System.

CSX owns a majority interest in Richmond, Fredericksburg & Potomac and Fruit Growers Express and also engages in non-rail activities such as real estate, oil and gas, aviation, and publishing.

Address of general offices: P. O. Box C-3222, Richmond, VA 23261
Date: March 1983

On January 1, 1983, the Seaboard Coast Line and the Louisville & Nashville merged to form the Seaboard System Railroad. Also included in the new railroad are the Clinchfield, the West Point Route, and the Georgia Railroad, all previously controlled by SCL and L&N.

SBD.

DARDANELLE & RUSSELLVILLE RAILROAD

The Dardanelle & Russellville was chartered in 1883 to connect Dardanelle, Arkansas — or actually a point opposite Dardanelle on the north bank of the Arkansas River — with the Little Rock & Fort Smith, now Missouri Pacific, at Russellville, 5 miles away. During World War One and for several years afterward coal deposits north of Dardanelle were mined, providing traffic for the railroad. The railroad is now owned by Richmond Leasing Co. and serves as a home road for a large fleet of leased covered hopper cars.

Address of general offices: P. O. Box 150, Dardanelle, AR 72834

Miles of road operated: 7
Reporting marks: DR
Number of locomotives: 4
Number of freight cars: 1240, all 4750-cubic-foot covered hoppers
Principal commodities carried: Feed, pulpwood, wood chips
Junctions with other railroads: Missouri Pacific: Russellville, Ark.
Recommended reading: *Short Line Railroads of Arkansas*, by Clifton E. Hull, published in 1969 by the University of Oklahoma Press, Norman, OK

DELAWARE & HUDSON RAILWAY

The Delaware & Hudson dates from 1823, when the Delaware & Hudson Canal Co. was chartered to build a canal from Honesdale, Pennsylvania, to Kingston, New York, to carry coal from the mines of Pennsylvania to New York City. Access to the mines near Carbondale was by a gravity railroad with stationary engines and ropes for the uphill portions. D&H sold the canal in 1899, and it was abandoned in 1904.

After the Civil War the D&H increased its coal holdings and contracted with the newly constructed Albany & Susquehanna Railroad (Albany-Binghamton, N.Y.) for access to the north. In 1871 the D&H opened a railroad line from Lanesboro, Pa., on the Erie, north to Nineveh, N.Y., to cut off the triangular route required to get to the A&S at Binghamton. D&H then leased the Rensselaer & Saratoga to gain access to Lake Champlain at Whitehall, N.Y. Soon the D&H system extended north to Montreal, and eventually it encompassed boats on Lake Champlain and Lake George and electric railways between Albany and Saratoga.

D&H sold the Hudson Coal Co. in 1960 and reincorporated in 1962. A condition of the 1964 Norfolk & Western merger was that Delaware & Hudson be allowed in, because the impending merger of the Pennsylvania and the New York Central would essentially surround and dry up the D&H. In 1968 Dereco, a subsidiary of N&W, acquired control of D&H and EL, but neither road was ever considered a part of the N&W system. EL entered Conrail in 1976; D&H remained independent. When Conrail was created, D&H purchased the former Pennsylvania Railroad line from Buttonwood, near Wilkes-Barre, to Sunbury, Pa., and acquired trackage rights over Conrail lines to Newark, New Jersey, Buffalo, Philadelphia, and Washington.

D&H subsidiary Napierville Junction Railway extends 28 miles north from Rouses Point, N.Y., to connections with Canadian Pacific and Canadian National at Delson, Quebec.

In 1983 Timothy Mellon's Guilford Transportation Industries purchased Delaware & Hudson.

Address of general offices: Delaware & Hudson Building, 40 Beaver St., Albany, NY 12207

Miles of road operated: 1699

Reporting marks: DH, DHNY
Number of locomotives: 134
Number of freight cars: 4796
Principal commodities carried: Pulp and paper, iron ore, grain
Major yards: E. Binghamton, N. Y. (Conklin)
Principal shops:
Locomotive: Watervliet, N. Y. (Colonie)
Car: Oneonta, N. Y.
Radio frequencies: 160.590 (road and dispatcher to train), 160.530
(train to dispatcher)
Passenger routes: Amtrak — Schenectady to Rouses Point (*Adirondack*) (Rouses Point-Montreal on subsidiary Napierville Junction)
Recommended reading: *Delaware & Hudson*, by Jim Shaughnessy, published in 1967 by Howell-North, P. O. Box 3051, La Jolla, CA 92038
Date: February 1983

In purchasing diesels, both new and secondhand, Delaware & Hudson favored on-line builder Alco (in Schenectady). A Binghamton-Allentown freight on former Erie trackage at Lanesboro, Pa., shows this preference with C424 453 (ex-Erie Lackawanna) and C420 411 (ex-Lehigh Valley) on the head end.

Scott Hartley.

DELAWARE OTSEGO SYSTEM
Central New York Railroad
Cooperstown & Charlotte Valley Railway
Fonda, Johnstown & Gloversville Railroad
Lackawaxen & Stourbridge Railroad
New York, Susquehanna & Western Railway

In 1966 the New York Central abandoned the western end of its Ulster & Delaware branch. The Delaware Otsego Corporation purchased 2.6 miles of the line at Oneonta, New York, and operated it as a tourist carrier with an 0-6-0 for power. DO also offered freight service, but there was

little market for it. In 1971 Delaware & Hudson wanted to abandon its Cooperstown branch, and DO found that its Oneonta operation was in the path of highway construction. DO bought the D&H branch and operated it as the Cooperstown & Charlotte Valley. The passenger operation was not a success, but DO management saw potential in acquiring low-traffic branches that larger roads couldn't operate profitably.

In 1973 DO purchased the Richfield Springs branch of the Erie Lackawanna to operate as the Central New York. The state of New York through the Rail Preservation Bond Act of 1974 provided funds to rehabilitate the line. In 1975 DO bought the Fonda, Johnstown & Gloversville, rehabilitated it, and turned it into a profitable operation.

One of the provisions under which Conrail was formed was that it could

Continued on next page.

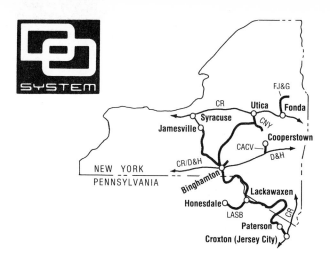

Jim Shaughnessy

In 1982 Delaware Otsego operated several excursion trains on the Northern Division of the Susquehanna. Here the July 5 train rolls down Schuyler Street in Utica, with a pair of Alco C420s and 4 full-length dome cars purchased from Auto-Train.

abandon low-traffic lines. One such route was the former Erie Lackawanna line between Lackawaxen and Honesdale, Pennsylvania. The commonwealth of Pennsylvania bought the line and contracted with Delaware Otsego to run it as a designated operator. For that purpose DO organized a subsidiary, Lackawaxen & Stourbridge.

Then the state of New Jersey asked DO to take over operation of the bankrupt and nearly dead New York, Susquehanna & Western. In 1980 DO purchased the NYS&W.

In 1981 Conrail proposed abandonment of the former EL line between Binghamton, N. Y., and Jamesville, just south of Syracuse, and the Utica branch of that line. Delaware Otsego purchased the lines and organized them as the Northern Division of the NYS&W. DO also purchased a por-

tion of the former Lehigh & Hudson River between Warwick, N. Y., and Franklin, N. J., from Conrail and secured trackage rights from Binghamton to Warwick and from Franklin to Sparta Jct. to connect the two divisions of NYS&W. Through interchange with Delaware & Hudson at Binghamton, Delaware Otsego's NYS&W offers the only non-Conrail access to northern New Jersey. The Central New York is now operated as part of the Northern Division of the NYS&W.

Address of general offices: 1 Railroad Avenue, Cooperstown, NY 13326
Miles of road operated: 524
Reporting marks: CACV, CNYK, FJG, LASB, NYSW
Number of locomotives: 20
Number of freight cars: 617
Principal commodities carried: Grain, chemicals, paper products, lumber

Principal shops: Fonda, N. Y.; Little Ferry, N. J.
Junctions with other railroads:
Conrail:
    Binghamton, N. Y.
    Croxton, N. J.
    Fonda, N. Y.
    Jamesville, N. Y.
    Hillside Jct., Pa.
    Utica, N. Y.
    Hawthorne, N. J.

    Passaic Jct., N. J.
    Lackawaxen, Pa.
    Suscon, Pa.
Delaware & Hudson:
    Binghamton, N. Y.
    Cooperstown, N. Y.
Radio frequencies: 160.485 (NYSW — New Jersey Division), 160.620 (LASB, FJG, NYSW — New York Division), 161.295 (CACV, CNYK)
Recommended reading: *The "DO" Lines*, by Edward A. Lewis, published in 1978 by The Baggage Car, P. O. Box 733, Morrisville, VT 05661

DENVER & RIO GRANDE WESTERN RAILROAD

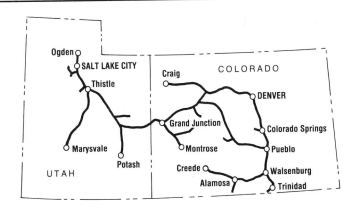

The Denver & Rio Grande was incorporated by William Jackson Palmer in 1870 to build a railroad from Denver south along the eastern edge of the Rockies to El Paso, Texas. Jackson chose 3-foot gauge for reasons of economy, and the line was completed to the new town of Colorado Springs in 1871. Palmer pushed his railroad south to Pueblo and then west to tap coal deposits near Canon City, Colorado, which remained the terminus of the line for a few years.

In 1878 Palmer's forces narrowly lost Raton Pass to the Santa Fe and battled with the Santa Fe in the Royal Gorge of the Arkansas River west of Canon City. Shortly afterward the D&RG was leased to the Santa Fe for a year. In 1879 the narrow gauge was on its own again under the management of Palmer and Jay Gould, and the D&RG and the Santa Fe agreed to go in separate directions: Santa Fe south into New Mexico and D&RG west into the Rockies. In 1881 the Rio Grande reached Gunnison

and Durango and added a third rail for standard-gauge trains to its Denver-Pueblo line.

In 1882 D&RG leased the Denver & Rio Grande Western, which was building and consolidating lines southeast from Salt Lake City; in 1883 the two railroads were joined near Green River, Utah, forming a narrow-gauge route from Denver to Salt Lake City. In 1890 a new standard

Continued on next page.

gauge route was completed over Tennessee Pass, the highest point reached by a standard gauge main line in North America. This route shared the Rio Grande Junction Railway between Rifle and Grand Junction with the standard gauge Colorado Midland. D&RG's narrow gauge "Chili Line" arrived in Santa Fe, N. Mex., in 1895.

The Rio Grande was deeply involved in financing the construction of the Western Pacific between Salt Lake City and San Francisco, which was completed in 1910. When WP went bankrupt, D&RG followed quickly. The railroad was sold in 1920, becoming the Denver & Rio Grande Western.

David Moffat's Denver, Northwestern & Pacific had built westward from Denver over Rollins Pass, eventually becoming the Denver & Salt Lake but getting no closer to its goal than Craig, in northwestern Colorado. The city of Denver constructed the 6-mile Moffat Tunnel under James Peak for the D&SL (and also to bring Western Slope water to Denver). The tunnel was opened in 1928. It let D&SL avoid the steep and often snowy climb over Rollins Pass, but D&SL had little traffic to send through the tunnel. At Bond, the D&SL was about 40 miles up the Colorado River from D&RGW's main line at Dotsero. D&RGW gained control of the D&SL and constructed a cutoff to connect the two routes. The Dotsero Cutoff was opened in 1934, placed Denver on a transcontinental main line for the first time, and cut 175 miles off D&RGW's route between Denver and Salt Lake City.

In 1947 D&RGW came out of receivership and merged with the D&SL. Denver soon received its transcontinental passenger train, the *California Zephyr*, operated by D&RGW, Western Pacific, and Chicago, Burlington & Quincy. The railroad began to abandon its remaining narrow-gauge lines; longest lived was the line from Alamosa west to Durango and Silverton, Colo., and Farmington, N. Mex. Two portions of that, Antonito, Colo.-Chama, N. Mex., and Durango-Silverton, still exist as tourist carriers. D&RGW developed into a fast-freight bridge route between Denver and Pueblo on the east and Salt Lake City and Ogden on the west. Much of D&RGW's tonnage consists of coal from northwestern Colorado.

Address of general offices: P. O. Box 5482, Denver, CO 80217
Miles of road operated: 1848
Reporting marks: DRGW

Tim Zukas.

Denver & Rio Grande Western chose to remain out of Amtrak in 1971 and continued to operate the triweekly Denver-Salt Lake City *Rio Grande Zephyr*, a remnant of the *California Zephyr*. The train is shown here at Tunnel 3 above Boulder, Colo., about an hour out of Denver. In April 1983 Rio Grande joined Amtrak. Amtrak moved the *San Francisco Zephyr* to D&RGW's line between Denver and Salt Lake City to supplant the *RGZ* and restored the *California Zephyr* name.

Number of locomotives: 282
Number of freight cars: 10,024
Number of passenger cars: 19
Principal commodities carried: Coal
Major yards: Denver (North Yard), Salt Lake City (Roper)
Principal shops: Denver (Burnham)
Radio frequencies: 160.455 and 160.920 (road frequencies in different zones), 161.490 (yard), 160.395 and 161.565 (Moffat Tunnel)
Passenger routes: Amtrak — Denver to Salt Lake City (*California Zephyr*)
Recommended reading: *Rio Grande to the Pacific*, by Robert A. Le Massena, published in 1974 by Sundance Limited, 100 Kalamath St., Denver, CO 80223

DETROIT & MACKINAC RAILWAY

The Detroit & Mackinac began operation in 1878 as the Lake Huron & Southwestern, a 38″-gauge logging railroad at Tawas City, Michigan. In 1883 the railroad made a connection with the Michigan Central (later New York Central) at Alger. In 1886 the road was standard-gauged and extended north along the west shore of Lake Huron to Alpena. It acquired its present name and its now-superseded turtle emblem in 1895. A year later the railroad was extended south to Bay City, and in 1904 it reached Cheboygan, near the northern tip of Michigan's lower peninsula.

In response to protests about its petition to discontinue passenger service, D&M teamed up with Grand Trunk Western in 1950 to offer through service between Alpena and Detroit. The arrangement lasted a year before D&M dropped its passenger train.

In 1976 D&M acquired portions of the former New York Central line from Bay City north through Cheboygan and on to Mackinaw City, essentially doubling its route mileage and creating a second line the length of the peninsula. The state of Michigan owns the ex-NYC line from near Linwood to Gaylord. D&M owns the remainder of the former NYC line and uses both that line and the "old" D&M line along the shore of Lake Huron as needed.

Address of general offices: 120 Oak Street, Tawas City, MI 48763
Miles of road operated: 405
Reporting marks: DM
Number of locomotives: 16
Number of freight cars: 1191
Principal commodities carried: Gravel, gypsum, shale, wood products, paper products
Principal shops: Tawas City, Mich.
Junctions with other railroads:
Chessie System: Bay City, Mich.
Grand Trunk Western: Bay City, Mich.
Michigan Northern: Mackinaw City, Mich.
Soo Line: Mackinaw City, Mich. (by ferry)
Radio frequencies: 161.310
Date: May 1983

James Pettinari

A black-and-gold Alco C425 numbered for the month and year of its acquisition leads a southbound freight through evening shadows near Indian River, Mich.

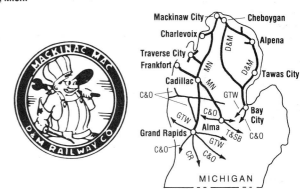

DULUTH, MISSABE & IRON RANGE RAILWAY

The Duluth & Iron Range Rail Road was chartered in 1874 to bring iron ore from the Vermilion Range of northeastern Minnesota down to ore docks at Two Harbors. The Duluth, Missabe & Northern Railway was incorporated in 1891, to link the open-pit iron mines of the Mesabi Range with docks at Duluth. Both railroads came under the ownership of U. S. Steel in 1901.

The Duluth, Missabe & Iron Range was incorporated in 1937 to consolidate the DM&N and the Spirit Lake Transfer Railway. In 1938 the company acquired the D&IR, which DM&N had leased since 1930, and the Interstate Transfer Railway.

In recent years as veins of high-grade ore have been depleted, mining companies have turned to lower-grade taconite. The taconite is processed into round pellets, which have a lower density than iron ore. DM&IR has built up the side of ore cars assigned to taconite service and permanently coupled them in groups of four, called "miniquads."

The DM&IR is the largest carrier of iron ore in the U. S. It is owned by U. S. Steel Corporation.

Address of general offices: Missabe Building, Duluth, MN 55802

Miles of road operated: 357
Reporting marks: DMIR
Number of locomotives: 66
Number of freight cars: 7405
Principal commodities carried: Iron ore
Major yards: Proctor, Minn.
Principal shops: Proctor, Minn.
Radio frequencies: 160.350, 160.800
Historical and technical society: Missabe Historical Society, 719 Northland Avenue, Stillwater, MN 55082
Recommended reading:
The Missabe Road, by Frank A. King, published in 1972 by Golden West Books, P. O. Box 8136, San Marino, CA 91108 (ISBN 87095-040-1)
RAILROADS YOU CAN MODEL, by Mike Schafer, published in 1976 by Kalmbach Publishing Co., 1027 North Seventh Street, Milwaukee, WI 53233 (ISBN 0-89024-526-6)
Date: February 1983

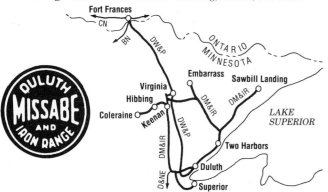

Howard Patrick.

Duluth, Missabe & Iron Range's arrowhead emblem stands out in yellow on the cabs of its maroon hood units at Keenan Junction, Minn. DM&IR keeps to the left on its double-track main line.

DELIVERED WITH PRIDE

David C. Schauer

Duluth, Winnipeg & Pacific owns only two diesel models. Representatives of both are shown here at West Duluth: RS11 3610 and SD40 5907.

DULUTH, WINNIPEG & PACIFIC RAILWAY

The first portion of the Duluth, Winnipeg & Pacific was the middle — a logging railroad, the Duluth, Virginia & Rainy Lake, opened in 1901 from Virginia, Minnesota, to nearby Silver Lake. The road was soon purchased by Canadian Northern interests and the name changed to Duluth, Rainy Lake & Winnipeg. In 1908 the line was extended north to a connection with Canadian Northern (see Canadian National, page 42) at Fort Frances, Ontario. In 1909 the road acquired its present name and built southward to Duluth, reaching there in 1912. In 1918 control of Canadian Northern passed to the Canadian government and the railroad became part of Canadian National Railway. The "Peg" is now a unit of the Grand Trunk Corporation.

Address of general offices: 72nd Avenue West and Raleigh Street, Duluth, MN 55807

Miles of road operated: 167

Reporting marks: DWC

Number of locomotives: 13

Number of freight cars: 2428

Principal commodities carried: Potash, lumber, paper

Junctions with other railroads:

Burlington Northern: Duluth, Minn.

Canadian National: Fort Frances, Ont.; Ranier, Minn.

Chicago & North Western: Duluth, Minn.

Chicago, Milwaukee, St. Paul & Pacific: Duluth, Minn.

Duluth, Missabe & Iron Range: Virginia, Minn.

Lake Superior Terminal & Transfer: Superior, Wis.

Minnesota, Dakota & Western: Ranier, Minn.

Soo Line: West Duluth, Minn.

Radio frequencies: 161.415, 161.205, 160.935

Map: See Duluth, Missabe & Iron Range, opposite

Date: February 1983

EASTERN SHORE RAILROAD

The New York, Philadelphia & Norfolk, a subsidiary of the Pennsylvania Railroad, completed a line down the Delmarva Peninsula from Wilmington, Delaware, to Cape Charles, Virginia, in 1884. In conjunction with a car ferry across the mouth of Chesapeake Bay to Norfolk the line formed a route to the south that bypassed the congestion and restrictive clearances of Baltimore and Washington.

In the 1960s the line's status declined, and Penn Central continued the process of neglect during its brief stewardship. At one point the Southern Railway was interested in the line for access to the chemical industry at Wilmington, but SR could not reach an agreement with one of the unions involved.

In 1976 Conrail took over the main line as far south as Pocomoke City, Maryland, and operated the line south of there with federal subsidy. On April 1, 1977, the Virginia & Maryland took over the line between Pocomoke City and Cape Charles and undertook extensive rehabilitation of the track. At the end of October 1981 a new company under local control, the Eastern Shore Railroad, took over.

Address of general offices: P. O. Box 312, Cape Charles, VA 23310
Miles of road operated: 96 (70 rail, 26 water)
Reporting marks: ESHR
Number of locomotives: 5
Number of freight cars: 290
Principal commodities carried: Coal, agricultural products
Junctions with other railroads:
Conrail: Pocomoke, Md.
Norfolk & Portsmouth Belt: Norfolk, Va.
Norfolk & Western: Norfolk, Va.
Norfolk, Franklin & Danville: Norfolk, Va.
Southern: Norfolk, Va.
Radio frequencies: 161.445
Recommended reading: *The "DO" Lines*, by Edward A. Lewis, published in 1978 by The Baggage Car, P. O. Box 733, Morrisville, VT 05661
Map: See Maryland & Delaware, page 115

Blue GP8 1600 is a product of the rebuilding program of Illinois Central Gulf's Paducah Shops.

Kent Griffith.

ELGIN, JOLIET & EASTERN RAILWAY

The Elgin, Joliet & Eastern was incorporated in 1888 in Illinois and 1889 in Indiana as a consolidation of the EJ&E of Illinois and the EJ&E of Indiana. In 1909 the railroad leased the Chicago, Lake Shore & Eastern, and in 1938 it merged with that road and with the Joliet & Blue Island.

The "J" is also known as the Chicago Outer Belt. Its line runs from Waukegan, Ill., on the shore of Lake Michigan north of Chicago to Porter, Ind., forming an arc about 30 to 40 miles from the center of Chicago. It intersects with every railroad entering Chicago. Chief among the industries served by the EJ&E is the Gary Works of United States Steel, the railroad's owner.

Address of general offices: P. O. Box 880, Joliet, IL 60434
Miles of road operated: 231

Continued on next page.

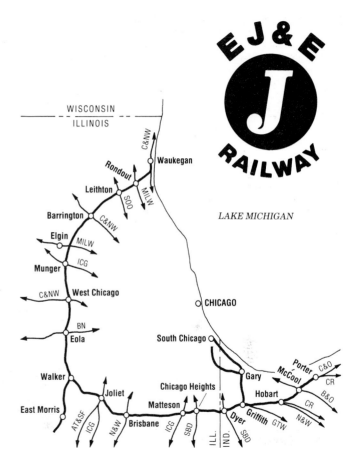

A bright orange EJ&E SD38 leads a train of coil-steel cars across the Grand Trunk Western and Chessie System (C&O) diamonds at Griffith, Ind.

Louis A. Marre

Reporting marks: EJE
Number of locomotives: 100
Number of freight cars: 10,193
Principal commodities carried: Coal, iron, steel
Major yards: Gary, Ind.; Joliet, Ill.
Principal shops: Joliet, Ill.
Connects with:
Atchison, Topeka & Santa Fe
Belt Railway of Chicago
Burlington Northern
Chessie System
Chicago & Illinois Western
Chicago & North Western
Chicago & Western Indiana
Chicago Heights Terminal Transfer
Chicago, Milwaukee, St. Paul & Pacific
Chicago Short Line
Chicago South Shore & South Bend
Chicago, West Pullman & Southern
Conrail
Grand Trunk Western
Illinois Central Gulf
Indiana Harbor Belt
Manufacturers Junction
Missouri Pacific
Norfolk & Western
Seaboard System
Soo Line
Radio frequencies: 160.350 (road and dispatcher), 160.260 (yard)
Date: January 1983

ESCANABA & LAKE SUPERIOR RAILROAD

The Escanaba & Lake Superior was incorporated in 1898. It constructed a line between Escanaba, Michigan, on the shore of Lake Michigan, and Channing, Mich., where it connected with the Milwaukee Road. For a time (before the Milwaukee Road-Chicago & North Western ore pooling agreement of the 1930s) Milwaukee Road ore trains moved to ore docks at Escanaba over the E&LS.

In 1980 E&LS took over operation of several Milwaukee Road lines — from Channing to Green Bay, Wisconsin, Republic, Mich., and Ontonagon, Mich. — and later purchased them.

Address of general offices: Wells, MI 49894
Miles of road operated: 325
Reporting marks: ELS
Number of locomotives: 8
Number of freight cars: 130
Principal commodities carried: Iron ore, paper, pulpwood, cranes
Shops: Wells, Mich.
Radio frequencies: 160.320

William S. Christopher.

In recent years the ex-Delaware & Hudson Baldwin shark-nose units were stored on the E&LS. Number 1216 was used briefly in October 1982.

Junctions with other railroads:
Chicago & North Western: Escanaba, Mich.; Iron Mountain, Mich.
Chicago, Milwaukee, St. Paul & Pacific: Green Bay, Wis.
Soo Line: North Escanaba, Mich.; Pembine, Wis.
Map: see Lake Superior & Ishpeming, page 103
Date: May 1983

FLORIDA EAST COAST RAILWAY

In 1885 Henry M. Flagler took over the Jacksonville, St. Augustine & Halifax, a 36-mile, 3-foot-gauge railroad extending south from Jacksonville, Florida. He standard-gauged the line, built a bridge across the St. Johns River to connect with other railroads at Jacksonville, and pushed the line southward, reaching Miami in 1896.

Then, to tap the Cuban trade and also because Key West was the closest port to the Panama Canal (then under construction), he decided to build a line south through the southern portion of the Everglades and across the Florida Keys to Key West. Construction was set back by hurricanes in 1906, 1909, and 1910, but the line reached Key West early in 1912, only months before Flagler's death.

The Florida Boom came in 1924, and FEC went whole hog: new cutoffs, branches, double track, signals, and 4-8-2s. The boom peaked and receded in 1926, the Seaboard Air Line Railway reached Miami in 1927, and the Depression hit. FEC entered receivership in 1931.

A hurricane in 1935 wiped out most of the Key West Extension. What remained was used as the right of way for U. S. highway 1 to Key West. In 1944 Atlantic Coast Line, whose streamliners FEC operated between Jacksonville and Miami, offered to purchase the FEC; later Seaboard Air Line and Southern Railway came up with a joint counterproposal. There was, however, considerable pressure to keep control of the railroad within the state of Florida.

The railroad was reorganized in 1960. Control was assumed by the St. Joe Paper Co. (which also owns Apalachicola Northern, page 14), owned by the Alfred I. duPont estate. In 1963 the nonoperating unions struck the railroad, which had refused to go along with an industry-wide pay increase. Within two weeks management was operating freight service. The strike became increasingly bitter, with bombings and destruction, and it was not settled until 1971. By then the railroad had instituted sweeping changes: no more passenger service; two-man freight crews running the length of the railroad (where formerly it had taken three five-man crews); extensive rebuilding of the railroad, including many miles of concrete ties; single track and CTC; and — a harbinger of the future — no cabooses.

Address of general offices: 1 Malaga Street, St. Augustine, FL 32084
Miles of road operated: 554
Reporting marks: FEC
Number of locomotives: 61
Number of freight cars: 2508
Principal commodities carried: Agricultural products, piggyback traffic
Major yards: Jacksonville (Bowden), Miami (Hialeah)

Continued on next page.

Principal shops: Jacksonville (cars), New Smyrna Beach (locomotives)
Junctions with other railroads:
Port of Palm Beach District: Port of Palm Beach Jct., Fla.
St. Johns River Terminal: Jacksonville, Fla.
Seaboard System:
  Jacksonville, Fla.
  Lake Harbor, Fla.
  Marcy, Fla.
  Miami, Fla.
  West Palm Beach, Fla.
Southern: Jacksonville, Fla.
Radio frequencies: 160.650 (train to dispatcher), 160.530 (road and dispatcher to train)
Recommended reading: *The Railroad that Died at Sea*, by Pat Parks, published in 1968 by Stephen Greene Press, P. O. Box 1000, Brattleboro, VT 05301

William J. Husa Jr.

A blue FEC GP9 leads a train of sugar cane cars from the U. S. Sugar Corp. refinery at Clewiston east out of Lake Harbor, Fla.

FORDYCE & PRINCETON RAILROAD

In 1981 the Fordyce & Princeton, a 2-mile switching railroad at Fordyce, Arkansas, took over the former Rock Island line from Fordyce to Crossett, Ark., providing an outlet to the St. Louis Southwestern for the Georgia Pacific mills in the Crossett area. The Georgia Pacific Corporation owns the Fordyce & Princeton and the Ashley, Drew & Northern. The two railroads share executives and general offices; F&P's operating headquarters is at Fordyce.

FP.

Fordyce & Princeton has two SW1500s, 1503 and 1504, and an Alco S3 numbered 662.

Address of general offices: P. O. Box 757, Crossett, AR 71635
Miles of road operated: 57
Reporting marks: FP
Number of locomotives: 3
Number of freight cars: 329
Principal commodities carried: Pulpwood, paper products
Radio frequencies: 160.770

Junctions with other railroads:
Arkansas & Louisiana Missouri: Crossett
Ashley, Drew & Northern: Crossett, Whitlow Jct.
St. Louis Southwestern: Fordyce
Warren & Saline River: Hermitage
Map: See Ashley, Drew & Northern, page 16
Date: February 1983

GOVERNMENT OF ONTARIO TRANSIT

Toronto, like most other large cities in the 1950s, faced related problems of commuter traffic and strangulation by highways. In 1959 Canadian National Railways announced its plan to build a large freight classification yard northwest of Toronto. Freight traffic would be rerouted onto a belt line, freeing CN's route along the shore of Lake Ontario for commuter trains. CN added that any such commuter service would have to be financed by someone else.

In 1965 the government of Ontario approved a plan to operate a 60-mile commuter service between Pickering on the east, Toronto, and Hamilton on the west. Government of Ontario Transit — GO Transit for short — began operation in 1967 and was immediately successful.

GO Transit added service to Georgetown on CN's secondary main line to London in 1974, north to Richmond Hill on CN's Bala Subdivision in 1978, and west to Milton on Canadian Pacific in 1981. In 1982 GO took over operation of two trains that VIA Rail Canada had inherited from CN: Toronto-Stouffville and Toronto-Bradford, the latter a truncation of the VIA service to Barrie, Ontario.

Continued on next page.

GO.

GO Transit's green-and-white bilevel cars, built by Hawker Siddeley in Thunder Bay, Ont., are doubtless North America's most distinctive commuter rolling stock. Seven appear here east of Toronto, sandwiched between a GP40TC, which is pushing the train, and an auxiliary power-cab unit, rebuilt from an F unit.

GO Transit also contracts with three bus companies for operation of bus service in the Toronto area.

Address of general offices: 555 Wilson Avenue, Downsview, ON, Canada M3H 5Y6

Miles of road operated: 212

Number of locomotives: 32, plus 14 auxiliary power units, some with cabs

Number of passenger cars: 272

Self-propelled passenger cars: 9

Major yards: Mimico (Willowbrook Maintenance Depot), Toronto (Bathurst North)

Principal shops: Mimico (Willowbrook Maintenance Depot)

Radio frequencies: 419.4375

Passenger routes:
Hamilton-Oakville-Toronto-Pickering (CN)
Toronto-Bradford (CN)
Toronto-Georgetown (CN)
Toronto-Milton (CP)
Toronto-Richmond Hill (CN)
Toronto-Stouffville (CN)

Date: March 1983

GRAND TRUNK CORPORATION

Grand Trunk Industries was incorporated in 1970 to consolidate the U. S. subsidiaries of Canadian National. The company was renamed Grand Trunk Corporation within two months, and at the end of 1971 it acquired the Central Vermont, the Duluth, Winnipeg & Pacific, and the Grand Trunk Western. The company is wholly owned by Canadian National Railways.

Address of executive offices: 466 Congress Street, Portland, ME 04111

Date: March 1983

The whole Grand Trunk Corporation family appears in this 1978 scene of a southbound freight passing Central Vermont's general office building at St. Albans, Vt. Leading are two M420s from parent Canadian National, and behind are three DW&P RS11s, a CV RS11, and a GTW GP9.

Ronald N. Johnson.

GRAND TRUNK WESTERN RAILROAD

The Grand Trunk Western's ancestor was Canada's Grand Trunk Railway, originally conceived in 1852 to connect Montreal and Toronto. To that was added a line from Montreal to the nearest seaport, Portland, Maine. Construction and acquisition at the west end of the line in 1858 put Grand Trunk across the St. Clair River between Sarnia, Ontario, and Port Huron, Michigan, first by ferries and later by a tunnel. The line was extended through Michigan and Indiana, reaching Chicago in 1880.

Canada's Grand Trunk stockholders guaranteed the bonds for the con-

Ernest L. Novak.

Grand Trunk Western freights meet in Detroit against a background of the General Motors Building (right) and the Fisher Building.

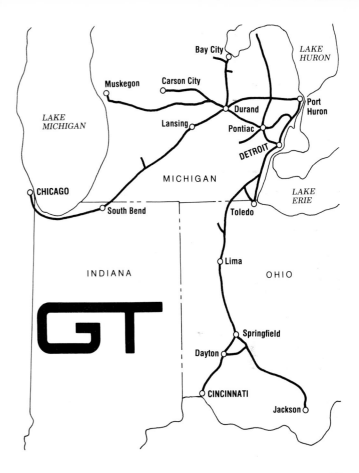

struction of the Grand Trunk Pacific from Winnipeg to Prince Rupert, British Columbia. The GTP proved expensive, though, and GT's financial problems brought it under Canadian government ownership and absorption into the nationalized Canadian National Railways in 1923.

The Grand Trunk Western was incorporated in 1928 by CN to consolidate the Grand Trunk properties in Michigan, Indiana, and Illinois. In 1980 the Grand Trunk Western purchased the 580-mile Detroit, Toledo & Ironton. DT&I's checkered history includes control by Henry Ford; an experiment in electrification; ownership by subsidiaries of the Pennsylvania Railroad and its successor, Penn Central; and ownership of the now-defunct Ann Arbor Railroad.

In 1981 GTW purchased the Norfolk & Western's half interest in the jointly owned Detroit & Toledo Shore Line. N&W had acquired its share of the D&TSL in the merger with the Nickel Plate. D&TSL has been merged into GTW, but DT&I retains some of its own identity. For marketing purposes GTW and DT&I are referred to as Grand Trunk Rail System.

Grand Trunk Western's main line extends from Port Huron, Mich., to

Continued on next page.

Chicago, and a secondary line crosses Michigan from Detroit to Muskegon, intersecting the main line at Durand. Until recently GTW operated a car ferry across Lake Michigan to Milwaukee. DT&I's line extends south from Detroit to Jackson, Ohio. DT&I acquired trackage rights into Cincinnati over Conrail to make direct connection with Louisville & Nashville (now Seaboard System) and Southern Railway.

In 1982 Grand Trunk Western agreed to purchase the Milwaukee Road. The matter is now before the Interstate Commerce Commission.

Address of general offices: 131 W. Lafayette Boulevard, Detroit, MI 48226
Miles of road operated: 1514
Reporting marks: DTI, DTS, GTW

Number of locomotives: 262
Number of freight cars: 11,867
Principal commodities carried: Automobiles and auto parts, fuel, chemicals
Major yards: Battle Creek; Durand, Mich.; Chicago (Elsdon); Ferndale, Mich.; Flat Rock, Mich; Toledo
Principal shops: Battle Creek, Port Huron
Radio frequencies: 160.590, 160.530, 160.845
Passenger routes:
Amtrak — Battle Creek-Port Huron, Mich. (*International*)
Southeastern Michigan Transportation Authority — Detroit-Pontiac
Date: March 1983

GREAT WESTERN RAILWAY

The Great Western Railway was incorporated in 1901 by the Great Western Sugar Co., which opened its first factory at Loveland, Colorado, that same year. The sugar company opened more factories in the next few years at Longmont, Windsor, Eaton, and Johnstown, Colo. The railroad was extended to connect the several factories and carry sugar beets from the surrounding farming area to the factories. The railroad reached its present extent in 1907. In 1917 GW purchased a portion of the defunct Denver, Laramie & Northwestern from Elm south to Wattenburg; that line was abandoned in 1948.

In the 1950s and 1960s Great Western was known for operating steam locomotives during the sugar beet harvest season. Four of these locomotives are still in existence. Consolidation No. 60 operates on the Black River & Western in New Jersey and has appeared in many TV commercials. The other two 2-8-0s, 51 and 75, have made movie appearances; both are kept in the Denver area. The best known of GW's steamers was Decapod No. 90, now at the Strasburg Railroad in Strasburg, Pennsylvania.

Address of general offices: P. O. Box 537, Loveland, CO 80539
Miles of road operated: 58
Reporting marks: GWR
Number of locomotives: 4
Number of freight cars: 153
Principal commodities carried: Sugar beets, sugar, coal, molasses
Shops: Loveland, Colo.
Junctions with other railroads:
Burlington Northern: Longmont, Loveland, Windsor
Union Pacific: Eaton, Kelim, Milliken
Radio frequencies: 160.260
Recommended reading: *Sugar Tramp*, by Gary Morgan, published in 1975 by Centennial Publications, 1400 Ash Drive, Fort Collins, CO 80521
Date: March 1983

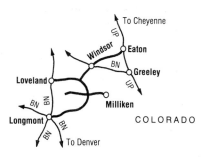

GWR

Great Western's locomotives are named for on-line towns and cities, and each wears a different version of the yellow, white, and blue livery. The road's principal business is carrying sugar beets and sugar for parent Great Western Sugar Co.

GREEN BAY & WESTERN RAILROAD

The Green Bay & Lake Pepin was chartered in 1866 to build westward from Green Bay, Wisconsin, to the Mississippi River. The road was to provide a market for Minnesota's wheat and serve the growing lumber industry of northern Wisconsin. The first spike was driven in 1871, and the road reached the Mississippi at East Winona, Wis., in 1873. After several name changes and a period of control by the Lackawanna Iron & Coal Co., an affiliate of the Delaware, Lackawanna & Western, the road was reorganized as the Green Bay & Western in 1896.

The railroad's eastern extension to Lake Michigan was incorporated in 1890 as the Kewaunee, Green Bay & Western. It was placed in service in 1891, providing a connection with the ferries that plied Lake Michigan between Frankfort and Ludington, Mich., and Kewaunee, Wis. The KGB&W came under GB&W control in 1897; its corporate existence lasted long enough that one of GB&W's Alco FA1s was lettered for the subsidiary.

The importance of GB&W's bridge traffic diminished in the late 1970s — Ann Arbor's ferries ceased running in 1982, and Chesapeake & Ohio was down to a single Ludington-Kewaunee run — and the importance of Wisconsin's paper industry increased to the point that Burlington Northern at one point expressed interest in acquiring the GB&W. The road has remained independent, however.

Address of general offices: P. O. Box 2507, Green Bay, WI 54306
Miles of road operated: 255
Reporting marks: GBW
Number of locomotives: 19

Continued on next page.

Green Bay & Western has been an all-Alco railroad since its dieselization. Here a pair of bright-red C424s prepare to leave the road's terminal at Green Bay with time freight No. 1 for Winona.

Otto P. Dobnick.

Number of freight cars: 2060
Principal commodities carried: Paper products
Shops: Green Bay, Wis.
Junctions with other railroads:
Ahnapee & Western: Casco Jct., Wis.
Burlington Northern: East Winona, Wis.; Winona, Minn
Chessie System (ferry): Kewaunee, Wis.
Chicago & North Western:
  Green Bay, Wis.
  Merrilan, Wis.
  New London, Wis.
  Winona, Minn.
  Wisconsin Rapids, Wis.
Chicago, Milwaukee, St. Paul & Pacific:
  Green Bay, Wis.
  Winona, Minn.
  Wisconsin Rapids, Wis.

Soo Line
  Black Creek, Wis.
  Stevens Point, Wis.
  Wisconsin Rapids, Wis.
Radio frequencies: 161.250, 161.070
Date: March 1983

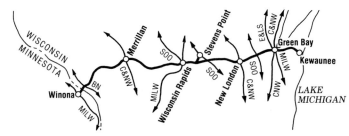

GREEN MOUNTAIN RAILROAD

After a strike in 1961 closed down the Rutland Railroad (see Vermont Railway, page 200) F. Nelson Blount proposed operating the excursion trains of his Steamtown, U. S. A. museum over some portion of the railroad's Bellows Falls-Rutland line. The state of Vermont asked if Blount would also operate freight service as needed on the line. The only major source of traffic was a pair of talc plants at Chester and Gassetts. Blount agreed to operate freight service between Bellows Falls and Ludlow, 27 miles.

In 1964 Steamtown moved from its former site in North Walpole, New Hampshire (across the Connecticut River from Bellows Falls), to a new location on the Vermont side of the river just north of Bellows Falls. Blount's freight operation began in 1965. Employees persuaded Blount to lease the line all the way from Bellows Falls to Rutland.

After Blount's death in 1967 the Green Mountain Railroad Co. emerged from Blount's tangle of museum, steam locomotives, passenger operations, and freight service as an independent, employee-owned company.

Because of customer preference most traffic is interchanged with Delaware & Hudson and Vermont Railway at Rutland rather than with Boston & Maine at Bellows Falls. In 1978 GMRC assumed operation of B&M's Keene, N. H., yard, and in early 1982 took over B&M's line between Brattleboro, Vt., and Keene via Dole Jct. In 1982 that operation was cut back from Keene to Hinsdale, N. H.

Address of general offices: P. O. Box 498, Bellows Falls, VT 05101
Miles of road operated: 50
Reporting marks: GMRC
Number of locomotives: 6

Scott Hartley.

Both the bridge at Cuttingsville and the number and paint scheme of the RS1 are unchanged from Rutland days as Green Mountain 405 leads a westbound freight train over Mount Holly.

Number of freight cars: 497
Principal commodities carried: Talc
Shops: North Walpole, N. H.
Junctions with other railroads:
Boston & Maine: Bellows Falls, Vt.
Delaware & Hudson: Rutland, Vt.
Vermont: Rutland, Vt.
Radio frequencies: 160.605, 161.445
Passenger routes: Steamtown, U. S. A. (tourist railroad) operates over part of the line
Recommended reading: *The Rutland Road* (second edition), by Jim Shaughnessy, published in 1981 by Howell-North, P. O. Box 3051, La Jolla, CA 92038
Date: March 1983

GUILFORD TRANSPORTATION INDUSTRIES

In 1977 Timothy Mellon of Guilford, Connecticut, teamed up with David Fink to form Perma Treat, a railroad tie treatment company. Mellon considered acquiring several railroads: Illinois Central Gulf; Pittsburgh & Lake Erie; and Detroit, Toledo & Ironton. None of those ventures worked out, but Mellon's interest in railroads continued.

In 1980 he discussed acquisition of Boston & Maine with its reorganization trustees, and in July 1981 he reached an agreement to purchase B&M. Meanwhile, Mellon purchased the Maine Central Railroad from its owner, United States Filter Corp., through his holding company, Guilford Transportation Industries. Then the state of New York approached Guilford about acquisition of the Delaware & Hudson, and in October 1981 Norfolk & Western agreed to sell to Guilford the Delaware & Hudson, which was controlled by N&W's subsidiary, Dereco, Inc.

The three railroads comprise approximately 4000 route-miles stretching from Calais, Maine, to Buffalo, New York, and from Montreal to Washington, D. C. The railroads will remain separate, but a common paint scheme has been devised to indicate their alliance.

Address of general offices: 171 Orange Street, New Haven, CT 06510

The first locomotive that was painted in Guilford's charcoal gray, orange, and white was Maine Central GP7R 470, rebuilt in 1982 at MEC's Waterville, Maine, shops.

Jerry Angier.

HILLSDALE COUNTY RAILWAY

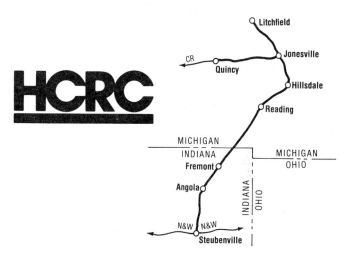

In the early 1970s the U. S. Economic Development Agency attracted many new industries to Hillsdale County in southwestern Michigan. Eight of these industries used rail service. United States Railway Association plans for Conrail did not include the former New York Central lines in Hillsdale County, and these industries and several others stated that they would have to move or close if rail service were discontinued.

John Marino, intermodal planning manager of USRA, concluded that a short line operation could be profitable. He resigned from USRA, helped incorporate the Hillsdale County Railway, and was elected its president.

The Michigan State Highway Commission and the Indiana Public Service Commission purchased the lines, and in April 1976 Hillsdale County Railway took over their operation. On-line industries include a food processing plant, a furniture factory, and several feed mills.

Address of general offices: 50 Monroe St., Hillsdale, MI 49242
Miles of road operated: 62
Number of locomotives: 3
Number of freight cars: 390
Reporting marks: HCRC
Principal commodities carried: Grain, agricultural products, manufactured goods
Junctions with other railroads:
Conrail: Quincy, Mich.
Norfolk & Western: Steubenville, Ind.
Passenger routes: Pleasant Lake-Angola-Fremont (Little River Railroad — tourist carrier)
Radio frequencies: 161.100
Recommended reading: *The "DO" Lines* by Edward A. Lewis, published in 1978 by The Baggage Car, P. O. Box 223, Strasburg, PA 17579

During the dedication ceremonies on April 10, 1976, Hillsdale County's NW2 1976, named *Chief Baw Beese*, and GP8 1600, *Capt. Moses Allen*, stand in front of the brick station at Hillsdale.

John B. Corns.

HOUSTON BELT & TERMINAL RAILWAY

The Houston Belt & Terminal was incorporated in 1905. It is owned by Missouri Pacific (50 percent), Santa Fe (25 percent), Burlington Northern (12½ percent), and the estate of the Rock Island (12½ percent). It built and owned the passenger station used by its owners — indeed, Amtrak's Chicago-Houston *Texas Chief/Lone Star* used the station until 1974. HB&T is now out of the passenger business but is nonetheless a busy railroad serving the fifth largest city in the U. S. and its deepwater port on Buffalo Bayou.

Address of general offices: 202 Union Station Building, Houston, TX 77002

Miles of road operated: 57

Reporting marks: HBT
Number of locomotives: 25
Connects with:
Atchison, Topeka & Santa Fe
Burlington Northern
Missouri-Kansas-Texas
Missouri Pacific
Port Terminal Railroad Association
Southern Pacific
Radio frequencies: 160.530
Date: March 1983

Houston Belt & Terminal 62, an MP15, poses on a highway overpass with Houston's impressive skyline as a backdrop.

HBT.

Illinois Central Gulf

ILLINOIS CENTRAL GULF RAILROAD

The Illinois Central was chartered in 1851 to build a line from Cairo, at the southern tip of Illinois — the confluence of the Ohio and Mississippi rivers — to Galena, in the extreme northwestern corner of the state, with a branch to Chicago. A previous undertaking had resulted in a few miles of grading north of Cairo but nothing else; the IC was aided, however, by a land grant act signed by President Millard Fillmore in 1850. Finished in 1856, the line was a Y-shaped railroad with its junction just north of Centralia (named for the railroad). The railroad gave Chicago an outlet to the Mississippi for north-south traffic, and indeed, the railroad operated a steamboat line between Cairo and New Orleans.

In 1867 the IC, which had been built beyond Galena and across the Mississippi to Dubuque & Sioux City, leased the Dubuque & Sioux City, extending its western line to Iowa Falls. The line reached Sioux City in 1870.

On the southern front, IC entered into an agreement with the New Orleans, Jackson & Great Northern and the Mississippi Central (which formed a through route between New Orleans and Jackson, Tennessee) to build a line between Jackson and Cairo, replacing a connection via the Mobile & Ohio. The new line was completed that same year, and in 1874 IC, principal bondholder of the other two lines, took them over. The route from Cairo south to New Orleans had been built to a 5-foot track gauge. The entire 550-mile route was converted to standard gauge in one day, July 29, 1881.

In the late 1880s IC undertook an expansion program that linked the western line directly with Chicago and put its rails into Sioux Falls, South Dakota, and Madison, Wisconsin. The road bridged the Ohio at

Continued on next page.

Cairo in 1889, purchased the Chesapeake, Ohio & Southwestern (Louisville to Memphis) in 1893, built into St. Louis from the southeast in 1895, and extended a branch of the western line into Omaha, Nebraska, in 1899.

In 1900 a minor train wreck at Vaughan, Mississippi, achieved worldwide fame because an engine-wiper named Wallace Saunders wrote a song about the incident. The engineer, the only person killed, was one John Luther Jones, nicknamed "Casey."

In 1906 the IC came under the control of E. H. Harriman. In 1908 it forged a route from Fulton, Kentucky, to Birmingham, Alabama, largely on trackage rights, and in 1909 it acquired, for a time, control of the Central of Georgia. In 1926 IC electrified its suburban line along the Chicago lakefront. In 1928 it constructed a cutoff line between Edgewood, Ill., and Fulton, Ky., to bypass congestion at Cairo, the waist of its system.

IC was known for its passenger trains, and at the top of its list was the *Panama Limited*, which ran between Chicago and New Orleans on a fast overnight schedule. Few trains were its peer when it came to class and punctuality.

In 1972 IC merged with the parallel Gulf, Mobile & Ohio to form Illinois Central Gulf. GM&O was itself the product of several mergers. In the beginning was the Gulf, Mobile & Northern (Mobile, Alabama-Jackson, Tennessee-Dyersburg, Tennessee). It was an independent line, but considered a friend of the IC. In 1926 GM&N negotiated trackage rights to Paducah, Ky., over the Nashville, Chattanooga & St. Louis and then later via Illinois Central. In 1930 GM&N acquired the New Orleans Great Northern, built by lumber interests, thereby obtaining access to New Orleans through Jackson, Mississippi.

In 1940 GM&N merged with Mobile & Ohio, a poor relation of the Southern Railway. M&O's line north from Mobile was more or less parallel to GM&N's; more important was M&O's line to East St. Louis, Illinois. The resulting Gulf, Mobile & Ohio merged in 1947 with the Alton, an old railroad whose principal lines ran from Chicago to St. Louis and Kansas City. Most recently it had been an unprofitable part of the Baltimore & Ohio. Thus GM&O became a north-south railroad through much the same general area as Illinois Central. In the 1960s the young management team that had put together the Gulf, Mobile & Ohio was no

George A. Forero Jr.

Illinois Central Gulf, continuing the program of predecessor Illinois Central, has rebuilt much of its diesel fleet at its Paducah, Ky., shops. Trademarks of the Paducah rebuilds are four exhaust stacks and an oxbow-like air filter structure atop the hood. Here, several products of the rebuilding program lead a piggyback train west through the hill country of northwestern Illinois.

longer young, and there were no replacements in sight. GM&O was a likely merger partner for the parallel Illinois Central.

Illinois Central Gulf is currently owned by IC Industries.

Address of general offices: 233 N. Michigan Avenue, Chicago, IL 60601

Miles of road operated: 7100

Reporting marks: GMO, IC, ICG

Number of locomotives: 1090

Number of freight cars: 40,120

Principal commodities carried: Coal, grain, lumber, paper products, chemicals, piggyback and container traffic

Major yards: Chicago (Markham); Jackson, Miss.; Memphis (Johnston)

Principal shops: Centralia, Ill.; Jackson, Tenn. (Iselin); McComb, Miss.; Paducah, Ky.; Woodcrest, Ill.

Radio Frequencies: 161.190 (road, IC), 160.920 (road, GM&O), 161.460 (yard), 161.025 (commuter)

Passenger routes:
Amtrak — Chicago-New Orleans (*City of New Orleans, Shawnee, Illini*); Chicago-St. Louis (*Ann Rutledge, State House, Eagle*)
Regional Transportation Authority — Chicago-Park Forest South, Chicago-Blue Island, Chicago-South Chicago

Historical and technical societies:
Gulf, Mobile & Ohio Historical Society, Box 3382, Springfield, IL 62708
Illinois Central Historical Society, 556 South Elizabeth Drive, Lombard, IL 60148

Recommended reading:
Main Line of Mid-America, by Carlton J. Corliss, published in 1950 by Creative Age Press, New York, NY
The Gulf, Mobile & Ohio, by James Hutton Lemley, published in 1953 by Richard D. Irwin, Inc., Homewood, IL 60430

Date: March 1983

INDIANA HARBOR BELT RAILROAD

R. B. Olson.

Three representatives of Indiana Harbor Belt's all-switcher roster, 2 of them in the road's new orange-and-black livery, pull a cut of cars out of the east end of Blue Island Yard.

The Indiana Harbor Belt was incorporated in 1896 as the East Chicago Belt. It received its present name in 1907, at which time it took over the Michigan Central's rights in the Chicago Junction Railway from Whiting, Indiana, to Franklin Park, Illinois. Until 1911 the railroad was jointly owned by Michigan Central and Lake Shore & Michigan Southern (both part of the New York Central System). At that time 20 percent interests were sold to Chicago & North Western and the Milwaukee Road. Penn Central and later Conrail inherited NYC's interest. Present ownership is divided equally between Conrail and the Milwaukee Road. IHB's main line extends from the industrial area at the southern end of Lake Michigan west and north through Blue Island and La Grange, Ill., to Franklin Park, Illinois.

Continued on next page.

Franklin Park, forming a belt line much of the way around Chicago. IHB's route bypasses the rail congestion of Chicago and reduces transit time through the Chicago gateway.

Address of general offices: P. O. Box 389, Hammond, IN 46325
Miles of road operated: 114
Reporting marks: IHB
Number of locomotives: 106
Number of freight cars: 33
Major yards: Hammond, Ind. (Gibson), Riverdale, Ill. (Blue Island)
Shops: Hammond, Ind.
Connects with:
Atchison, Topeka & Santa Fe
Belt Railway of Chicago
Burlington Northern
Chessie System
Chicago & Illinois Western
Chicago & North Western
Chicago, Milwaukee, St. Paul & Pacific
Chicago Short Line
Chicago South Shore & South Bend
Conrail
Elgin, Joliet & Eastern
Grand Trunk Western
Illinois Central Gulf
LaSalle & Bureau County
Missouri Pacific
Norfolk & Western
Seaboard System
Soo Line
Radio frequencies: 160.980, 161.070, 160.665 (Gibson hump), 161.565 (Blue Island hump)
Date: March 1983

IOWA RAILROAD COMPANY

The Iowa Railroad began operation in November 1981 on the former Rock Island main line between Council Bluffs and Stuart, Iowa. In mid-1982 the railroad's operations were extended east to Bureau, Illinois, sharing trackage rights with the Milwaukee Road between Iowa City and West Davenport in an interesting arrangement — Iowa Railroad uses the track from 8 p.m. to 8 a.m. and Milwaukee Road uses it from 8 a.m. to 8 p.m.

Address of general offices: P. O. Box 10355, Des Moines, IA 50306
Miles of road operated: 456
Reporting marks: IRRC
Number of locomotives: 12
Number of freight cars: 296
Principal commodities carried: Grain
Junctions with other railroads:
Burlington Northern:
    Council Bluffs, Iowa

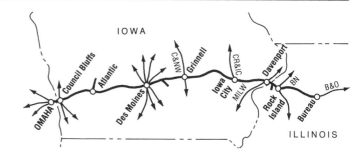

Des Moines, Iowa
Rock Island, Ill.
Cedar Rapids & Iowa City: Iowa City, Iowa
Chessie System: Bureau, Ill.

Chicago & North Western:
   Council Bluffs, Iowa
   Des Moines, Iowa
   Grinnell, Iowa
Chicago, Milwaukee, St. Paul & Pacific:
   Iowa City, Iowa
   Rock Island, Ill.
Davenport, Rock Island & North Western: Rock Island, Ill.
Des Moines Union: Des Moines, Iowa
Illinois Central Gulf: Council Bluffs, Iowa
Norfolk & Western: Council Bluffs, Iowa; Des Moines, Iowa
Union Pacific: Council Bluffs, Iowa
Radio frequencies: 161.220

David Harris.

A pair of bright-yellow ex-Illinois Central Gulf U30Bs lead a westbound Iowa Railroad freight through Tiskilwa, Ill., on former Rock Island track.

KANSAS CITY SOUTHERN RAILWAY

In 1890 Arthur Stilwell began construction of the Kansas City, Pittsburg & Gulf, building as directly southward as possible from Kansas City to create the shortest route to the Gulf of Mexico. In 1897 the line was completed to Port Arthur, Texas — which Stilwell also built. The purpose of the railroad was to carry agricultural products to the Gulf. Within two years the road entered receivership. Stilwell was squeezed out (he then built the Kansas City, Mexico & Orient — see Chihuahua Pacific, page 62) and the road was reorganized as the Kansas City Southern.

Discovery of oil in eastern Texas changed things for KCS: Northbound petroleum and chemical traffic supplemented southbound grain. Leonor F. Loree was brought in to build up the railroad. He served from 1906 to 1936 as chairman of the executive committee, and for almost all of that same period he was president of Delaware & Hudson (accounting, perhaps, for the similarity of the steam locomotive rosters of the two railroads).

Between 1896 and 1907 William Edenborn built the Louisiana Railway & Navigation Co. between New Orleans and Shreveport. It formed the shortest route between the two cities. In 1923 Edenborn extended his line west to McKinney, Texas, within hailing distance of Dallas, by purchase of a Missouri-Kansas-Texas branch.

William Buchanan started a logging line in 1896; by 1906 it had become the Louisiana & Arkansas Railway, from Hope, Ark., to Alexandria, La., with a branch to Shreveport.

The LR&N and the L&A were merged in 1928 as the Louisiana & Arkansas by Harvey Couch, and that railroad was merged with Kansas City Southern in 1939. Its New Orleans-Shreveport route and its line to Dallas were natural extensions of the Kansas City Southern.

The 1940s and 1950s saw KCS rebuilt with heavy rail, new ties, CTC, and diesels under the leadership of William N. Deramus, who was succeeded in 1961 by his son, William N. Deramus III.

To prepare for unit coal trains KCS undertook extensive rebuilding of its track in the 1970s. It teamed up with Burlington Northern in the movement of unit coal trains from the Powder River Basin in Wyoming to power plants in Arkansas, Louisiana, and Texas. In spite of the storm of

Continued on next page.

mergers surrounding it, the road remains independent, and Louisiana & Arkansas still retains some measure of a separate existence within Kansas City Southern Lines.

Address of general offices: 114 W. 11th Street, Kansas City, MO 64105

Miles of road operated: 1663

Reporting marks: KCS, LA

Number of locomotives: 301

Number of freight cars: 7129

Principal commodities carried: Coal, chemicals, paper products

Major yards: Shreveport, La. (Deramus)

Principal shops: Shreveport, La.

Radio frequencies: 160.260 (road and dispatcher to train), 160.350 (train to dispatcher)

Historical and technical society: Kansas City Southern Historical Society, 9825 Bellaire, Kansas City, MO 61571

Date: March 1983

Fred W. Frailey.

Once known for glossy black passenger cars trimmed in red and yellow, Kansas City Southern is now the road of white diesels — with the same trim colors. Four of them, a GP30 and 3 GP38s, lead a northbound freight across Big Cypress Bayou at Jefferson, Texas.

KANSAS CITY TERMINAL RAILWAY

The Kansas City Terminal was incorporated in 1906. In 1910 it absorbed the Kansas City Belt Railway and the Union Depot Co. of Kansas City. The company built Kansas City Union Station, opened in 1914, and still operates it, though the only tenant is, of course, Amtrak. KCT is owned equally by Santa Fe, Burlington Northern, Chicago & North Western, Milwaukee Road, Illinois Central Gulf, Kansas City Southern, Missouri-Kansas-Texas, Missouri Pacific, Union Pacific, Norfolk & Western, and Cotton Belt.

Address of general offices: 207 Union Station, 30 W. Pershing Road, Kansas City, MO 64108
Miles of road operated: 27
Reporting marks: KCT
Number of locomotives: 10
Connects with:
Atchison, Topeka & Santa Fe
Burlington Northern
Chicago & North Western
Chicago, Milwaukee, St. Paul & Pacific
Illinois Central Gulf
Kansas & Missouri Railway & Terminal Co
Kansas City Southern
Missouri-Kansas-Texas
Missouri Pacific
Norfolk & Western
St. Louis Southwestern (Cotton Belt)
Union Pacific
all at Kansas City, Mo., or Kansas City, Kans.
Radio frequencies: 161.310 (road and yard), 161.010 (dispatcher)
Date: March 1983

The visors over the rear windows of SW1200s 73 and 78 are a feature unique to KCT.

Louis A. Marre.

101

LAKE ERIE, FRANKLIN & CLARION RAILROAD

The Lake Erie, Franklin & Clarion was incorporated in 1913 to consolidate the Pennsylvania Northern; Pennsylvania Southern; and Pittsburg, Clarion & Franklin railroads. The principal commodity carried by the railroad is coal from mines in the area. The road also brings in raw materials and carries out the finished products of a glass factory. The large fleet of freight cars assures a good supply of cars to on-line shippers. The railroad is privately owned.

Address of general offices: P. O. Box 430, Clarion, PA 16214
Miles of road operated: 15

Reporting marks: LEF
Number of locomotives: 6
Number of freight cars: 1121
Principal commodities carried: Coal, glass, bricks, lumber
Junctions with other railroads: Conrail: Summerville, Pa., Sutton, Pa.
Radio frequencies: 160.650, 160.335
Map: See Pittsburg & Shawmut, page 151
Date: May 1983

Ken Kraemer.

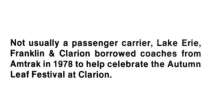

Not usually a passenger carrier, Lake Erie, Franklin & Clarion borrowed coaches from Amtrak in 1978 to help celebrate the Autumn Leaf Festival at Clarion.

LAKE SUPERIOR & ISHPEMING RAILROAD

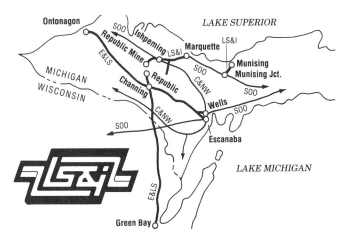

In 1896 the Cleveland Cliffs Iron Mining Co. opened the Lake Superior & Ishpeming Railway. The purpose of the railroad was to transport iron ore from Cleveland Cliffs' mines in Michigan's Upper Peninsula to the docks on Lake Superior at Marquette, Mich. Previously the ore had been handled by the Duluth, South Shore & Atlantic; the mining company saw economies in having its own railroad. In 1927 the LS&I was merged with the Munising, Marquette & Southeastern Railway, also a Cleveland Cliffs operation and a product of a merger of two small roads between Marquette and Munising, Mich. The new road was the Lake Superior & Ishpeming Railroad.

In 1979 LS&I abandoned its trackage east of Marquette, except for a five-mile segment between Munising and the Soo Line at Munising Junction. LS&I continues to haul iron, both as ore and as taconite pellets for its owner, Cleveland Cliffs Iron Co.

Address of general offices: 105 East Washington Street, Marquette, MI 49855

Miles of road operated: 60

Reporting marks: LSI

Number of locomotives: 23

Number of freight cars: 2175

Principal commodities carried: Iron ore

Shops: Eagle Mills, Mich.

Junctions with other railroads:

Chicago & North Western: Ishpeming, Mich.

Soo Line:

Ishpeming, Mich.

Marquette, Mich.

Munising Jct., Mich.

Radio frequencies: 160.230

Date: April 1983

Stanley H. Mailer.

Three Lake Superior & Ishpeming diesels, a General Electric U23C and a pair of Alco RSD15s, bring empty ore cars past Empire Mine en route to Tilden Mine in the iron ore country of Michigan's Upper Peninsula. Most of the ore cars have extended sides for carrying taconite pellets.

LAMOILLE VALLEY RAILROAD

Edward A. Lewis.

Two yellow-and-green RS3s bring a freight train through Fisher Bridge, now a state historic site, east of Wolcott.

In 1869 ground was broken for the Portland & Ogdensburg-Vermont Division at St. Johnsbury, Vermont. The railroad's destination was Lake Champlain; it was to be part of a bridge route between Portland, Maine, and the Great Lakes. The Portland & Ogdensburg Railroad building northwest from Portland met the independent Vermont Division at Lunenburg, Vt., east of St. Johnsbury on the New Hampshire boundary, in 1875. The line was pushed through to Swanton, Vt., almost to Lake Champlain, in 1877. Receivership followed within months.

The railroad was reorganized as the St. Johnsbury & Lake Champlain by its bondholders in 1880, and it built the last few miles to the shore of Lake Champlain at Maquam that year. In 1883, with the encouragement of the Ogdensburg & Lake Champlain, it built a short extension from Swanton to Rouses Point, New York, to connect with the O&LC, the last link in the Portland-to-Ogdensburg route. In the meantime the Central Vermont took over the O&LC and refused to interchange traffic with the StJ&LC at Rouses Point, and the now-useless new extension was abandoned.

In 1880 Maine Central acquired the Portland & Ogdensburg and leased the portion of the StJ&LC that lay east of St. Johnsbury. Boston & Lowell obtained control of the StJ&LC in 1885; that control passed to Boston & Maine in 1895 when B&M took over B&L.

The StJ&LC was returned to local management in 1925 and it struggled on into bankruptcy in 1944. It was reorganized in 1948 as the St. Johnsbury & Lamoille County Railroad. Boston & Maine soon sold the

railroad to local interests. They in turn sold it in 1956 to the H. E. Salzberg Co.; it was sold again in 1967 to Samuel M. Pinsly, who like Salzberg was the owner of a group of short lines. Pinsly's rehabilitation of the railroad included abandonment of the western end of the railroad between Swanton and East Swanton, including the three-span covered bridge over the Missisquoi River at Swanton, and replacement of two more covered bridges at Cambridge Jct. and west of Wolcott, with steel bridges. The Fisher Bridge east of Wolcott was preserved with concealed reinforcement, retaining its appearance as a covered bridge, and it became the emblem of the railroad.

Pinsly had no more financial success with the road than had previous management. He petitioned for abandonment, embargoed the line, and proposed that the state of Vermont purchase it as it had the Rutland Railway. In 1973 the state purchased the railroad from Pinsley and awarded the operating contract to Bruno Loati of Morrisville, Vt. The road began operation as the Lamoille County Railroad and then reassumed its former name. Because of a dispute with the state over required track rehabilitation, the state announced that Vermont Northern, a subsidiary of Morrison-Knudsen, would take over in October 1976.

Vermont Northern took over, but the state was still not satisfied with the operation of the railroad. A local group that included the line's major shippers formed the Northern Vermont Corporation, bid in on the operation, and incorporated the Lamoille Valley Railroad, which took over the railroad on January 1, 1978.

In 1980 the Lamoille Valley and the Central Vermont agreed to interchange traffic at St. Albans rather than Fonda Jct., with LVRC operating between Sheldon Jct. and St. Albans on CV track and CV in turn serving the road's customers at Swanton and East Swanton.

Address of general offices: R. F. D. 1, Stafford Ave., Morrisville, VT 05661

Miles of road operated: 99

Reporting marks: LVRC
Number of locomotives: 4
Number of freight cars: 50
Principal commodities carried: Talc, asbestos, grain, paper, lumber
Shops: Morrisville, Vt.
Junctions with other railroads:
Canadian Pacific: St. Johnsbury, Vt.
Central Vermont: Sheldon Jct., Vt.; Swanton (Fonda Jct.), Vt.
Maine Central: St. Johnsbury, Vt.
Radio frequencies: 161.340, 160.230
Recommended reading: RAILROADS YOU CAN MODEL, by Mike Schafer, published in 1976 by Kalmbach Publishing Co., 1027 North Seventh Street, Milwaukee, WI 53233 (ISBN 0-89024-526-6)
Map: See Vermont Railway, page 200
Date: April 1983

LITTLE ROCK & WESTERN RAILWAY

The Little Rock & Western is one of several short lines created from the remains of the Rock Island upon its death on March 31, 1980. The LR&W bought the Perry-Pulaski, Arkansas, portion of RI's Choctaw Route (Little Rock-Oklahoma City-Amarillo, Texas-Tucumcari, New Mexico) to provide a rail outlet for the Arkansas Kraft Paper Mill 3 miles east of Perry. The railroad is owned by Green Bay Packaging.

Address of general offices: P. O. Box 386, Perry, AR 72125
Miles of road operated: 54
Number of locomotives: 2
Number of freight cars: 350
Reporting marks: LRWN
Principal commodities carried: Paper products
Junctions with other railroads:
Missouri Pacific: Little Rock (Pulaski), Ark.
St. Louis Southwestern: North Little Rock, Ark.
Radio frequencies: 161.025
Date: April 1983

Bill Folsom

Little Rock & Western 101 is an Alco C420 formerly listed on the Long Island Rail Road's roster as No. 207. It was rebuilt by the Green Bay & Western and replaced one of LR&W's leased GB&W RS3s. A similar unit will replace the other leased RS3.

The Long Island Rail Road Company

LONG ISLAND RAIL ROAD

The Long Island Rail Road was chartered in 1834. It was intended to be a link in a complex New York-Boston route: ferry from Manhattan to Brooklyn; rail to Greenport, New York, at the northeastern tip of Long Island; steamer across Long Island Sound to Stonington, Connecticut; and rail to Boston. The line was completed to Greenport in 1841, but by 1850 the engineers who had assured the LIRR backers that a railroad could never be built along the Connecticut shore had been proven wrong — an all-rail route between New York and Boston was capturing most of the business. The Long Island entered receivership and turned its attention away from Boston and to local matters for several decades.

In 1880 Austin Corbin gained control of the railroad. He planned to make Montauk, N. Y., at the eastern tip of Long Island, a port for transatlantic shipping. The capital he provided was useful to the railroad, even if his plans came to naught. The LIRR absorbed its competitors, such as the New York & Flushing and the South Side Railway, and became the only railroad on the island. In 1885 the railroad began operating trains of flatcars to carry farmers' wagons into New York City — the first piggyback service.

Under Alexander J. Cassatt the Pennsylvania Railroad acquired control of the Long Island in 1900 and included it in plans for Pennsylvania Station in New York City. Because of its involvement in the Penn Station project, LIRR was able to boast of mainline electrification with 600-volt DC third rail (1905), the first steel passenger car (1905), and the first all-steel passenger fleet (1927). The suburban boom on Long Island began in the early 1920s, and LIRR's access to a terminal in Manhattan was a decided asset in building its commuter business.

The Long Island Rail Road found it was difficult to make money in the commuter business. Commuter service requires large amounts of rolling stock and correspondingly large numbers of employees to run it for two short periods each day, plus, of course, the track and stations to handle large crowds. Nor was the railroad helped by a New York Public Service Commission freeze on commuter fares from 1918 to 1947. LIRR went into the red in 1935. Taxes, the cost of grade-crossing elimination projects, and the maintenance required by the heavy World War Two traffic drove the railroad into bankruptcy.

The Long Island Transit Authority and LIRR's owner, the Pennsylvania Railroad, both proposed plans for bringing the road out of bankruptcy, and the two reached agreement in 1954. The plan adopted called for a 12-year rehabilitation period during which Pennsy would receive no dividends (indeed, Pennsy had received a return on its investment for perhaps 10 of the 50 years it had owned the Long Island) and fares could be increased to cover expenses. The plan also included relief from property taxes. Rehabilitation included modernization of cars and purchase of new ones, dieselization of the non-electrified portion of the line, plant improvements, and increased service. LIRR's passengers were happy even if the accountants soon found themselves looking at balance sheets similar to those they had seen before.

In 1965 the Metropolitan Commuter Transportation Authority was created; it purchased the railroad from the Pennsylvania Railroad in 1966. In 1968 the Metropolitan Transportation Authority was formed; it is now the owner of the Long Island Railroad.

The Long Island is the busiest passenger railroad in the U. S. It operates trains from three western terminals — Penn Station in Manhattan, Flatbush Avenue in Brooklyn, and Hunterspoint Avenue in Queens — through the eight tracks of Jamaica station, busiest through station in the U. S., to destinations on nine branches, plus New York-Port Washington trains that branch off the main line west of Jamaica. Most of LIRR's revenue comes from carrying passengers; freight business accounts for only one tenth of LIRR's revenue.

Address of general offices: Jamaica Station, Jamaica, NY 11435

Miles of road operated: 322

Reporting marks: LI

Number of locomotives: 72, plus 23 auxiliary power-control cab units

Number of passenger cars: 227

Number of self-propelled passenger cars: 809

Principal commodities carried: Foodstuffs, copper, rock salt

Shops: Morris Park, N. Y.

Junctions with other railroads: Conrail: Fresh Pond Jct., N. Y.

Radio frequencies: 160.380 (road and towers), 161.445 (dispatcher), 161.265 (yard)

Passenger routes: New York (Penn Station), Brooklyn (Flatbush Avenue), and Hunterspoint Avenue via Jamaica to Far Rockaway, Long Beach, Babylon, West Hempstead, Hempstead, Oyster Bay, Port Jefferson, Greenport, and Montauk; New York (Penn Station) to Port Washington

Recommended reading: *Steel Rails to the Sunrise*, by Ron Ziel and George Foster, published in 1965 by Hawthorn Books, 260 Madison Ave., New York, NY 10016 (ISBN 0-8015-7147-2)

Passenger service in Long Island's electrified zone is provided by Budd-built *Metropolitan* M. U. cars, such as this New York-bound train at Woodside. Directly above LIRR's station is the 61st Street station of New York City's subway system.

William D. Middleton.

LOUISIANA & NORTH WEST RAILROAD

The Louisiana & North West was incorporated in 1889 as successor to the Louisiana North & South Railroad. It was in receivership from 1913 to 1927. In 1948 the L&NW abandoned its line south of Gibsland — at one time it had extended south to Natchitoches, where it connected with Texas & Pacific — but North Louisiana & Gulf (page 143) purchased the portion of the line between Bienville and Gibsland to maintain its connections with L&NW and Illinois Central.

In 1958 L&NW was purchased from its owner, Middle States Petroleum Co., by the H. E. Salzberg company, which then also owned Wellsville, Addison & Galeton; Fort Dodge, Des Moine & Southern; Des Moines & Central Iowa; and St. Johnsbury & Lamoille County. Recently Lousiana & North West has acquired a following among enthusiasts for its half-dozen F units originally owned by Southern Pacific and Western Pacific.

Address of general offices: P. O. Box 89, Homer, LA 71040
Miles of road operated: 62
Reporting marks: LNW
Number of locomotives: 7
Number of freight cars: 36
Principal commodities carried: Pulpwood, wood chips, paper products, chemicals
Shops: Gibsland, La.
Junctions with other railroads:
Illinois Central Gulf: Gibsland, La.
North Louisiana & Gulf: Gibsland, La.
St. Louis Southwestern: McNeil, Ark.
Radio frequencies: 160.530, 160.650
Date: April 1983

Two Louisiana & North West trains meet at Athens, La. The southbound train (left) includes several carloads of pulpwood ahead of its caboose; the northbound is powered by ex-Southern Pacific F7 No. 46.

R. T. Sharp.

LOUISIANA MIDLAND RAILWAY

The Louisiana Midland was incorporated in 1945 to purchase a branch of the Louisiana & Arkansas between Packton, Louisiana, and Vidalia, La., on the west bank of the Mississippi River opposite Natchez, Mississippi. The railroad was absorbed by Illinois Central on March 28, 1967, and it resumed independent operation on March 28, 1974, exactly seven years later. For a brief period in late 1980 and early 1981 the road operated the former Rock Island line between Hodge and Winnfield, La. That line is now operated by the Central Louisiana & Gulf (see North Louisiana & Gulf, page 143). As this book went to press the Louisiana Midland was embargoed because of flood and fire damage.

Address of general offices: P. O. Box 110, Jena, LA 71342
Miles of road operated: 75
Reporting marks: LOAM
Number of locomotives: 2
Number of freight cars: 54
Principal commodities carried: Pulpwood and wood products
Junctions with other railroads:
Illinois Central Gulf: Natchez, Miss. (by ferry)
Louisiana & Arkansas (Kansas City Southern): Packton, La.
Missouri Pacific:
   Concordia Jct., La.
   Ferriday, La.
   Georgetown, La.
   Vidalia, La.
Radio frequencies: 160.680
Date: May 1983

Louis Saillard.

Louisiana Midland RS1 1111, ex-Gulf, Mobile & Ohio, wore LOAM's purple and white livery. The unit has been sold to Chattahoochee Industrial.

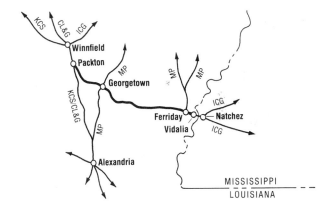

LOUISVILLE, NEW ALBANY & CORYDON RAILROAD

The Louisville, New Albany & Corydon Railroad was incorporated in 1888 as a reorganization of the LNA&C Railway, which was completed in 1883. It is now owned by U. S. Railway Manufacturing Co., which builds freight cars. Many of LNA&C's freight cars are assigned to special service; others are "free runners" (they need not be sent toward their home road but can be dispatched in any direction) earning per diem charges for their owner. The railroad connects Corydon, Indiana, which is about 20 miles west of Louisville, Kentucky, with the Louisville-St. Louis line of the Southern Railway.

Address of general offices: P. O. Box 10, Corydon, IN 47112
Miles of road operated: 8
Reporting marks: LNAC
Number of locomotives: 1
Number of freight cars: 1259
Principal commodities carried: Feed, lumber, furniture, battery separators
Junctions with other railroads Southern: Corydon Junction, Ind.
Date: May 1983

Louisville, New Albany & Corydon's 45-tonner *Betty-Sue* is dwarfed by the standard 40-foot boxcar behind it.

R. T. Sharp.

110

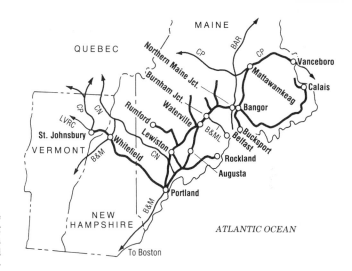

MAINE CENTRAL RAILROAD

The Maine Central was incorporated in 1862 as the consolidation of the Androscoggin & Kennebec and Penobscot & Kennebec railroads, forming a 5′6″-gauge route from Portland to Bangor, Maine, in conjunction with the Atlantic & St. Lawrence (now Canadian National) between Portland and Danville Jct. The new company soon absorbed most of the other railroads in the area between Portland and Bangor and standard-gauged its lines. Further expansion involved leasing the Portland & Ogdensburg from Portland to St. Johnsbury, Vermont, and the grandly named European & North American from Bangor east to the Canadian border at Vanceboro, Maine.

The Maine Central took over Maine's most prosperous 2-foot-gauge railroads, the Sandy River & Rangeley Lakes and the Bridgton & Saco River in 1911 and 1912; the narrow gauge lines regained their independence in 1923 and 1927, respectively.

In 1933 MEC entered an agreement with the Boston & Maine for joint employment of some officers and personnel. The cooperative arrangement, providing the benefits of merged operation, continued until 1952, when MEC resumed independent operation and replaced B&M maroon on its cars and locomotives with pine needle green. Separation from B&M was completed on December 29, 1955.

In December 1980 U. S. Filter Corporation purchased the railroad. Almost immediately Ashland Oil took over U. S. Filter and in June 1981 sold the railroad to Timothy Mellon's Guilford Transportation Industries. GTI has also acquired the Boston & Maine and the Delaware & Hudson.

Maine Central owns the Portland Terminal Company, a switching road at Portland.

Address of general offices: 242 St. John Street, Portland, ME 04102
Miles of road operated: 819
Number of locomotives: 65
Number of freight cars: 4377
Reporting marks: MEC
Principal commodities carried: Paper products
Principal shops: Waterville, Maine

Continued on next page.

The most scenic part of Maine Central's track is the line through Crawford Notch in the White Mountains of New Hampshire. U18B 401 and three GP38s lead freight YR-1 (St. Johnsbury, Vt.-Rigby Yard, South Portland, Maine) south through the notch in September 1979.

Ronald N. Johnson.

Major yards: Bangor, Maine, Waterville, Maine, South Portland, Maine (Rigby)

Junctions with other railroads:

Bangor & Aroostook: Northern Maine Jct., Maine
Belfast & Moosehead Lake: Burnham Jct., Maine
Boston & Maine: Portland, Maine, Whitefield, N. H.
Canadian National:
   Danville Jct., Maine
   Portland, Maine
   Yarmouth Jct., Maine
Canadian Pacific
   Mattawamkeag, Maine

   Milltown Jct., Maine (Milltown, N. B.)
   St. Johnsbury, Vt.
   Vanceboro, Maine
Lamoille Valley: St. Johnsbury, Vt.
Portland Terminal: Portland, Maine

Radio frequencies: 160.620 (road), 160.380 (yard), 161.250 (Portland Terminal)

Historical and technical society: Railroad Historical Society of Maine, Box 8057, Portland, ME 04104

Recommended reading: *Meet the Maine Central*, published in 1981 by The 470 Railroad Club, P. O. Box 641, Portland, ME 04104

Date: February 1983

MANUFACTURERS RAILWAY

The Manufacturers Railway is a switching and terminal road serving the southeast part of St. Louis, Missouri. It is owned by Anheuser-Busch Companies, Inc., maker of Budweiser beer.

Address of general offices: 2850 S. Broadway, St. Louis, MO 63118
Miles of road operated: 42
Reporting marks: MRS
Number of locomotives: 11
Number of freight cars: 1177
Principal commodities carried: Beer, grain, chemicals
Connects with:
Alton & Southern
Burlington Northern
Chessie System
Chicago & North Western
Conrail
Illinois Central Gulf
Missouri-Kansas-Texas
Missouri Pacific
Norfolk & Western
St. Louis Southwestern
Seaboard System
Southern Railway
Terminal Railroad Association of St. Louis
all within the St. Louis-East St. Louis Switching Districts
Radio frequencies: 160.740
Date: April 1983

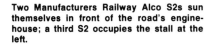

Two Manufacturers Railway Alco S2s sun themselves in front of the road's enginehouse; a third S2 occupies the stall at the left.

MRS.

Rhinelander

Bradley

SOO

Tomahawk

SOO

Wisconsin Dam

MILW

Merrill

WISCONSIN

Wausau

MARINETTE, TOMAHAWK & WESTERN RAILROAD

The Marinette, Tomahawk & Western Railway was incorporated in 1894 and opened in 1895. It purchased the Wisconsin & Chippewa Railway in 1898. The railroad was reorganized in 1912 with its present name. It is owned by Owens-Illinois, Inc., whose paper mill at Tomahawk accounts for outbound paper products and inbound coal on the road's ledgers. The MT&W also serves a Georgia Pacific mill. In recent years MT&W's bright green boxcars have become a familiar sight on railroads across the country.

Address of general offices: P. O. Box 315, Tomahawk, WI 54487
Miles of road operated: 13
Reporting marks: MTW
Number of locomotives: 3
Number of freight cars: 595
Principal commodities carried: Paper products, coal
Junctions with other railroads:
Chicago, Milwaukee, St. Paul & Pacific: Tomahawk, Wis.
Soo Line: Bradley, Wis.
Radio frequencies: 160.290
Date: May 1983

Phillip Tygum.

A lake forms a reflecting pool for Marinette, Tomahawk & Western NW2 No. 62 and for the road's office building.

114

MARYLAND & DELAWARE RAILROAD

The New York, Philadelphia & Norfolk, a subsidiary of the Pennsylvania Railroad, completed a line down the Delmarva Peninsula from Wilmington, Delaware, to Cape Charles, Virginia, in 1884. In conjunction with a car ferry across the mouth of Chesapeake Bay to Norfolk the line formed a route to the south that bypassed the congestion and restrictive clearances of Baltimore and Washington.

In the 1960s the line's status declined, and Penn Central continued the process of neglect during its brief stewardship. At one point the Southern Railway was interested in the line for access to the chemical industry at Wilmington, but SR could not reach an agreement with one of the unions involved.

In 1976 Conrail took over the main line as far south as Pocomoke City, Maryland, but the branches on the Delmarva Peninsula were classified as light density by the United States Railway Association and therefore not included in Conrail. However, Conrail operated the branches for a time with federal subsidy.

Rail Services Associates proposed operating all the branches as a single entity, and in August 1977 the Maryland & Delaware Railroad assumed operating responsibility for three branches: Townsend, Del., to Chestertown and Centreville, Md.; Clayton, Del., to Easton, Md., with a spur from Queen Anne to Denton, Md.; and Seaford, Del., to Cambridge, Md., with a branch from Preston to Hurlock, Md. In May 1982 the railroad

Continued on next page

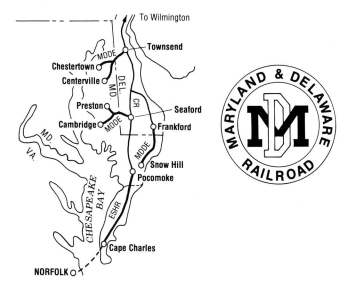

MDDE

Typical of Maryland & Delaware's operation is Alco RS1 No. 20 at the head of a freight train. The ballast tamper on the spur and the fresh ballast under the locomotive are evidence of track rehabilitation.

took over the line from Frankford, Del., to Snow Hill, Md. Maryland & Delaware abandoned the Clayton-Easton branch in February 1983 because of lack of business and bridge deterioration.

Address of general offices: P. O. Box 2596, Salisbury, MD 21801
Miles of road operated: 120
Reporting marks: MDDE
Number of locomotives: 4

Number of freight cars: 125
Principal commodities carried: Printing paper, plastic and paper cups, fertilizer, foodstuffs
Shops: Federalsburg, Md.
Junctions with other railroads: Conrail: Frankford, Seaford, and Townsend, Del.
Date: April 1983

MARYLAND & PENNSYLVANIA RAILROAD

The Maryland & Pennsylvania — the Ma & Pa, for short — used to be the quintessential, archetypal short line. It had to go 77 miles to get from Baltimore, Maryland, to York, Pennsylvania — cities that are less than 50 miles apart. Its steam locomotives were small and old, and its passenger cars were innocent of such characteristics as all-steel construction, cast trucks, and vestibules.

The Maryland Central Railroad was chartered in 1867. In 1884 it reached Delta, Md., 44 rail miles northeast of Baltimore, and it entered receivership about the time its three-foot-gauge track entered Delta. It was reorganized in 1888 as the Maryland Central Railway.

The Peach Bottom Railway was opened in 1874 from York, Pennsylvania, to Peach Bottom, about 35 miles away on the Susquehanna River. By

Paul J. Dolkos.

A Ma & Pa shop crew assembles freight car trucks at the road's shop.

1881 the narrow gauge railroad was in receivership; it was reorganized in 1882 as the York & Peach Bottom. In 1891 the York & Peach Bottom and the Maryland Central were merged as the Baltimore & Lehigh Railroad, which went bankrupt in 1892.

In 1894 the Pennsylvania portion of the road was reorganized as the York Southern and the Maryland portion as the Baltimore & Lehigh Railway. They were standard-gauged in 1895 and 1900, respectively, and merged in 1901 to form the Maryland & Pennsylvania.

The Ma & Pa eked out an existence for more than half a century on local traffic, most of it on the northern part of the line. In 1958 the railroad abandoned the Maryland portion of its line, from Delta to Baltimore. In 1969 the road restored its Peach Bottom branch, which had been pulled up in 1903. Philadelphia Electric Co. was constructing a nuclear power plant at Peach Bottom, and inbound construction materials furnished revenue for the road for several years.

Emons Industries purchased the railroad in 1971, primarily as a means for entering the freight car leasing field. The railroad built a new shop at York in 1977 and began building new freight cars. When Conrail was formed, Ma & Pa picked up the former Pennsylvania Railroad line from York to Walkersville, Md., plus a three-mile segment of the old Northern Central, Pennsy's direct route from Harrisburg through York to Balti-more. The Walkersville line was cut back to Hanover, Pa., in 1978, and the original Ma & Pa line was abandoned south of Red Lion, Pa., that same year. In 1983 Ma & Pa abandoned the rest of its original line between York and Red Lion.

Address of general offices: 490 E. Market Street, York, PA 17403
Miles of road operated: 66
Number of locomotives: 6
Number of freight cars: 2192
Reporting marks: MPA
Principal commodities carried: Paper products, foodstuffs, furniture
Shops: York, Pa.
Junctions with other railroads:
Chessie System: Hanover, Pa.; York, Pa.
Conrail: York, Pa.
Radio frequencies: 160.335, 160.695
Recommended reading:
MORE RAILROADS YOU CAN MODEL, by Mike Schafer, published in 1978 by Kalmbach Publishing Co., 1027 North Seventh Street, Milwaukee, WI 53233 (ISBN 0-89024-534-6)
The Ma & Pa, by George Hilton, second edition published in 1980 by Howell-North, P. O. Box 3051, La Jolla, CA 92038

MARYLAND DEPARTMENT OF TRANSPORTATION

The Maryland Department of Transportation subsidizes commuter service on Chessie System (Baltimore & Ohio) from Washington, D. C., west through the Potomac Valley to Brunswick, Md. (49 miles, 5 weekday trains, one of which continues to Martinsburg, West Virginia, 73 miles from Washington, unsubsidized by MDOT), and northeast to Baltimore (38 miles, three weekday trains for commuters to Washington and one for commuters to Baltimore). The latter is the oldest rail passenger route in the U. S. MDOT also underwrites two Baltimore-Washington trains each weekday operated by Amtrak using leased New Jersey Department of Transportation *Jersey Arrow* cars on the former Pennsylvania Railroad line (40 miles).

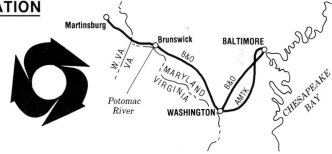

Continued on next page.

Address of general offices: P. O. Box 8755, Baltimore-Washington International Airport, Baltimore, MD 21240
Miles of road operated: 151
Number of locomotives: 5
Number of passenger cars: 22
Number of self-propelled passenger cars: 10
Radio frequencies: Chessie System: 160.230, 160.320
Passenger routes:
Amtrak: Washington-Baltimore (ex-Pennsylvania Railroad)
Chessie System (Baltimore & Ohio): Washington-Baltimore, Washington-Brunswick, Md.
Date: April 1983

A rebuilt F7 leads four rebuilt coaches, originally Norfolk & Western and Pennsylvania Railroad sleepers, past Baltimore & Ohio's old brick depot at Point of Rocks, Maryland, junction of B&O's Old Main Line (the line directly west from Baltimore) and its line from Washington to Cumberland, Md.

Jim Popson.

MASSACHUSETTS BAY TRANSPORTATION AUTHORITY

In 1947 the Metropolitan Transit Authority of Massachusetts took over the Boston Elevated Railway, a transit system serving Boston and 13 surrounding cities and towns with subway and elevated trains, streetcars, trackless trolleys, and buses. The MTA was succeeded in 1964 by the Massachusetts Bay Transportation Authority, whose scope encompassed 79 municipalities in eastern Massachusetts.

In 1964 three railroads operated commuter service to Boston: Boston & Maine to North Station and New Haven and New York Central (Boston & Albany) to South Station. None of the three was financially healthy, and in 1965 MBTA made its first assistance payment to Boston & Maine for operating commuter trains. Soon MBTA was underwriting all rail commuter service into Boston. In 1973 MBTA purchased former New Haven commuter lines to Attleboro, Stoughton, and Franklin, Mass., and a segment of the former New York Central line between Riverside and Framingham, Mass. In 1975 MBTA purchased Boston & Maine's locomo-

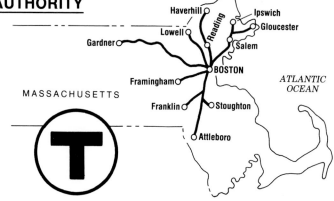

Massachusetts Bay Transportation Authority's equipment includes new push-pull trains made up of Pullman-Standard-built cars and EMD F40s. The distinctive livery is purple and silver with yellow trim.

Tom Nelligan.

tives, cars, and physical plant used for commuter service; B&M continued to operate the service for MBTA as before.

Penn Central operated the service out of South Station for MBTA; PC was succeeded by Conrail on April 1, 1976. In 1977 Conrail asked for a large subsidy increase for the ex-New Haven and ex-New York Central commuter service it had inherited from Penn Central. MBTA sought another operator and chose Boston & Maine, which took over the south side (ex New Haven and New York Central) operations.

MBTA's commuter equipment included B&M's fleet of Budd RDCs (the world's largest), long-distance coaches from the New Haven, and an assortment of ex-NH diesels and RDCs. Some of the coaches have been rebuilt and refurbished, and many of the RDCs have been de-engined and made into non-powered coaches. The old diesels have been traded in on rebuilt ex-Gulf, Mobile & Ohio F3s and F7s, now designated FP10 and equipped with head-end electrical power for train heating and lighting. MBTA has also purchased new coaches and locomotives.

MBTA also operates Boston's transit system, which extends well into the suburbs, and an extensive suburban bus system.

Address of general offices: 50 High Street, Boston, MA 02110
Miles of road operated: 244 (does not include transit)
Number of locomotives: 37
Number of passenger cars: 158
Number of self-propelled passenger cars: 92
Radio frequencies: 161.310
Passenger routes:
Boston (North Station) to Gardner, Lowell, Haverhill, Reading, Ipswich, and Rockport, Mass.; Boston (South Station) to Stoughton, Attleboro, Franklin, and Framingham, Mass.
Recommended reading:
Route of the Minute Man, by Tom Nelligan and Scott Hartley, published in 1980 by Quadrant Press, New York, NY (ISBN 0-915276-26-7)
Change at Park Street Under, by Brian J. Cudahy, published in 1972 by Stephen Greene Press, P. O. Box 1000, Brattleboro, VT 05301 (ISBN 0-8289-0173-2)
Date: April 1983

McCLOUD RIVER RAILROAD

The McCloud River Railroad was incorporated in 1897 to provide access to the forests east of Mt. Shasta in northern California. It was and still is essentially a lumber railroad. It connects with Southern Pacific at Mt. Shasta City and with Burlington Northern (ex-Great Northern) at Hambone (BN owns the line from Hambone east to Lookout, but McCloud River maintains and operates it). The line from Mt. Shasta over Signal Butte to McCloud has a single switchback east of the summit about 5 miles west of McCloud and 1000 feet higher — trains departing from Mt. Shasta in normal fashion arrive McCloud in reverse.

The McCloud River was owned for many years by the McCloud Lumber Company and later U. S. Plywood; it is now owned by the ITEL Corporation. The line was completely rehabilitated in 1982 with the help of a grant from the Federal Railroad Administration.

Address of general offices: 325 Main Street, McCloud, CA 96057

Miles of road operated: 100

Reporting marks: MR

Number of locomotives: 5 (4 diesel, 1 steam)

Number of freight cars: 250

Principal commodities carried: Forest products

Shops: McCloud, Calif.

Junctions with other railroads:

Burlington Northern: Hambone, Calif.

Southern Pacific: Mt. Shasta, Calif.

Radio frequencies: 160.695 (road), 161.025 (switching), 161.860 (switching)

Passenger routes: Excursion trains operate over the line occasionally.

Recommended reading:

Pine Across the Mountain, by Robert M. Hanft, published in 1970 by Golden West Books, P. O. Box 8136, San Marino, CA 91108 (ISBN 0-87095-038-X)

MORE RAILROADS YOU CAN MODEL, by Mike Schafer, published in 1978 by Kalmbach Publishing Co., 1027 North Seventh Street, Milwaukee, WI 53233 (ISBN 0-89024-534-6)

Date: August 1982

Ted Benson.

Red-and-white SD38s 36 and 37 tug gondolas full of wood chips up the 4.4% grade between McCloud and the switchback at Signal Butte. The road's other two diesels are SD38 No. 38 and SD38-2 No. 39.

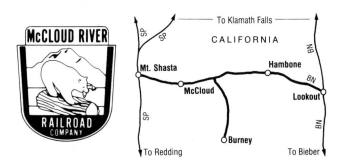

J. P. Lamb Jr.

A GP9-GP7 duo brings a Meridian & Bigbee freight through a shallow cut a few miles south of Meridian, Miss.

MERIDIAN & BIGBEE RAILROAD

The Meridian & Bigbee was incorporated in 1917 as the Meridian & Bigbee River Railway. Operation began in 1928 between Meridian, Mississippi and Cromwell, Alabama, and the line was completed through from Meridian to Myrtlewood, Ala., in 1935.

A trustee was appointed to manage the line in 1933, and the railroad was reorganized under its present name in 1952. From 1955 to 1982 it was owned by American Can Co., which has a large paper products plant on the line near Naheola, Ala. On July 1, 1982, the railroad was purchased by the James River Corporation.

Address of general offices: P. O. Box 551, Meridian, MS 39301
Miles of road operated: 51
Number of locomotives: 5
Number of freight cars: 477
Reporting marks: MB
Principal commodities carried: Pulp, chemicals, paper products
Shops: Meridian, Miss.
Junctions with other railroads:
Burlington Northern: Cromwell, Ala.
Illinois Central Gulf: Meridian, Miss.
Seaboard System: Myrtlewood, Ala.
Southern: Meridian, Miss.
Radio frequencies: 160.350
Date: April 1983

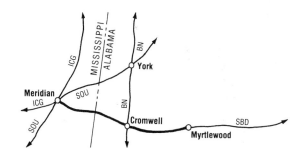

121

METRO-NORTH COMMUTER RAILROAD CO.

The Northeast Rail Service Act of July 1981 instructed Conrail to divest itself of its commuter operations by the end of 1982. The Metropolitan Transportation Authority of the state of New York established Metro-North Commuter Railroad as a subsidiary to operate the services that Conrail had inherited through Penn Central from New York Central and New Haven — the trains serving New York and Connecticut from Grand Central Terminal in New York City.

MTA provides operating subsidies for service on the Hudson (New York-Poughkeepsie) and Harlem (New York-Brewster-Dover Plains) lines; MTA and the Connecticut Department of Transportation jointly subsidize service on the New Haven line. Metro-North began operation on January 1, 1983.

MTA also subsidizes service operated by NJ Transit on former Erie-Lackawanna lines from Hoboken, New Jersey, to Spring Valley and Port Jervis, N. Y.

Other Metropolitan Transportation Authority subsidiaries are the Long Island Rail Road, the New York City Transit Authority, and the Staten Island Rapid Transit Operating Authority.

Address of general offices: 347 Madison Avenue, New York, NY 10017

Miles of road operated: 262

Reporting marks: MNCW, MNCX

Number of locomotives: 51 (48 diesel, 3 electric)

Number of passenger cars: 156

Number of self-propelled passenger cars: 554 (526 electric, 28 diesel)

Number of freight cars: 159

Radio frequencies: 161.280

Passenger routes: New York (Grand Central Terminal) to Poughkeepsie and Dover Plains, N. Y., and New Haven, Waterbury, Danbury, and New Canaan, Conn.

Date: May 1983

J. W. Swanberg.

Drawing power from the third rail, blue and silver Metro-North M. U. cars roll north along the Hudson River at Scarborough, N. Y., bound for Croton-Harmon. Both cars and track are former New York Central property.

MICHIGAN INTERSTATE RAILWAY

The history of the Ann Arbor Railroad began with two companies organized in 1869 and 1872 to build a railroad between Toledo, Ohio, and Ann Arbor, Michigan, about 45 miles. The Panic of 1873 killed at least one of those companies; it took another 20 years and 12 companies — most of them named Toledo, Ann Arbor & something — for the railroad to reach the eastern shore of Lake Michigan at Frankfort, Mich., where it connected with car ferries to Kewaunee, Wisconsin.

The Panic of 1893 caused yet another reorganization of the railroad; it became the Ann Arbor Railroad. In 1925 the Wabash (which was controlled by Pennsylvania Railroad interests) acquired control of the Ann Arbor, and in 1963 Wabash sold it to the Detroit, Toledo & Ironton (which was owned by the Wabash and the Pennsy). The Ann Arbor entered reorganization in 1973. The state of Michigan purchased it, and it was operated in its entirety for a while by the Michigan Interstate Railway Co. Dispute arose over terms and payment, and in 1983 operation of the Ann Arbor was split among three railroads: Michigan Interstate: Toledo to Ann Arbor plus a short branch to Saline, Mich; Tuscola & Saginaw Bay: Ann Arbor to Alma, with trackage rights from Durand to Ashley over Grand Trunk Western, and a 27-mile branch from Owosso to Swan Creek; and Michigan Northern: Alma to Frankfort. Operation of the Lake Michigan ferry has ceased.

Address of general offices: P. O. Box 619, Owosso, MI 48867
Miles of road operated: 49
Reporting marks: AA
Number of locomotives: 3
Number of freight cars: 524
Principal commodities carried: Auto parts, automobiles, cement
Shops: Toledo, Ohio
Junctions with other railroads:
Chessie System: Toledo, Ohio
Conrail: Ann Arbor, Mich., Toledo, Ohio
Grand Trunk System: Diann, Mich., Toledo, Ohio
Norfolk & Western: Milan, Mich., Toledo, Ohio
Toledo Terminal: Toledo, Ohio

David P. Oroszi

Two bright orange RS2s purchased from the Green Bay & Western in 1979 bring a Michigan Interstate/Ann Arbor train across the Norfolk & Western crossing at Milan, Mich., in April 1980.

Radio frequencies: 161.490
Historical and technical society: Ann Arbor Railroad Technical & Historical Association, P. O. Box 51, Chesaning, MI 48616
Date: May 1983

123

MICHIGAN NORTHERN RAILWAY

The Michigan Northern was formed in December 1975 to take over operation of the former Pennsylvania Railroad Grand Rapids & Indiana line between Grand Rapids and Mackinaw City, Michigan. The line was not slated for inclusion in Conrail and it was purchased by the Michigan State Highway Commission to maintain rail service in the area. Michigan Northern began operation on April 1, 1976, which was also start-up day for Conrail. In 1982 Michigan Northern inaugurated seasonal passenger service into the resort areas along its line. In 1983 the railroad purchased the Chesapeake & Ohio lines from Grawn to Williamsburg and from Petoskey to Charlevoix and took over operation of the state-owned Ann Arbor Railroad from Alma to Frankfort.

Address of general offices: P. O. Box 359, Cadillac, MI 49601
Miles of road operated: 248
Reporting marks: MIGN
Number of locomotives: 8
Number of freight cars: 22

Principal commodities carried: Sand, lumber, LP gas, foodstuffs
Shops: Cadillac, Mich.
Junctions with other railroads:
Cadillac & Lake City: Missaukee Jct.
Chessie System: Alma, Clare, Reed City
Conrail: Grand Rapids
Detroit & Mackinac: Mackinaw City
Soo Line: Mackinaw City
Tuscola & Saginaw Bay: Alma
Radio frequencies: 160.650
Passenger routes: Cadillac-Mackinaw City, Cadillac-Charlevoix, Traverse City-Williamsburg
Recommended reading: *The "DO" Lines*, by Edward A. Lewis, published in 1978 by The Baggage Car, P. O. Box 733, Morrisville, VT 05661
Map: see Detroit & Mackinac, page 77
Date: April 1983

Michigan Northern clears away the snows of yesteryear, 1979 to be exact, north of Howard City, Mich., with a Jordan spreader, an Alco RS3, and a Baldwin RS12.

William S. Christopher.

MISSOURI-KANSAS-TEXAS RAILROAD

The Katy was born as the Union Pacific Railway, Southern Branch, which was incorporated in 1865 to build south from Junction City, Kansas, along the Neosho River through Emporia and eventually to New Orleans (the road had no corporate connection with the Union Pacific proper). The railroad received a land grant, and construction began in 1869. The railroad changed its name to Missouri, Kansas & Texas Railway the following year, and late in 1870 it reached the southern boundary of Kansas at Chetopa ahead of two rival lines, thereby earning the right to build south through what is now Oklahoma. Also in 1870 the MK&T absorbed the Tebo & Neosho, a line from Sedalia, Missouri, southwest to Parsons, Kans.

Katy rails reached Denison, Texas, in 1872. Other significant events in the 1870s included a battle with the Atlantic & Pacific (a Frisco predecessor) over a crossing at Vinita, Okla., in 1871; extension from Sedalia to a junction with the Burlington at Hannibal, Mo., in 1873; and control of the road by Jay Gould, who saw it as a feeder to his Missouri Pacific system.

Katy reached Dallas and Fort Worth in 1881, the latter on trackage rights over the Texas & Pacific from Whitesboro, Tex. That same year the road purchased the International & Great Northern, another Gould road; the MK&T and the I&GN met at Taylor, Tex., in 1882. Katy purchased the Galveston, Houston & Henderson in 1883; Gould promptly leased the GH&H to the I&GN. In 1886 MK&T built north from Parsons, Kans., to Paola, and negotiated trackage rights for an entrance to Kansas City over the Kansas City, Fort Scott & Gulf (later Frisco). Jay Gould was thrown out in 1888, Missouri Pacific's lease of the Katy was canceled, and control of I&GN passed to MP.

In 1886 Texas passed a law compelling railroads operating in that state to maintain general offices there. Accordingly in 1891 the Missouri, Kansas & Texas of Texas was created to hold all of Katy's Texas trackage. The MK&T emerged from receivership that same year and began a period of expansion which put its rails into Houston (1893), St. Louis (1896), Shreveport, Louisiana (1900), San Antonio (1900), Tulsa (1903), and Oklahoma City (1904). In 1910 Katy acquired the Texas Central, which reached out toward Abilene from Waco, and in 1911 took over the Wich-

Continued on next page.

ita Falls & Northwestern and the Wichita Falls & Southern. By 1915 the sprawling system had 3865 miles of railroad that reached south from St. Louis, Hannibal, and Kansas City, Mo., and Junction City, Kans., to Galveston and San Antonio, Tex., and extended east to Shreveport, La., and west into the Oklahoma panhandle.

In 1923 the Katy was reorganized as the Missouri-Kansas-Texas Railroad. It pruned back the Hannibal line, sold the Shreveport line to the Louisiana Railway & Navigation Co. (now part of Kansas City Southern), and sloughed off the line to Oklahoma City, which became the Oklahoma City-Ada-Atoka Railway (now part of Santa Fe). In 1931 Katy purchased the Beaver, Meade & Englewood, which reached almost to the west end of the Oklahoma panhandle.

Through the 1930s and into World War Two Katy's image was one of classic American railroading tempered with individuality — embossed red and white heralds on the tenders of its Pacifics and Mikados, and bright yellow cabooses and boxcars. The war brought increased traffic to the Katy; oil moving north furnished an exception to Katy's customary pattern of southbound traffic.

Not everything associated with the war was beneficial to the Katy: The increased traffic was hard on the track, and in a three-month period in 1945 Katy's top three officers died. Dieselization helped the road briefly — it had purchased no new locomotives since 1925 — but Katy's diesel maintenance program was insufficient. Track deterioration continued, and drought in the 1950s held traffic down. Suddenly, in 1957, Katy was in the red. William N. Deramus III was brought in from the Chicago Great Western to take over the presidency. He rationalized the locomotive roster, repowering non-EMD units with EMD engines; abandoned the Junction City branch, Katy's original line; trimmed the payroll; consolidated offices; and cut most of the road's passenger service.

Katy's decline resumed in a few years, and in 1965 John W. Barriger was brought in to save the railroad. In the 1940s he had rebuilt the Monon; more recently he had retired after several years as president of Pittsburgh & Lake Erie. Barriger faced the same situation that he had on the Monon: almost complete deterioration of the physical plant and equally complete lack of employee morale. Barriger set to work as Traveling Freight Agent and President (his own description of his job) and did

Maurice B. Quirin.

Green-and-yellow GP38-2s lead a Katy freight north past the depot at Vinita, Okla. Two long-time traits of Katy stations are the road's herald and the state name on the station sign.

what he had done before and would do again (for Boston & Maine and Rock Island). He reopened the railroad's office in St. Louis (where he lived); discontinued the remaining passenger service; and found money for a rehabilitation program by liquidating bonds, applying for loans that had been approved but not made, and even cleaning up scrap around the railroad. His program included rebuilding the track, purchasing new motive power, and purchasing and leasing new freight cars. After a long period of economizing itself to death, Katy spent more than one year's gross receipts for new equipment.

A lean, rejuvenated Katy returned to profitability in 1971 under the leadership of Reginald Whitman. Much of its business is now in unit trains of grain and coal moving southbound from off-line connections. Interline traffic accounts for 71 percent of Katy's traffic, and therefore the current crop of mergers, particularly that of Missouri Pacific and Union Pacific, are of some concern to Katy management. In answer to MKT's opposition to the MP-UP merger, the ICC granted Katy trackage rights to Lincoln and Omaha, Nebraska, Council Bluffs, Iowa, and Atchison, Kans.

The railroad embarked upon a program of diversification with the incorporation of Katy Industries in 1967. Katy Industries acquired most of the stock of the railroad in exchange for its own stock.

Katy owns the Galveston, Houston & Henderson (a "paper" or "invisible" railroad) jointly with Missouri Pacific and owns Texas City Terminal jointly with MP and Santa Fe. Katy subsidiary Oklahoma, Kansas & Texas operates the former Rock Island line between Salina, Kans., and Dallas.

Address of general offices: 701 Commerce Street, Dallas, TX 75202
Miles of road operated: 2175
Reporting marks: BKTY, MKT
Number of locomotives: 200
Number of freight cars: 5514
Principal commodities carried: Coal, grain
Major yards: Denison, Tex., Parsons, Kans.
Principal shops: Denison, Tex., Parsons, Kans.
Radio frequencies: 160.590
Passenger routes: Amtrak: Temple-Taylor, Tex. (*Eagle*)
Historical and technical society: Katy Railroad Historical Society, 6832 East Mockingbird Lane, Dallas TX 75214
Date: April 1983

MISSOURI PACIFIC SYSTEM

To explain its history, the Missouri Pacific Railroad can be divided into three parts: the lines west of St. Louis, the lines south and southwest of St. Louis, and the lines in Texas.

Ground was broken for the Pacific Railroad at St. Louis, Missouri, on July 4, 1851, the nation's 75th birthday. The road had been chartered two years previously to build west from St. Louis through Jefferson City, Mo., to the Pacific. The first four miles of the railroad were opened the next year, and its train was the first to operate west of the Mississippi River. The railroad reached Sedalia, Mo., in 1860; because of the Civil War it did not reach Kansas City until 1865. The railroad was reorganized as the Missouri Pacific Railway in 1876.

Two early railroads formed the nucleus of the southern part of the Missouri Pacific: the St. Louis & Iron Mountain, chartered in 1851 to build southwest from St. Louis, and the Cairo & Fulton, chartered in 1854 to build a railroad from Birds Point, Mo., across the Mississippi River from Cairo, Illinois, to Fulton, Arkansas, near the Texas border. The two railroads were consolidated in 1874.

The Texas portion of MP took shape in 1873 when the International & Great Northern was formed by consolidation of the Houston & Great Northern (Houston to Palestine, Tex.) and the International Railway (Longview-Palestine-Hearne). The Texas & Pacific was chartered by an act of Congress in 1871 to build a railroad from the eastern border of Texas to San Diego, California.

Jay Gould bought control of Missouri Pacific in 1879. By then MP extended beyond Kansas City to Atchison, Kans. He soon added to his portfolio St. Louis & Iron Mountain; Missouri, Kansas & Texas; International & Great Northern; Texas & Pacific; Galveston, Houston & Henderson; Wabash; and Central Branch, Union Pacific (now MP's line west from

Continued on next page.

Atchison, Kans.). He began an expansion program that extended Missouri Pacific to Omaha, Nebraska, and Pueblo, Colorado; I&GN to Laredo, Tex., on the Mexican border; SL&IM to Memphis, Tennessee, Lake Charles, Louisiana, and Fort Smith, Ark.; and T&P west to a connection with Southern Pacific at Sierra Blanca, Tex., 90 miles east of El Paso. Gould transferred control of the Iron Mountain to Missouri Pacific in 1881. Then his empire began to fall apart. Wabash entered receivership in 1884, T&P in 1885, MK&T in 1888, and I&GN in 1889. T&P and I&GN remained in the Missouri Pacific family, MK&T remained independent, and Wabash eventually became part of the Pennsylvania Railroad system.

In the early 1900s Missouri Pacific constructed several new lines along rivers to bypass stiff grades on its older routes. Among them were the Illinois Division along the Mississippi south of St. Louis and the Jefferson City-Kansas City line along the Missouri. In 1917 the Missouri Pacific Railroad was incorporated to consolidate the Missouri Pacific Railway and the Iron Mountain, which had entered receivership in 1915.

Missouri Pacific acquired Gulf Coast Lines in 1924; the expanded system was known as Missouri Pacific Lines. At various times this entity also included the Texas & Pacific. Gulf Coast Lines was an agglomeration of railroads between New Orleans and Brownsville, Tex. They had been assembled by B. F. Yoakum when he was chairman of the board of the Rock Island and the Frisco. It included the St. Louis, Brownsville & Mexico; the Beaumont, Sour Lake & Western; and the New Orleans, Texas & Mexico. They were divorced from the Frisco in 1913, at which time they acquired the Gulf Coast Lines name. Later GCL purchased the International & Great Northern, which returned to the Missouri Pacific fold in 1923 when MP purchased GCL.

In more recent times, MoPac acquired an interest in the Chicago & Eastern Illinois (Chicago to Evansville, Ind., Joppa, Ill., and St. Louis and Chaffee, Mo.) in 1961. In 1967 MoPac took control of C&EI, in 1969 sold the Evansville line to Louisville & Nashville, and in 1976 merged C&EI into MP. Texas & Pacific was also merged into Missouri Pacific in 1976. In 1968 MP purchased a half interest in Alton & Southern from Alcoa; Chicago & North Western was the other owner but has since sold its half to St. Louis Southwestern. Several smaller subsidiaries, among them the

MP.

Three General Electric B30-7As bring a Missouri Pacific freight south on elevated track along the St. Louis waterfront. Each of the diesel units has a 3000-h.p. 12-cylinder engine. Overhead is the Martin Luther King Memorial Bridge.

MP.

An assortment of EMD power — an SD40-2, two GP35s, and a GP18 — heads a MoPac train at Kansas City.

Fort Worth Belt and the Missouri-Illinois, were merged into MP in 1977. That same year MP was reincorporated and became a wholly owned subsidiary of Missouri Pacific Corporation.

Merger of MP, Western Pacific, and Union Pacific is under way.

Address of general offices: Missouri Pacific Building, 210 N. 13th Street, St. Louis, MO 63103

Miles of road operated: 11,547

Reporting marks: ARDP, ARMH, ARMN, CEI, CHTT, DKS, MI, MOD, MP, TNM, TP

Number of locomotives: 1439

Number of freight cars: 52,989

Principal commodities carried: Chemicals, coal, farm products, automobiles and parts

Major yards: Fort Worth, Tex., Houston, Tex., Kansas City, Mo., North Little Rock, Ark., St. Louis, Mo.

Principal shops:

Locomotive: North Little Rock, Ark., Kansas City, Mo., Fort Worth, Tex.

Car: DeSoto, Mo.; Sedalia, Mo.

Radio frequencies: 160.410 (road), 160.470 (yard)

Passenger routes: Amtrak — St. Louis-Fort Worth and Taylor, Tex.-San Antonio (*Eagle*); St. Louis-Kansas City (*Ann Rutledge, Missouri Mule, Kansas City Mule*)

Historical and technical society: Missouri Pacific Historical Society, P. O. Box O, Camp Point, IL 62320

Recommended reading: *Mopac Power*, by Joe G. Collias, published in 1980 by Howell-North, P. O. Box 3051, La Jolla, CA 92038 (ISBN 0-8310-7117-6)

Date: May 1983

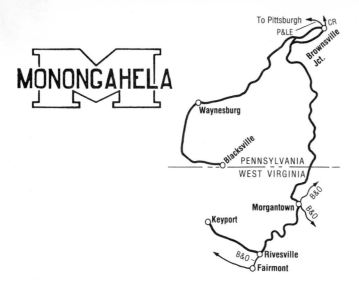

J. J. Young Jr.

Three Monongahela GP38s bring a unit coal train out of a tunnel on the Waynesburg Southern.

MONONGAHELA RAILWAY

The Monongahela Railway was incorporated in 1915 as a consolidation of the Monongahela Railroad and the Buckhannon & Northern Railroad. In the 1920s and 1930s it absorbed several shorter railroads in the area, and it has operated the Waynesburg Southern Railroad since it was opened in 1968 to tap new coal mines.

The Monongahela extends south from Brownsville, Pennsylvania, along its namesake river. It serves the coal mining area of southwestern Pennsylvania and adjacent portions of West Virginia. The railroad is jointly owned by Chessie System (Baltimore & Ohio), Conrail (formerly Pennsylvania Railroad), and Pittsburgh & Lake Erie.

Address of general offices: 53 Market Street, Brownsville, PA 15417

Reporting marks: MGA
Miles of road operated: 136
Number of locomotives: 6
Principal commodities carried: Coal
Shops: Brownsville, Pa.
Junctions with other railroads:
Chessie System: Rivesville, W. Va.
Conrail: Brownsville Jct., Pa.
Pittsburgh & Lake Erie: Brownsville Jct., Pa.
Radio frequencies: 161.265
Date: May 1983

MONTREAL URBAN COMMUNITY TRANSPORTATION COMMISSION
(Commission de Transport de la Communaute Urbaine de Montreal)

At one time Montreal, Quebec, was served by commuter trains from all points of the compass operated by Canadian National, Canadian Pacific, and New York Central. By the 1970s, though, service was down to two routes, Canadian National's line through the Mount Royal tunnel to Deux Montagnes and Canadian Pacific's "Lakeshore" route west to Vaudreuil and Rigaud. Both routes had a long history of commuter service.

When the Canadian Northern arrived at Montreal it found that the routes of easy access to the center of the city had already been taken by Canadian Pacific and Grand Trunk. CN made do with a station in the eastern part of the city and set about planning a downtown terminal. Part of the terminal project was a 3.2-mile tunnel under Mount Royal; another part was the laying out of a model community, the Town of Mount Royal, at the west portal of the tunnel. The length of the tunnel and the ascending grade to the west required electrification of the line, Canada's first mainline electrification.

Work began in 1912, but World War One delayed the opening of the tunnel and the terminal until 1918. Canadian Northern was absorbed by Canadian National Railways in 1919, and in 1943 Canadian National consolidated its Montreal passenger facilities in a new station, Central Station, at the site of Canadian Northern's terminal. For the expanded terminal electrification (through trains were hauled in and out of the new station with electric power) CN augmented the six boxcab electrics built in 1914 and 1916 with nine English Electric locomotives acquired from the National Harbours Board. Three General Electric steeplecabs were added in 1950, and in 1952 CN bought 18 multiple-unit cars, 12 trailers and 6 motors, from Canadian Car & Foundry.

With the dieselization of CN passenger service some of the electrification was pruned, leaving only one route under wires. The electric locomotives also pull VIA's Chicoutimi and Senneterre trains out of Central Station and through the tunnel.

Commuters were part of the passenger business on Canadian Pacific's

Andre St-Amant.

The first locomotive to wear MUCTC's two-tone blue and white was FP7 1303, formerly CP Rail 4073, shown at Windsor Station in Montreal on April 7, 1983.

route west of Montreal as early as 1889. The area along the line made a gradual transition from rural to suburban until the end of World War Two, when the rate of change accelerated. Although automobile ownership increased correspondingly, commuter business held up well enough that Canadian Pacific purchased 40 new coaches for the Montreal-Rigaud, Que., trains in 1953 and 9 gallery cars in 1969. (Canadian National discontinued its parallel commuter service in 1957.)

As the 1980s began, the usual progression of increased fares and decreased service affected patronage on both routes, and it was clear that some kind of government subsidy was necessary. On July 1, 1982, MUCTC took over management and funding of the CN service between Montreal and Deux Montagnes, 17 miles. Frequency of service increased

Continued on next page.

and fares were reduced so they were uniform with bus fares over the same route. On November 1, 1982, MUCTC acquired Canadian Pacific's commuter service and the equipment necessary to operate it, making the same initial fare reductions and service increases that it did on the CN route. The railroads continue to operate the service, but now for MUCTC, not for themselves. MUCTC also operates subway and bus systems in Montreal.

Address of general offices: 159 St. Antoine St., W., Montreal, PQ, Canada H2Z 1H3
Miles of road operated: 57
Number of locomotives: 2 diesel, 14 electric
Number of passenger cars: 70
Number of self-propelled passenger cars: 11 electric
Passenger routes: Montreal (Central Station)-Deux Montagnes, Que.; Montreal (Windsor Station)-Rigaud, Que.

Two of the 1950 General Electric steeplecabs bring a commuter train of rebuilt heavyweight coaches out of the west portal of Canadian National's Mount Royal tunnel.

William D. Middleton.

NATIONAL RAILWAYS OF MEXICO (Ferrocarriles Nacionales de Mexico)

The National Railways of Mexico is an amalgamation of several railroads built separately and at different times.

The line from Ciudad Juarez south to Mexico City through the cities of Torreon, Aguascalientes, and Queretaro was built by Atchison, Topeka & Santa Fe interests as the Mexican Central. It was completed in 1884.

The route south from Laredo was built as the 3-foot-gauge Mexican National. It was begun in 1881 by Gen. William Jackson Palmer (of Denver & Rio Grande fame) and completed to Mexico City via Monterrey, Saltillo, San Luis Potosi, Acambaro, and Toluca, with branches from Monterrey east to Matamoros and from Acambaro southwest to Uruapan. The main line was standard-gauged as far south as Escobedo in 1903, and

a new line was built from there to Mexico City roughly parallel to the Mexican Central, forming what is now known as the B line between Queretaro and Mexico City. (The former Mexican Central is the A line.) The line from Escobedo through Toluca to Mexico City was widened to standard gauge in 1949.

The line from Mexico City to Veracruz via Jalapa is the former 3-foot-gauge Interoceanic Railway, standard-gauged in 1948. A branch of this line from Oriental to Teziutlan is still 3-foot gauge.

The Mexico City-Veracruz line through Orizaba is the former Mexican Railway (Ferrocarril Mexicano), built with British capital. It was absorbed by NdeM in 1959. The portion of this line between Esperanza and Paso del Macho — the Maltrata Incline with grades in excess of 4 percent — was electrified in the 1920s; electric operation ceased in the 1970s.

In recent years NdeM has undertaken several line relocations and built

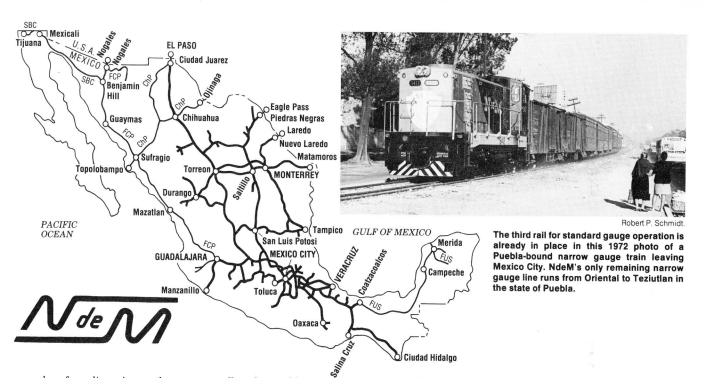

SBC — Mexicali
Tijuana
U.S.A.
MEXICO
SBC
FCP
Benjamin Hill
Nogales
Nogales
ChP
EL PASO
Ciudad Juarez
Ojinaga
ChP
Guaymas
FCP
ChP
Chihuahua
Eagle Pass
Piedras Negras
Laredo
Nuevo Laredo
Matamoros
Sufragio
Torreon
MONTERREY
Topolobampo
Saltillo
Durango
Mazatlan
PACIFIC OCEAN
FCP
GUADALAJARA
Tampico
GULF OF MEXICO
San Luis Potosi
MEXICO CITY
Manzanillo
Toluca
VERACRUZ
Coatzacoalcos
Merida
FUS
Campeche
Oaxaca
FUS
Salina Cruz
Ciudad Hidalgo

Robert P. Schmidt.

The third rail for standard gauge operation is already in place in this 1972 photo of a Puebla-bound narrow gauge train leaving Mexico City. NdeM's only remaining narrow gauge line runs from Oriental to Teziutlan in the state of Puebla.

a number of new lines. Among them are a cutoff northeast of Queretaro for traffic moving between Monterrey and Mexico City; extensive reconstruction of the line between the north end of that cutoff and Saltillo; a new line from a point south of Uruapan to the Pacific port city of Lazaro Cardenas; a new double-track electrified line from Mexico City to Queretaro, already partly in use, to replace the steep, twisting A and B lines; and, still under construction, a line bypassing the severest grade on the former Mexicano. This last will include the world's highest double-track railroad bridge.

Address of general offices: Avenida Central No. 140, Mexico 3, D. F.
Miles of road operated: 12,396 standard gauge, 263 narrow gauge
Reporting marks: FCM, NDM
Number of locomotives: 1,068 standard gauge, 16 narrow gauge
Number of freight cars: 37,528 standard gauge, 213 narrow gauge

Continued on next page.

133

National Railways of Mexico train 7, _El Fronterizo_, pauses at Aguascalientes for servicing on its two-night-and-one-day journey from Mexico City to Ciudad Juarez. On the head end is a pair of GP38-2s whose high short hoods accommodate steam generators for heating passenger cars.

An SW1504, a diesel model unique to NdeM, switches a large cement plant at Monterrey.

Number of passenger cars: 1,014 standard gauge, 34 narrow gauge
Number of self-propelled passenger cars: 39 standard gauge
Major yards: Mexico City (Valle de Mexico)
Principal shops: Aguascalientes, Mexico City, Monterrey, San Luis Potosi
Junctions with other railroads:
Atchison, Topeka & Santa Fe: Ciudad Juarez, Chihuahua
Chihuahua Pacific: Ciudad Juarez, Chih.; Tabalaopa, Chih.
Pacific: Guadalajara, Jalisco
United Southeastern: Coatzacoalcos, Veracruz
Missouri Pacific: Matamoros, Tampaulipas; Nuevo Laredo, Tamps.
Southern Pacific:

Ciudad Juarez, Chih.
Matamoros, Tamps.
Piedras Negras, Coahuila
Texas Mexican: Nuevo Laredo, Tamps.
Radio frequencies: 173.225, 173.325, 172.450, 173.600
Passenger routes:
Mexico City-Nuevo Laredo, Mexico City-Ciudad Juarez, Mexico City-Guadalajara-Manzanillo, Mexico City-Toluca-Uruapan, Mexico City-Oaxaca, Mexico City-Ciudad Hidalgo, Mexico City-Coatzacoalcos, Mexico City-Veracruz, Saltillo-Piedras Negras, Monterrey-Torreon-Durango, Monterrey-Matamoros, Monterrey-Tampico, San Luis Potosi-Tampico, plus mixed train service on most other lines

NEVADA NORTHERN RAILWAY

Mining in Nevada meant gold or silver — until the electrical industry began to grow. Then copper, which had been treated almost as a waste material, became valuable. A large deposit of copper ore was discovered near Ely, in eastern central Nevada many miles from the nearest railroad. Proposals for a railroad to Ely involved standard gauging the Eureka & Palisade and extending it 75 miles eastward from Eureka, Nev., to Ely over four intervening mountain ranges. In 1905 the Nevada Consolidated Copper Co., which had been created the previous year by merger of several companies active in the area, incorporated the Nevada Northern Railway to build a line from Ely north through the Steptoe Valley to a connection with the Southern Pacific's line between Reno, Nev., and Ogden, Utah. NN's route was almost twice as long as the proposed line from Eureka, but the only obstacle was sagebrush. The railroad was completed in 1906.

Nevada Consolidated Copper Co. became a subsidiary of Utah Copper Co. in 1909; Kennecott Copper Corp. acquired control in 1923 and is still owner of the Nevada Northern. In the Ely area the Nevada Northern is used by the mine trains of its parent, but the major portion of the road sees only a triweekly freight train. In mid-1983 Kennecott shut down its smelter at McGill, Nev.; for lack of traffic, NN suspended operation.

Address of general offices: P. O. Box 767, East Ely, NV 89315
Miles of road operated: 148
Reporting marks: NN
Number of locomotives: 1
Number of freight cars: 76
Principal commodities carried: Copper concentrate (outbound), general merchandise (inbound)
Shops: East Ely, Nev.
Junctions with other railroads:
Southern Pacific: Cobre, Nev.
Union Pacific (Western Pacific): Shafter, Nev.
Radio frequencies: 462.125 (dispatcher), 462.150 (road)
Recommended reading: *Railroads of Nevada and Eastern California*, by David F. Myrick, published in 1962 by Howell-North, P. O. Box 3051, La Jolla, CA 92038
Date: July 1983

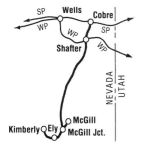

Nevada Northern's lone diesel, an SD7, leads three gondolas and a caboose north through the sagebrush near Goshute, Nev.

Ted Benson.

135

NJ TRANSIT RAIL OPERATIONS

The Department of Transportation of the state of New Jersey was subsidizing rail commuter service as early as 1968 by furnishing equipment for the railroads that ran the commuter trains. That year NJDOT purchased a group of GP40Ps for service on the Central of New Jersey. In the early 1970s the state DOT bought more locomotives, this time U34CHs for service on Erie Lackawanna's non-electrified routes, and cars to go with them. More equipment was purchased — secondhand passenger diesels and long-distance coaches, largely for use on the North Jersey Coast route, the New York & Long Branch Railroad, which was jointly owned and operated by the Pennsylvania and the Central of New Jersey. Later purchases have included a batch of F40PHs, *Jersey Arrow* M. U. cars for service on former Pennsylvania Railroad track and also to eventually replace the original rolling stock of the Lackawanna electrification, nonpowered *Comet II* coaches for ex-CNJ lines, re-electrification of the former Lackawanna lines to Montclair, Dover, and Gladstone, and extension of electrification to Matawan on the NY&LB. Gradually the services operated by the railroads began to look more and more like an operation of the state than of the railroads (eventually they all became part of Conrail).

Then Conrail shed its commuter services. The NJ Transit Rail division of NJ Transit Corporation (the operating arm of the New Jersey Department of Transportation; there is an NJ Transit Bus division, and NJ Transit also operates the Newark subway) was formed in April 1982 to take them over. It began operation on January 1, 1983.

NJ Transit operates the New York portion of the former Erie Lackawanna Hoboken-Port Jervis, N. Y., line for New York's Metropolitan Transportation Authority. NJ Transit owns all the lines on which it provides commuter service except for the former Pennsylvania line between New York and Trenton, which is owned by Amtrak.

Address of general offices: P. O. Box 10009, Newark, NJ 07101
Miles of road operated: 490
Number of locomotives: 97 diesel, 13 electric
Number of passenger cars: 489
Number of self-propelled passenger cars: 653 electric, 22 diesel

Tom Nelligan.

NJ Transit 4112 is a GP40P originally built for the Central of New Jersey. Here it heads a New York-Bay Head train through Elizabeth, N. J., on the former Pennsylvania Railroad line. The clock tower in the background belongs to the old CNJ station at Elizabeth.

Shops: Elizabethport, Hoboken
Radio frequencies: 161.400
Passenger routes: (NJ Transit's route name and former operator in parentheses)
Newark-Phillipsburg (Raritan Valley — CNJ)
New York-Trenton, Princeton Jct.-Princeton (Northeast Corridor — PRR)

New York-Bay Head (North Jersey Coast — PRR and CNJ)
Hoboken-Dover, Hoboken-Gladstone, Hoboken-Montclair (Morris & Essex — Lackawanna)
Hoboken-Netcong (Boonton Line — Lackawanna)
Hoboken-Port Jervis (Main Bergen Line — Erie)
Hoboken-Spring Valley (Pascack Valley — Erie)
Date: May 1983

NEW ORLEANS PUBLIC BELT RAILROAD

The New Orleans Public Belt is a switching railroad owned and operated by the city of New Orleans. It was formed by a city ordinance in 1900 to provide rail service to the port area. Operation of the line, which extends along the Mississippi River waterfront and the Industrial Canal, began in 1908. Like most such railroads it goes about its business unnoticed, but a couple of items are worth noting. First, NOPB once owned a trio of 900-h.p. Baldwin diesel switchers built in 1937, the only ones of their type. They were among the earliest Baldwin diesels, and they have long since been scrapped. Second, NOPB owns the Huey P. Long Bridge across the Mississippi River. It was opened in December 1935. Including approach trestles it is nearly 4½ miles long; the eight main spans total 3524 feet. Flanking the tracks on each side is a pair of highway lanes.

Address of general offices: P. O. Box 51658, New Orleans, LA 70151
Miles of road operated: 47

Continued on next page.

SP.

The Huey P. Long bridge was still under construction when this view was taken from the west bank of the Mississippi River.

Reporting marks: NOPB
Number of locomotives: 9
Number of freight cars: 1250
Connects with:
Illinois Central Gulf
Louisiana & Arkansas (Kansas City Southern)
Missouri Pacific
New Orleans Terminal Co.
Seaboard System
Southern Pacific
Southern Railway
all in the New Orleans switching district
Radio frequencies: 160.320, 160.530
Date: May 1983

TRAINS: J. David Ingles.

Red-and-white SW1000s and SW1500s congregate at New Orleans Public Belt's engine terminal.

NORFOLK & PORTSMOUTH BELT LINE RAILROAD

The Norfolk & Portsmouth Belt Line Railroad was incorporated in 1896 as the Southeastern & Atlantic Railroad. It received its present name in 1898. The N&PBL is a switching road serving Norfolk, Virginia. It is jointly owned by Chessie System, Norfolk & Western, Seaboard System, and Southern Railway.
Address of general offices: P. O. Box 3667, Norfolk, VA 23514
Miles of road operated: 30
Reporting marks: NPB
Number of locomotives: 15
Connects with:
Chessie System
Eastern Shore
Norfolk & Western
Seaboard System
Southern
all within the Norfolk-Portsmouth-Chesapeake switching district
Radio frequencies: 160.980
Date: May 1983

EMD.

Norfolk & Portsmouth Belt Line 106 is an SW1200, shown here fresh out of the shops of its builder, Electro-Motive Division of General Motors.

NW

NORFOLK & WESTERN RAILWAY

Norfolk & Western's oldest ancestor was a line from Petersburg, Virginia, to City Point, a few miles away on the James River. In 1850 the Norfolk & Petersburg Railroad was chartered to build a railroad between the cities of its name. It reached Petersburg in 1858 after crossing part of the Dismal Swamp on a roadbed laid on a mat of trees and logs. Other N&W forebears were the Southside Railroad, opened in 1854 from Petersburg to Lynchburg, Va., and the Virginia & Tennessee, completed in 1856 from Lynchburg to Bristol on the Virginia-Tennessee line.

The three railroads were consolidated in 1867 but maintained their identities until 1870, when they were organized as the Atlantic, Mississippi & Ohio. The AM&O was sold in 1881 to the Clark family, which ran a banking house in Philadelphia and owned a railroad through the Shenandoah Valley. The Clarks moved the headquarters of their old railroad to Big Lick, which was renamed Roanoke. Roanoke also became the headquarters of their new line, which they renamed the Norfolk & Western Railroad.

The N&W was extended northwest into coalfields and in 1890 began an extension to the Ohio River. It reached the Ohio in 1892 where it connected with an existing road to Columbus, Ohio; purchase of another railroad put the N&W in Cincinnati in 1901. That plus branches to Winston-Salem and Durham, North Carolina, constituted the major part of the "old N&W" — essentially an Ohio River-to-tidewater coal road. The Pennsylvania Railroad began purchasing N&W stock in 1900. By 1964 Pennsy owned about one-third of N&W's stock, either directly or through a subsidiary holding company.

Continued on next page.

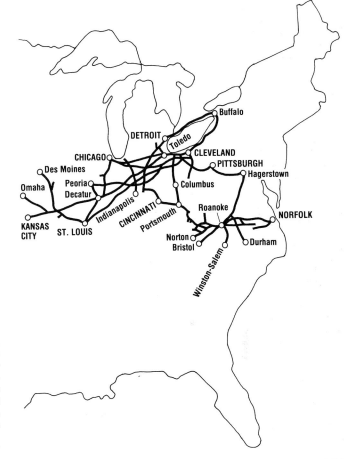

The old N&W was the epitome of coal railroading, and longer than any other coal road — well into the late 1950s — it burned in its locomotives what it hauled in its hopper cars. N&W built many of its steam locomotives in its Roanoke Shops, experimented with a steam turbine-electric locomotive, and explored what modern servicing facilities could do for steam locomotive operating efficiency. Even today more than 60 percent of the road's tonnage is coal.

The Virginian Railway, which N&W merged with in 1959, was a coal carrier whose main line ran from Deepwater, West Virginia, south of Charleston, south and east through Roanoke to Norfolk, paralleling the N&W much of the way. It was only a marginal passenger carrier, but it made up for that in coal, using such hardware as 2-10-10-2s, 12-wheel gondolas, and a long stretch of electrified line to carry millions of tons of coal to tidewater.

In 1962 N&W purchased the Atlantic & Danville, a line running west from Norfolk to Danville, Va., 211 miles, and reorganized it as the Norfolk, Franklin & Danville. The western third of this line has since been abandoned.

In 1964 the Norfolk & Western merged with the Nickel Plate Road (more formally, the New York, Chicago & St. Louis Railroad), leased the Wabash Railroad and the Pittsburgh & West Virginia Railway, and purchased the Akron, Canton & Youngstown Railroad and the Columbus-Sandusky, Ohio, line of the Pennsylvania Railroad. The Pennsy line was necessary to connect the N&W with the Nickel Plate.

The Nickel Plate was begun in 1880 as a nuisance railroad to parallel (and draw traffic away from) William H. Vanderbilt's Lake Shore & Michigan Southern (New York Central System) from Buffalo through Cleveland to Chicago. It was opened in 1882, whereupon Vanderbilt purchased it, shutting out Jay Gould, who was trying to assemble a transcontinental system. The Nickel Plate went bankrupt and was reorganized in 1887, but it never became part of the New York Central System. It was purchased in 1916 by two Cleveland real estate men, Oris and Mantis Van Sweringen.

The Van Sweringens added to it the Toledo, St. Louis & Western (the Clover Leaf), a former narrow gauge line from Toledo to St. Louis; the Clover Leaf's half interest in the Detroit & Toledo Shore Line; and the

Curt Tillotson Jr.

Norfolk & Western prefers to run its diesels long hood foremost, as exemplified by this SD45 on a coal train at Burkeville, Va. The position-light signal at right is characteristic of the "old" N&W, the Pennsy-controlled coal carrier.

Lake Erie & Western, a line from Sandusky, Ohio, to Peoria, Illinois. They later added Wheeling & Lake Erie to the Nickel Plate. W&LE was an X-shaped system with lines from Cleveland to Zanesville and from Toledo to Wheeling, W. Va. The Nickel Plate emerged as a fast freight railroad, and it was one of the last major operators of steam locomotives in the U. S.

Pittsburgh & West Virginia was the successor to Gould's ill-fated Wabash Pittsburgh Terminal. Its line ran from Pittsburgh Junction on the Wheeling & Lake Erie near Jewett, Ohio, straight east to Pittsburgh, cutting off the great northward sweep of the Ohio River between Pittsburgh and Steubenville. The line was extended east to a connection with the Western Maryland at Connellsville, Pa., in 1931.

Akron, Canton & Youngstown was a short line serving Akron, Ohio.

In 1920 it took over the Northern Ohio Railway, which extended west from Akron across most of the width of Ohio to Delphos, passing through no town that requires anything other than the smallest typeface in the *Rand-McNally Road Atlas*. Like the P&WV and the Virginian it favored Fairbanks-Morse diesels.

The Wabash Railroad had essentially two main lines, Chicago-St. Louis and Detroit/Toledo-Kansas City, that crossed at Decatur, Ill., a third route from St. Louis to Council Bluffs, Iowa, and trackage rights over Canadian National between Detroit and Buffalo. It had been part of Jay Gould's empire and later was under George Gould's control. At the time of the N&W merger and lease 84 percent of its stock was owned by the Pennsylvania Co., a subsidiary of the Pennsylvania Railroad.

The Interstate Commerce Commission ordered Norfolk & Western to take over the Erie Lackawanna and the Delaware & Hudson as a condition of the 1964 merger. Both roads were purchased by N&W's Dereco subsidiary. EL was pushed into bankruptcy by hurricane damage in 1972; D&H's problems began later when it found itself surrounded by Conrail. Both roads appeared as heavy lines on N&W system maps, but neither was considered a part of N&W. In 1981 N&W purchased the Illinois Terminal, the remnant of an interurban system that once connected Peoria and Danville, Ill., with St. Louis.

In 1982 the Interstate Commerce Commission approved the acquisition of the N&W and the Southern Railway by the Norfolk Southern Corporation, effectively merging the two roads.

Address of general offices: 8 N. Jefferson Street, Roanoke, VA 24042
Miles of road operated: 7454
Reporting marks: ACY, ITC, NKP, NW, PWV, VGN, WAB
Number of locomotives: 1409
Number of freight cars: 77,882
Principal commodities carried: Coal, foodstuffs, farm products
Major yards: Bellevue, Ohio; Chicago; Decatur, Ill.; Kansas City, Mo.; Portsmouth, Ohio; Roanoke, Va.; St. Louis
Principal shops: Decatur, Ill.; Roanoke, Va.
Radio frequencies: 161.190, 161.250, 160.440, 161.490
Passenger routes:
Amtrak — Champaign-Decatur, Ill. (*Illini*) (discontinued July 10, 1983)

George A. Forero Jr.

The western end of the N&W is much different — distinctly granger-country railroading on the former Wabash line at Mansfield, Illinois.

Regional Transportation Authority — Chicago-Orland Park, Ill.
Historical and technical societies:
Illinois Terminal Railroad Historical Society, c/o A. Gill Siepert, Illinois Central College, East Peoria, IL 61635
Nickel Plate Road Historical & Technical Society, Box 10069, Cleveland, OH 44110
Wabash Railroad Historical Society, 3005 Softwind Trail, Fort Worth, TX 76116
Recommended reading:
The Norfolk & Western: A History, by E. F. Pat Striplin, published in 1981 by the Norfolk & Western Railway, 8 N. Jefferson St., Roanoke, VA 24042
THE NICKEL PLATE STORY, by John A. Rehor, published in 1965 by Kalmbach Publishing Co., 1027 North Seventh Street, Milwaukee, WI 53233
THE VIRGINIAN RAILWAY, by H. Reid, published in 1961 by Kalmbach Publishing Co., 1027 North Seventh Street, Milwaukee, WI 53233
Date: May 1983

141

NORFOLK SOUTHERN CORPORATION

On March 25, 1982, the Interstate Commerce Commission approved the acquisition of two railroads by Norfolk Southern Corporation, a newly organized holding company: the Norfolk & Western Railway and the Southern Railway. Actual merger took place on June 1, 1982.

Don't confuse the Norfolk Southern of 1982 with the old Norfolk Southern, which ran from Norfolk, Virginia, south and west to Charlotte, North Carolina — a road noted for ACF Motorailers, Vanderbilt-tendered 2-8-4s, and Baldwin diesels. That Norfolk Southern was acquired by the Southern Railway in 1974 and merged with Carolina & Northwestern, another Southern subsidiary, under the name Norfolk Southern. The name of that subsidiary was changed to Carolina & Northwestern in 1981 so the new holding company could take the name Norfolk Southern.

Address of general offices: P. O. Box 3609, Norfolk, VA 23514
Date: May 1983

Curt Tillotson Jr.

Symbolic of Norfolk Southern is this mix of Norfolk & Western and Southern diesels leading a freight west through Crewe, Va., on N&W's main line.

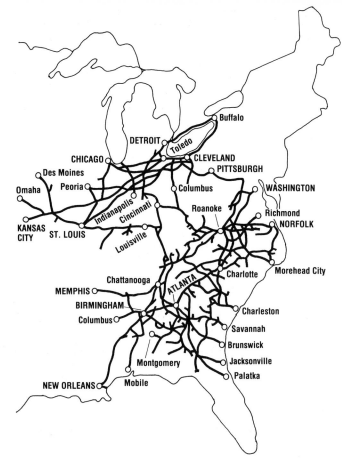

NORTH LOUISIANA & GULF RAILROAD

The North Louisiana & Gulf was incorporated in 1906 and reorganized with the same name in 1927 and again in 1928. The road is owned by Continental Can Co., which has a large paper mill at Hodge, Louisiana. The NL&G provides an outlet for the products of that mill to the Illinois Central Gulf and Louisiana & North West and through the latter to the St. Louis Southwestern at McNeil, Arkansas.

Upon the demise of the Rock Island in 1980, the Continental Group, parent company of Continental Can, purchased the Hodge-Winnfield, La., portion of the Rock and acquired the Rock's trackage rights over Lousiana & Arkansas (Kansas City Southern Lines) from Winnfield to Alexandria, La. Continental formed the Central Louisiana & Gulf Railroad to operate between Hodge and Alexandria. The officers of the CL&G are the same as those of the NL&G.

Address of general offices: P. O. Drawer 550, Hodge, LA 71247

Miles of road operated: 40
Reporting marks: NLG
Number of locomotives: 6
Number of freight cars: 994
Principal commodities carried: Pulpwood, paper products, wood chips
Shops: Hodge, La.
Junctions with other railroads:
Central Louisiana & Gulf: Hodge, La.
Illinois Central Gulf: Gibsland, La.
Louisiana & North West: Gibsland, La.
Radio frequencies: 160.230, 160.755
Date: April 1983

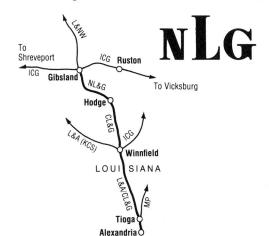

William J. Husa Jr.

Three of North Louisiana & Gulf's four MP15DCs roll south through Bryceland, La., en route from Gibsland to the line's headquarters at Hodge. The pulpwood is bound for the paper products plant of NL&G's owner, Continental Can Co.

OCTORARO RAILWAY

A washout in 1971 stopped service on Penn Central's Octoraro Branch from Wawa, Pennsylvania, southwest of Philadelphia near Media, to Colora, Maryland. The line served a rural area — one of the top mushroom-producing regions of the U. S., incidentally — and in earlier years it had extended all the way to Port Deposit, Md., where it connected with PRR's line along the Susquehanna River between Perryville, Md., and Columbia, Pa.

The Southeastern Pennsylvania Transportation Authority purchased the line for possible transit use, and Rail Development Incorporated agreed to lease the line and operate it as the Octoraro Railway for freight service. However, operation was impossible until the line had an interchange with other railroads, either by replacement of the washed-out bridge at the east end of the line or through construction of a connection to Reading's Wilmington & Northern branch, which crossed the line at Chadds Ford, Pa. The latter connection was made in June 1977, by which time the Octoraro had also become the designated operator for the Reading branch between Modena, Pa., just south of Coatesville, and Wilmington, Delaware.

The Octoraro also operates freight service on the former Baltimore & Ohio Landenberg Branch from Landenberg Jct., near Marshallton, Del., to Hockessin, Del. The line is owned by Historic Red Clay Valley, Inc., which as the Wilmington & Western Railroad operates excursion trains on the ex-B&O branch and the ex-Reading Wilmington & Northern line.

Address of general offices: P. O. Box 146, Kennett Square, PA 19348
Miles of road operated: 82
Reporting marks: OCTR
Number of locomotives: 4
Number of freight cars: 142
Principal commodities carried: Steel, scrap, fertilizers
Shops: Kennett Square, Pa.
Junctions with other railroads:
Brandywine Valley: Modena, Pa.
Chessie System: Elsmere Jct., Del., Landenberg Jct., Del.
Conrail: Wilmington, Del.
Radio frequencies: 160.545
Recommended reading: *The "DO" Lines*, by Edward A. Lewis, published in 1978 by The Baggage Car, P. O. Box 733, Morrisville, VT 05661
Date: June 1983

Herbert H. Harwood Jr.

Octoraro Railway No. 4, an Alco S2, leads a string of company gondolas across the Elkview steel trestle near Lincoln University, Pa.

ONTARIO CENTRAL RAILROAD/ONTARIO MIDLAND RAILROAD

Rail Management Services was selected by the New York Department of Transportation to operate several branch lines cast off by Conrail and purchased by the counties in which they were located: the former Pennsylvania Railroad line from Newark, N. Y., north to Sodus Point on Lake Ontario; a branch of that line from Newark to Marion, formerly the Marion Railway; a portion of the former New York Central "Hojack" line from West Webster, near Rochester, to Hannibal, crossing the Newark-Sodus Point line at Wallington; and a portion of the former Lehigh Valley from East Shortsville to West Victor. The lines intersecting at Wallington were designated the Ontario Midland, and the former Lehigh Valley track was designated the Ontario Central. The two roads are considered one for operating purposes.

The Ontario Midland began operation on October 1, 1979. The same management also operates the Ontario Eastern, a piece of the former New York Central between Ogdensburg and DeKalb Jct., N. Y., which connects with Conrail at the latter point. In September 1982 the same management group began operation of the Allegheny Southern Railway over a former Pennsylvania Railroad branch from Roaring Spring, south of Altoona, to Martinsburg and Curryville, Pennsylvania.

Address of general offices: P. O. Box 248, Sodus, NY 14551
Miles of road operated: 13 (ONCT), 65 (OMID)
Reporting marks: ONCT, OMID
Number of locomotives: 4
Principal commodities carried: Frozen food, distillery grain, ceramic insulators
Shops: Sodus, N. Y.
Junctions with other railroads: Conrail: Shortsville, N. Y. (ONCT); Newark, N. Y. (OMID)
Radio frequencies: 161.370
Date: May 1983

George W. Hockaday.

Three Ontario Midland Alco hood units pose in front of the road's shop at Sodus, N. Y.: RS36 86, ex-Nickel Plate 865; RS11 36, ex-Norfolk & Western 361; and RS36 40, ex-Norfolk & Western 408.

ONTARIO NORTHLAND RAILWAY

Shortly after the boundary between the Canadian provinces of Ontario and Quebec was defined in 1884, the people settling in Ontario just west of that boundary near Lake Temiskaming began to demand year-round transportation. A railway was needed, both for colonization and to tie the area to Toronto. Canadian Pacific had a branch to Lake Temiskaming, but it was from Montreal. In 1902 the legislative assembly of Ontario passed an act creating a commission to construct and operate the Temiskaming & Northern Ontario Railway. The commission chose to create a government railway rather than finance construction by a private corporation or build a railway for eventual operation by one of the existing carriers.

Construction began at North Bay, Ont., on the Canadian Pacific line between Montreal and Sudbury, Ont., and at the end of a Grand Trunk line from Toronto. The railway reached Englehart in 1906 and a junction with the National Transcontinental Railway, still under construction, at Cochrane, 252 miles from North Bay, in 1909. Some of the T&NO's traffic in its early days was supplies for construction of the NTR, and for a period T&NO formed part of a through route west from Toronto in conjunction with Grand Trunk from Toronto to North Bay and NTR west of Cochrane. Much more traffic was occasioned by the discovery of silver at Cobalt, Ont., in 1903 and the discovery of gold in the Porcupine area, near what is now Timmins, in 1909. The land through which the T&NO was built included forests and the Clay Belt agricultural area; the railway was instrumental in their development.

In 1928 the Nipissing Central, a T&NO subsidiary, constructed a branch east from Swastika to the gold-mining area at Noranda and Rouyn, Que. In 1931 T&NO completed a line from Cochrane north to the shore of James Bay at Moosonee. The name of the railway was changed in

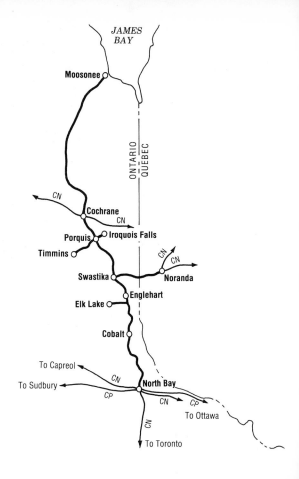

In 1977 Ontario Northland leased four used Trans Europe Express trainsets for Toronto-North Bay-Timmins *Northlander* service. The power cars were replaced in 1979 with rebuilt FP7s. One of the trains is shown here leaving Toronto Union Station. It will travel 228 miles on Canadian National track before it reaches home rails at North Bay; terminus of the run is at Timmins, 259 miles beyond North Bay.

Brian C. Nickle.

1946 to Ontario Northland to better reflect the area served and also to avoid confusion with the Texas & New Orleans, the Texas and Louisiana lines of Southern Pacific.

Ontario Northland Transportation Commission, parent company of the railway, also operates buses, trucks, boats, airplanes, and communications services in northern Ontario.

Address of general offices: 195 Regina Street, North Bay, ON P1B 8L3, Canada

Miles of road operated: 574

Reporting marks: ONT, ONTA

Number of locomotives: 42

Number of freight cars: 917

Number of passenger cars: 30

Principal commodities carried: Newsprint, pulpwood, lumber, ores and concentrates

Shops: Cochrane, Ont.; Englehart, Ont.; North Bay, Ont.; Rouyn, Que.; Timmins, Ont.

Junctions with other railroads:

Canadian National:

Cochrane, Ont.

Noranda, Que.

North Bay, Ont.

Canadian Pacific: North Bay, Ont.

Radio frequencies: 160.545

Passenger routes: North Bay-Cochrane-Moosonee, Ont.; Porquis-Timmins, Ont.

Recommended reading: *Steam Into Wilderness*, by Albert Tucker, published in 1978 by Fitzhenry & Whiteside, 150 Lesmill Road, Don Mills, ON M3B 2T5, Canada (ISBN 0-88902-444-8)

Date: May 1983

OREGON & NORTHWESTERN RAILROAD

The Oregon & Northwestern was incorporated in 1934 to take over the railroad properties of the Edward Hines Western Pine Co. The railroad had been using the Oregon & Northwestern name for several years. The line extends from Hines, Oreg., north through Burns, where it connects with a long branch of the Union Pacific from Ontario, Oreg., to Seneca. The road is owned by the Edward Hines Lumber Co.

Address of general offices: Hines, OR 97738
Miles of road operated: 51

Reporting marks: ONW
Number of locomotives: 4
Number of freight cars: 441
Principal commodities carried: Lumber
Shops: Hines, Oreg.
Junctions with other railroads: Union Pacific: Burns, Oreg.
Radio frequencies: 153.170, 153.290

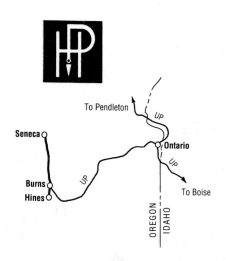

William J. Husa Jr.

Oregon & Northwestern's locomotive roster is exclusively Baldwin. Number 1 is shown here with empties in tow leaving Hines, Oreg., for Seneca.

OREGON, CALIFORNIA & EASTERN RAILWAY

In 1915 Robert E. Strahorn arrived in Klamath Falls, Oregon, eager to build a railroad. The city's first railroad, a branch of the Southern Pacific from Weed, California, had arrived only six years before, and most of central Oregon was still untouched by railroads. Strahorn formulated a system that would include a line from Klamath Falls north to Bend, Oreg., via Silver Lake; a line from Silver Lake southeast to Lakeview, Oreg.; and a line from Bend southeast to Crane, Oreg. Bend was the end of the Oregon Trunk, Crane was on a Union Pacific branch from Ontario, Oreg., and Lakeview was the northern terminal of the narrow gauge Nevada-California-Oregon. Strahorn hoped to eventually sell his system to one of these railroads.

Construction began in 1917 assisted by a municipal bond issue. The railroad reached Sprague River in 1923 and Bly in 1928. Southern Pacific purchased the line in 1927 and in 1928 sold a half interest to Great Northern. The two roads operated the OC&E for alternate five-year periods until 1975 when it was purchased by Weyerhaeuser Timber Co.

Over the years OC&E connected with a number of logging railroads; the only one remaining is Weyerhaeuser's line north from Sycan, near Bly. OC&E has a double switchback southwest of Sprague River.

Address of general offices: P. O. Box 1088, Klamath Falls, OR 97601
Miles of road operated: 66
Reporting marks: OCE
Number of locomotives: 5
Number of freight cars: 147
Principal commodities carried: Logs
Shops: Sycan, Oreg.
Junctions with other railroads:
Burlington Northern: Klamath Falls, Oreg.
Southern Pacific: Klamath Falls, Oreg.
Radio frequencies: 160.860
Date: May 1983

A trio of rebuilt U25Bs spliced by a pair of slugs (a slug has traction motors but no engine; it draws power from the locomotive to which it is coupled) brings an Oregon, California & Eastern train into Klamath Falls, Oreg. Most of the road's tonnage is logs bound for parent Weyerhaeuser Timber Co.'s mill at Klamath Falls.

Karol Miller.

149

PACIFIC RAILROAD (Ferrocarril del Pacifico)

The Ferrocarril del Pacifico was built by the Santa Fe in 1881 and 1882 as the Sonora Railway from Guaymas, the principal Gulf of California port in the Mexican state of Sonora, to Nogales, Son., on the U. S. border. In 1897 Santa Fe traded the railroad to the Southern Pacific for the line SP had built between Mojave and Needles, California.

Because of revolutions and Indian uprisings, it was not until 1927 that the Southern Pacific of Mexico was extended south to a connection with the National Railways of Mexico at Guadalajara, Jalisco. Construction of the southern part of the line through the barrancas south of Tepic in the state of Nayarit was very difficult. In 1951 SP sold the railroad to the Mexican government. It was renamed Ferrocarril del Pacifico. Although FCP's newest diesels, like those of the other smaller Mexican railroads, are painted in National Railways of Mexico colors, they bear FCP initials and the railroad is still considered a separate entity.

FCP does a considerable business in fruits and vegetables moving northward in solid piggyback trains at passenger-train speeds, and it teams up with National of Mexico to operate first-class passenger service between the U. S. border at Nogales and Mexico City.

Address of general offices: Apartado Postal 15-M, Guadalajara, Jalisco, Mexico

Reporting marks: FCP
Miles of road operated: 1435
Number of locomotives: 165
Number of freight cars: 5135
Number of passenger cars: 192
Number of self-propelled passenger cars: 6
Principal commodities carried: Wheat, corn, fertilizer, cement
Major yards: Ciudad Obregon, Son.; Culiacan, Sinaloa; Empalme, Sin.; Guadalajara, Jal.; Mazatlan, Sin.
Principal shops: Empalme, Sin.
Junctions with other railroads:
Chihuahua Pacific: Sufragio, Sin.
Sonora-Baja California: Benjamin Hill, Son.
National Railways of Mexico: Guadalajara, Jal.
Southern Pacific: Agua Prieta, Son.; Nogales, Son.
Radio frequencies: 167.100, 167.150
Passenger routes: Nogales-Guadalajara, Nogales-Cananea-Agua Prieta-Nacozari, Son. (mixed), Guadalajara-Etzatlan-Ameca, Jal. (mixed)
Map: See National Railways of Mexico, page 132
Date: April 1983

FCP train 2, *El Costeño*, leaves the border town of Nogales, Son., on its 26½-hour run to Guadalajara. Behind the baggage car are four new Japanese-designed coaches that were built in Mexico.

Robert A. Michalka

PITTSBURG & SHAWMUT RAILROAD

In 1903 the Brookville & Mahoning Railroad was incorporated by Edward Searles, who in 1882 had married the widow of Mark Hopkins (one of the four men who built the Central Pacific) and in 1891 had inherited her fortune. The first portion of the line was built south from Brookville, Pennsylvania, to Knoxdale, 9 miles; soon the railroad also had a line from Brookville east to Brockway. From 1908 to 1916 the railroad was leased and operated by the Pittsburg, Shawmut & Northern (which expired in 1947 after a long period of receivership). In 1910 the Brookville & Mahoning changed its name to Pittsburg & Shawmut; "Shawmut" is said to be a reference to a Boston bank which had an interest in the railroad.

Continued on next page.

Three SW9s team up to bring empty hopper cars across Mahoning Creek at Colwell, Pa.

Richard J. Cook.

151

The railroad prospered on coal traffic, some of which comes from mines of the Allegheny River Mining Co., owned by the railroad. The Shawmut dieselized in 1953 with nine SW9s; to celebrate the nation's bicentennial in 1976 these were repainted, renumbered, and given patriotic names or names of men famous in the gun industry.

Control of the railroad passed from Searles to his secretary, Arthur T. Walker, and then to Walker's estate. It is now controlled by the Dumaine family, which has long been connected with New England railroading.

Address of general offices: 1 Glade Park East, R. D. 3, Kittanning, PA 16201

Miles of road operated: 96

Reporting marks: PS
Number of locomotives: 11
Number of freight cars: 1291
Principal commodities carried: Coal
Shops: Brookville, Pa.
Junctions with other railroads:
Chessie System: Dellwood, Pa.; West Mosgrove, Pa.
Conrail: Brookville, Pa.; Freeport, Pa.
Radio frequencies: 161.160
Date: May 1983

PITTSBURGH & LAKE ERIE RAILROAD

The Pittsburgh & Lake Erie was chartered in 1875 and opened from Pittsburgh, Pennsylvania, to Youngstown, Ohio, in 1879. Cornelius Vanderbilt of the New York Central subscribed to 15 percent of the railroad's stock, because he saw the P&LE as the route by which his New York Central system could enter Pittsburgh to compete with the Pennsylvania Railroad. NYC gained control of P&LE in 1889, and from then on it was for all practical purposes a division of the NYC, albeit a very profitable one.

The portion of the P&LE south of Pittsburgh was incorporated in 1881 as the Pittsburgh, McKeesport & Youghiogheny. It was jointly owned by P&LE and NYC and was operated as part of P&LE. In 1965 P&LE bought NYC's half interest in the road. In 1972 Penn Central, successor to New York Central and rival Pennsylvania, owned 92.6 percent of P&LE's stock.

When PC went bankrupt in 1970 it owed P&LE $15 million. Officials who held positions with both PC and P&LE were replaced with new management, and P&LE began to chart an independent course. Local congressmen were persuaded by P&LE management, labor, and shippers to amend the Regional Rail Reorganization Act of 1973 to allow solvent subsidiaries of Penn Central to stay out of Conrail. Later negotiations gave P&LE access to Norfolk & Western's ex-Nickel Plate line at Ashtabula,

Ohio, via trackage rights on Conrail north from Youngstown. On February 27, 1979, Penn Central sold the Pittsburgh & Lake Erie Railroad to the new Pittsburgh & Lake Erie Company, which subsequently became a private corporation.

P&LE has few branch lines but has several subsidiary railroads: the wholly owned Montour Railroad (P&LE bought PC's half interest in 1975), which in turn owns the Youngstown & Southern; the Monongahela Railway, owned jointly with Chessie System (Baltimore & Ohio) and Conrail (the former Pennsylvania Railroad interest); and the Lake Erie & Eastern and the Pittsburgh, Chartiers & Youghiogheny, both owned jointly with Conrail.

In 1934 Baltimore & Ohio arranged for trackage rights over P&LE between McKeesport and New Castle Junction, Pa., bypassing the steep grades and sharp curves of B&O's own line west of Pittsburgh. Most of B&O's passenger trains moved to P&LE's station in Pittsburgh; the commuter trains stayed at B&O's station, where they remain, now under the aegis of the Port Authority of Allegheny County. In 1969 the B&O trackage rights were extended through McKeesport, moving B&O's trains from downtown streets to P&LE's line along the Monongahela River.

P&LE still operates one passenger train, a state-subsidized weekday commuter run between College, Pa., and Pittsburgh.

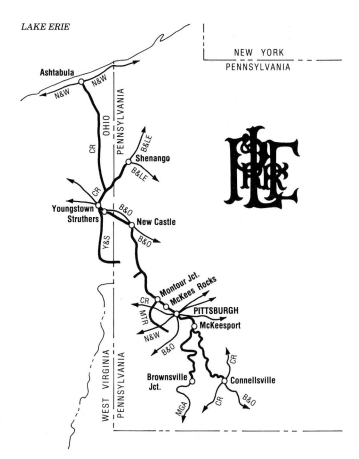

LAKE ERIE

William Metzger.

Pittsburgh & Lake Erie train AL-1 is a unit train operated in conjunction with Conrail. The train carries hot steel slabs between Wheeling-Pittsburgh Steel's Monessen and Allenport plants. It is shown here at Belle Vernon, Pa., about to pass under the Monongahela River bridge of the Norfolk & Western (ex-Pittsburgh & West Virginia).

Address of general offices: 4 Station Square, Pittsburgh, PA 15219
Miles of road operated: 273
Reporting marks: PLE
Number of locomotives: 95
Number of freight cars: 17,380
Number of passenger cars: 5
Principal commodities carried: Coal, iron ore, coke, limestone, steel
Major yards: Youngstown, Ohio (Gateway), McKees Rocks, Pa. (Riverton)
Principal shops: McKees Rocks, Pa.

Radio frequencies: 160.890 (road), 161.070 (yard)
Passenger routes:
Pittsburgh-College, Pa.
Port Authority of Allegheny County — Rankin-McKeesport, Pa.
Historical and technical society: New York Central System Historical Society, P. O. Box 10027, Cleveland, OH 44110
Recommended reading: *Pittsburgh and Lake Erie R. R.*, by Harold H. McLean, published in 1980 by Golden West Books, P. O. Box 8136, San Marino, CA 91108 (ISBN 0-87095-080-0)
Date: June 1983

PORT AUTHORITY OF ALLEGHENY COUNTY

For years Baltimore & Ohio operated a modest commuter service from Pittsburgh, Pennsylvania, south into the Monongahela Valley. These trains used B&O's station on the east side of the Monongahela River in Pittsburgh even after B&O's through trains moved across the river to the Pittsburgh & Lake Erie line in 1934. In 1953 B&O equipped the trains with Budd Rail Diesel Cars, and in 1956 the railroad built a new station at the foot of Grant Street for its commuter trains. Most of the trains operated from Pittsburgh to Versailles, Pa., 18 miles; the last commuter train that continued south to Connellsville, 58 miles, was discontinued in 1965. In 1969 the commuter trains — along with all other B&O trains — moved from B&O rails to P&LE tracks from Rankin to McKeesport so the B&O line through downtown McKeesport (which had numerous grade crossings) could be abandoned.

On February 1, 1975, the trains came under the supervision of the Port

Gordon Lloyd Jr.

A PATrain headed by one of the two rebuilt F7As owned by Port Authority of Allegheny Country pauses at McKeesport, Pa.

Authority of Allegheny County, which also operates the bus and streetcar system in Pittsburgh. With funding from the Pennsylvania Department of Transportation, the agency refurbished several former Chesapeake & Ohio coaches, purchased two locomotives, reduced fares, and increased frequency of service. Present schedules show seven trains between Pittsburgh and Versailles Monday through Friday plus another round trip between Pittsburgh and Port Vue/Liberty, 2 miles short of Versailles. Amtrak's Chicago-Washington *Capitol Limited* stops at Port Authority of Allegheny County's McKeesport station.

Address of general offices: Beaver and Island Avenues, Pittsburgh, PA 15233
Miles of road operated: 18
Number of locomotives: 2
Number of passenger cars: 9
Radio frequencies: 160.230 (road), 160.320 (dispatcher)
Passenger routes: Pittsburgh-Versailles, Pa.

PRAIRIE CENTRAL RAILWAY

In 1978 the Wabash Valley Railroad, a division of Morrison-Knudsen (the locomotive builder) took over operation of a former Pennsylvania Railroad line between Paris and Decatur, Illinois. Wabash Valley discontinued operation when the state of Illinois withdrew its operating subsidy. The line was then taken over by Craig Burroughs' Trans-Action Lines Limited as the Prairie Central. In 1982 PACY leased the Paris-Lawrenceville, Ill., segment of the former New York Central line from Chicago to Cairo, Ill., from the Penn Central. That same year the road applied to acquire the Lawrenceville-Mt. Carmel, Ill., portion of the line.

Address of general offices: P. O. Box 2249, Decatur, IL 62526
Miles of road operated: 165
Reporting marks: PACY
Number of locomotives: 7
Number of freight cars: 158
Principal commodities carried: Grain, grain products, fertilizer
Junctions with other railroads:
Chessie System: Decatur, Ill., Lawrenceville, Ill.
Conrail: Paris, Ill.
Illinois Central Gulf: Decatur, Ill.
Missouri Pacific: Arthur, Ill.
Norfolk & Western: Decatur, Ill., Oakland, Ill.
Radio frequencies: 160.425
Map: See Prairie Trunk, page 156
Date: May 1983

Allen Rider.

A Conrail U25B hastily restenciled with Prairie Central's reporting marks leads a train into Decatur, Illinois, on Illinois Central Gulf track.

PRAIRIE TRUNK RAILWAY

The southern part of the Baltimore & Ohio line from Springfield, Illinois, to Shawneetown, Ill., was constructed as the Illinois & Southeastern and opened in 1871. In 1977 (to leap over more than a century of history) the ICC approved the purchase of the portion of the line southeast of Flora, Ill., where it crossed B&O's Cincinnati-St. Louis main line, by Craig Burroughs' Trans-Action Lines Limited. The last five miles into Shawneetown are owned jointly with Seaboard System (ex-Louisville & Nashville).

Address of general offices: P. O. Box 690, Shawneetown, IL 62984
Miles of road operated: 180
Reporting marks: PARY
Number of locomotives: 4
Number of freight cars: 29

Principal commodities carried: Grain, grain products, fertilizer, fluorspar
Junctions with other railroads:
Chessie System: Flora, Ill.
Chicago & Illinois Midland: Springfield, Ill., Taylorville, Ill.
Conrail: Altamont, Ill.
Illinois Central Gulf: Edgewood, Ill., Springfield, Ill.
Missouri Pacific: Altamont, Ill.
Norfolk & Western: Cowden, Ill., Springfield, Ill., Taylorville, Ill.
Seaboard System: Enfield, Ill.
Southern: Fairfield, Ill., Norris City, Ill.
Radio frequencies: 161.265
Date: May 1983

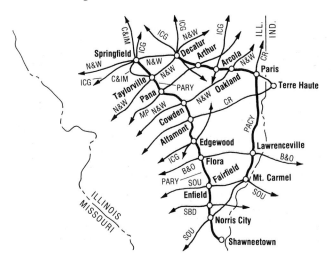

William A. Raia.

Prairie Trunk GP7 No. 475 is shown at the shops of its former owner, Belt Railway of Chicago.

PROVIDENCE & WORCESTER RAILROAD

The Providence & Worcester was chartered in 1844 and put in operation between its namesake cities in 1847. In 1889 it was leased to the New York, Providence & Boston, which was in turn leased to the New Haven in 1892. The road was operated thereafter as part of the New Haven.

In 1968, just before the New Haven was merged into Penn Central, the Providence & Worcester reincorporated and in 1970 requested independence from Penn Central. On February 3, 1973, P&W resumed independent operation. In that same year P&W purchased a line from Worcester to Gardner, Massachusetts, from the Boston & Maine. In 1980 P&W bought the Warwick Railway, a railroad at Cranston, Rhode Island, only nine-tenths of a mile long. In 1981 P&W purchased the Moshassuck Valley Railroad — twice as long as the Warwick, stretching from Woodlawn (Pawtucket) to Saylesville, R. I. P&W has acquired freight rights on Amtrak trackage from Attleboro, Mass., to Westbrook, Connecticut, and has purchased several other former New Haven lines in southeastern New England from Conrail.

Address of general offices: P. O. Box 1490, Woonsocket, RI 02895
Miles of road operated: 371
Number of locomotives: 14
Number of freight cars: 759
Reporting marks: PW, WRWK
Principal commodities carried: Chemicals, newsprint, foodstuffs, sand and gravel, pulp board
Junctions with other railroads:
Boston & Maine: Gardner, Mass.; Worcester, Mass.
Central Vermont: Willimantic, Conn.
Conrail: Old Saybrook, Conn.; Providence, R. I.; Worcester, Mass.
Radio frequencies: 160.650 (road), 161.100 (yard)
Passenger routes: Worcester-Uxbridge, Mass. (weekend excursion trains)
Date: May 1983

Bruce S. Nelson.

Providence & Worcester is the only U. S. railroad that uses Montreal Locomotive Works' M420R units. A pair of them are shown here leading a night freight out of Worcester, Mass.

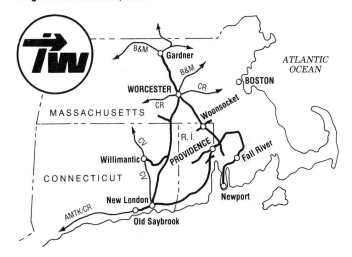

QUEBEC NORTH SHORE & LABRADOR RAILWAY

The area north of the St. Lawrence River along the Quebec-Newfoundland border — the Ungava tract in the Labrador Peninsula — was known to contain iron ore as early as the 1890s, but not until the 1930s and 1940s did exploration reveal a large enough deposit — one of the world's largest — to make mining and transportation of the ore economically feasible. In 1949 the Iron Ore Company of Canada (IOC) was formed with the backing of a number of U. S. steelmakers. One of its first projects was the construction of a railroad north from Sept-Iles, Quebec, about 356 miles. Much of the surveying for the line was done from helicopters, and most of the construction machinery and supplies was brought in by air. Construction began in 1951 and the road was completed in 1954. The southern half of the line is in Quebec; the northern half is in Newfoundland, except for the last few miles into Schefferville, Que.

In 1960 a branch was completed from Ross Bay Junction, Newfoundland, 224 miles from Sept-Iles, west 36 miles to the Carol Lake mining area near Labrador City and Wabush Lake. The branch is jointly owned by IOC and Wabush Lake Railway Co. An automated electrically operated railroad serves the mines in the Carol Lake area. Ore trains from that area move south on the QNS&L to Arnaud Junction, 8 miles north of Sept-Iles. From there the Arnaud Railway takes them to ore docks at Pointe-Noire, Que., 21 miles west of Sept-Iles. Like the nearby Cartier Railway, QNS&L and Arnaud have no rail connection to the rest of the North American rail system.

QNS&L is a heavy-duty single-track railroad characterized by such current technology as welded rail, long sidings, centralized traffic control, roller bearings, and radio control of mid-train helper locomotives. QNS&L's trains are among the longest and heaviest in the world — usually 230 cars, or about 1.6 miles and 28,000 tons.

Because ore freezes, the railroad carries raw ore only during the summer and autumn, but trains run year round to carry beneficiated (processed) ore in the form of concentrate or pellets.

QNS&L is a common carrier, and it operates biweekly passenger trains; there are no highways north of Sept-Iles. In November 1982 IOC announced the closing of its mining operations at Schefferville.

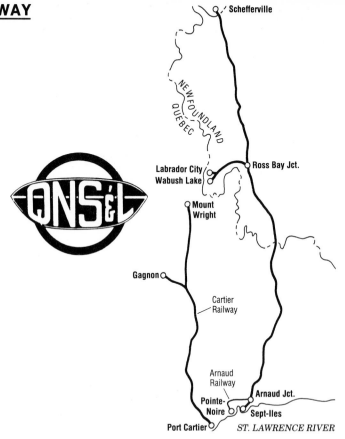

Address of general offices: P. O. Box 1000, Sept-Iles, PQ G4R 4L5
Miles of road operated: 397
Reporting marks: QNSL, IOCC
Number of locomotives: 76
Number of freight cars: 4238
Principal commodities carried: Iron ore
Major yards: Sept-Iles, Que., Labrador City, Newfoundland
Shops: Sept-Iles, Que.
Junctions with other railroads: Arnaud Railway, Arnaud Junction, Que.
Radio frequencies: 160.215, 160.290
Passenger routes: Sept-Iles to Schefferville, Ross Bay Jct.-Labrador City
Date: June 1983

Greg McDonnell.

A short train leaves the bank of the St. Lawrence River at Sept-Iles, Que., with tank and covered hopper cars of chemicals bound for the iron-mining area to the north.

REGIONAL TRANSPORTATION AUTHORITY (CHICAGO)

Regional Transportation Authority oversees and coordinates Chicago-area commuter service. It subsidizes operating expenses for commuter service on Burlington Northern, Chicago & North Western, Illinois Central Gulf, Norfolk & Western, and — jointly with Northern Indiana Commuter Transportation District — Chicago South Shore & South Bend. RTA subsidiary Northeast Illinois Railroad Corporation operates commuter service with its own crews on the Milwaukee Road and the former Rock Island line to Joliet, Ill., which NIRC purchased in December 1982. Several local transit districts own the rolling stock and stations used in the service: Chicago South Suburban Mass Transit District — ICG's ex-Illinois Central electrified lines; West Suburban Mass Transit District — Burlington Northern; and Northwest Suburban, North Suburban, and Greater Lake County Mass Transit Districts — Milwaukee Road.
Address of general offices: 300 N. State Street, Chicago, IL 60610

Miles of road operated: 429
Reporting marks: RTA
Number of locomotives: 132
Number of passenger cars: 692
Number of electric M. U. cars: 211 (including 8 for South Shore service)
Shops:
Locomotive: 47th Street, Chicago (ex-Rock Island); 40th Street, Chicago (Chicago & North Western); Western Avenue, Chicago (Milwaukee Road); 14th Street, Chicago (Burlington Northern)
Car: 49th Street, Chicago (ex-Rock Island); California Avenue, Chicago (Chicago & North Western); Western Avenue, Chicago (Milwaukee Road); 14th Street, Chicago (Burlington Northern)
Radio frequencies: BN: 161.100, C&NW: 161.040, CSS: 161.355, ICG:

Continued on next page.

(ex-GM&O): 160.920, ICG (ex-IC): 161.025, MILW: 160.770, N&W: 160.440, NIRC (ex-RI): 161.610

Passenger routes:

Chicago (North Western Station) to Geneva, Harvard, and McHenry, Ill., and Kenosha, Wis. (Chicago & North Western)

Chicago (Union Station) to Elgin and Fox Lake, Ill. (Milwaukee Road)

Chicago (Union Station) to Orland Park, Ill. (Norfolk & Western, ex-Wabash)

Chicago (Union Station) to Aurora, Ill. (Burlington Northern)

Chicago (Union Station) to Joliet, Ill. (Illinois Central Gulf, ex-Gulf, Mobile & Ohio)

Chicago (LaSalle St. Station) to Joliet, Ill. (NIRC, ex-Rock Island)

Chicago (Randolph St.) to Park Forest South, Blue Island, and South Chicago, Ill. (Illinois Central Gulf, ex-Illinois Central — electrified)

Chicago (Randolph St.) to South Bend, Ind. (Chicago South Shore & South Bend — electrified)

Date: May 1983

New York Central's *20th Century Limited* used to pose in Chicago's LaSalle Street Station with the Board of Trade building as a backdrop. Now what is left of the station sees only RTA F40s on commuter trains. Number 101 is shown on its first revenue trip in September 1977; trailing it are companion unit No. 100 and ex-Chicago & North Western bilevel cars leased from Amtrak.

Joe McMillan.

RICHMOND, FREDERICKSBURG & POTOMAC RAILROAD

The Richmond, Fredericksburg & Potomac was chartered in 1834 to build northward from Richmond, Virginia, to a point on the Potomac River to connect with steamboats to Washington, D. C. The rail route from Richmond to Washington was opened in 1872 with the completion of the Alexandria & Fredericksburg, a subsidiary of the Pennsylvania Railroad, south to a connection with the RF&P at Quantico — the northernmost portion of the route was the Alexandria & Washington, also a Pennsylvania subsidiary. In 1890 the two Pennsy properties were consolidated as the Washington Southern, and in 1901 the Richmond-Washington Company was formed to operate the WS and the RF&P as one railroad. In 1920 the RF&P absorbed the Washington Southern.

The Richmond-Washington Company owns about three-fourths of RF&P's common stock; the remainder of the common stock is owned by the Virginia Supplemental Retirement System and the public. Richmond-Washington was equally owned by Seaboard Air Line, Atlantic Coast Line, Chesapeake & Ohio, Baltimore & Ohio, Southern, and Pennsylvania. Penn Central relinquished its ex-Pennsylvania share in 1978, and mergers among the other owners have occurred, leaving ownership now in the hands of CSX Corporation (80 percent) and Norfolk Southern (20 percent).

RF&P is almost purely a bridge road, doing little local business between its terminals. It is double track all the way and basically a one-speed road. One interesting trait of its operations is that odd-numbered RF&P diesels usually face south and even-numbered ones face north.

Address of general offices: P. O. Box 11281, Richmond, VA 23230
Miles of road operated: 114
Reporting marks: RFP

Continued on next page.

Alex M. Mayes.

Three RF&P hood units, a GP40 and two GP35s, lead a fast freight south over Neabsco Creek near Woodbridge, Va. Note that the odd-numbered units face south and the even-numbered one faces north.

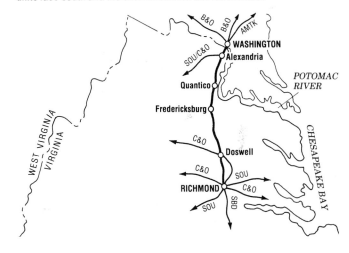

Number of locomotives: 39
Number of freight cars: 1883
Principal commodities carried: TOFC, pulp and paper products, foodstuffs, chemicals
Major yards: Alexandria (Potomac Yard), Richmond (Acca Yard)
Shops: Richmond (Bryan Park)
Junctions with other railroads:
Chessie System: Doswell, Potomac Yard
Conrail: Potomac Yard

Delaware & Hudson: Potomac Yard
Seaboard System: Richmond
Southern: Potomac Yard
Virginia Central: Fredericksburg
Radio frequencies: 161.550 (road and dispatcher to train), 161.490 (train to dispatcher)
Passenger routes: Amtrak: Washington-Richmond (*Silver Meteor*, *Silver Star*, *Colonial*, *Tidewater*, *Palmetto*)
Date: April 1983

ROBERVAL & SAGUENAY RAILROAD

The Roberval & Saguenay was incorporated in 1911 as the Ha! Ha! Bay Railway. It built a line about 20 miles long between Bagotville, Quebec, on the shores of an inlet of the Saguenay River just east of Chicoutimi, and Arvida, where it connected with the Canadian Northern. Within a few years it was renamed Roberval-Saguenay, and at some time in the 1920s the hyphen in the name was replaced by an ampersand. In 1968 the road purchased the nearby Alma & Jonquiere Railway; it was merged into the R&S in 1974.

The Roberval & Saguenay is owned by the Aluminum Company of Canada, and its chief purpose is to carry bauxite (aluminum ore) from the docks at Port Alfred to Alcan's plant at Arvida.
Address of general offices: P. O. Box 277, Arvida, PQ G7S 4K8
Miles of road operated: 55
Reporting marks: RS
Number of locomotives: 14
Number of freight cars: 292
Principal commodities carried: Bauxite
Shops: Arvida, Que.
Junctions with other railroads: Canadian National: Arvida, Que.; Saguenay Power, Que.
Radio frequencies: 160.185 and 161.145 (road), 160.725 and 160.605 (yard), 160.350 and 160.995 (plant switching)

David M. More.

A brand-new M420TR teams up with an older MLW hood unit to lift a train out of the Saguenay River valley at Port Alfred, Que.

ST. LAWRENCE RAILROAD

When the defunct Rutland Railroad was dismembered in 1963 (see Vermont Railway, page 200) there was little question about abandoning its Ogdensburg & Lake Champlain line between Rouses Point, New York, at the north end of Lake Champlain, and Ogdensburg, N. Y., 118 miles west on the St. Lawrence River. Only the 26-mile segment from the junction with the New York Central at Norwood to Ogdensburg escaped the scrappers, and that largely because the Ogdensburg State Hospital used heating coal delivered by rail.

In 1966 the Ogdensburg Bridge and Port Authority received a federal grant to purchase the Norwood-Ogdensburg line and contracted for operation of the line. The Ogdensburg & Norwood Railway started service the next year but ceased in 1968, having had little more success in obtaining traffic than the Rutland. The OBPA resumed operation under its own management in 1970.

In 1974 the St. Regis Paper Co. no longer needed its Norwood & St. Lawrence Railroad. The St. Lawrence Seaway made the boats that brought pulpwood to the N&StL obsolete, so St. Regis gave the entire railroad operation to the OBPA. In 1976 OBPA took over operation of the former New York Central branch from DeKalb Junction, N. Y., to Ogdensburg, a line that Conrail didn't want. That operation was discontinued in 1978, and the line has since become the Ontario Eastern (see page 145).

In 1977 National Railway Utilization Corp. leased OBPA's railroad operation and organized it as the St. Lawrence Railroad. NRUC has established a freight car plant at Norfolk, a few miles north of Norwood. NRUC has two other plants in South Carolina that build freight cars, at Pickens and Greenville. A good portion of the St. Lawrence's business is trucked to the railroad at Ogdensburg from Canadian points.

Address of general offices: 1 Park St., Norwood, NY 13668
Miles of road operated: 43
Reporting marks: NSL
Number of locomotives: 3
Number of freight cars: 1140 (all 50-foot boxcars)
Principal commodities carried: Paper, silica sand, coal

Shops: Norfolk, N. Y.
Junctions with other railroads: Conrail: Norwood, N. Y.
Radio frequencies: 160.215
Recommended reading: *The Rutland Road* (second edition), by Jim Shaughnessy, published in 1981 by Howell-North, P. O. Box 3051, La Jolla, CA 92038
Date: June 1983

NRUC.

Typical of St. Lawrence Railroad's fleet — and indeed of most of today's short-line boxcars — is this car. Note the use of the initials of predecessor Norwood & St. Lawrence.

ST. MARIES RIVER RAILROAD

In 1980 the Potlatch Corporation, a forest products company, purchased 115 miles of line in Idaho from the bankrupt Milwaukee Road — 64 miles of the former main line from Plummer to Avery (once the western terminal of Milwaukee's electrification through the Rocky Mountains) and 52 miles of a branch from St. Maries (pronounced "St. Marys") to Bovill. The company's purpose was to ensure continued rail service at its facilities at St. Maries and Santa. Potlatch began operation in May 1980. At the same time Potlatch began to renovate the track and right of way with financial assistance from the state of Idaho and the Federal Railroad Administration.

The former main line from Plummer to St. Maries and the branch to Bovill constitute the St. Maries River Railroad, a common carrier operated by Kyle Railways of San Diego, California, through its subsidiary Idaho Western Inc. The remainder of the main line that Potlatch purchased — St. Maries to Avery — is a private logging railroad.

Address of general offices: P. O. Box 619, St. Maries, ID 83861
Miles of road operated: 71
Reporting marks: STMA
Number of locomotives: 5
Number of freight cars: 517
Principal commodities carried: Logs, plywood, wood chips
Junctions with other railroads:
Burlington Northern: Bovill, Idaho
Union Pacific: Plummer, Idaho
Radio frequencies: 160.275
Date: June 1983

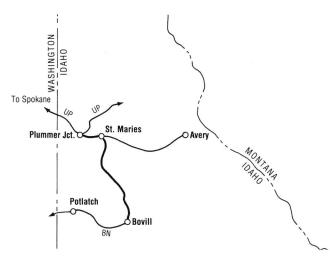

STMA.

Three low-nose GP9s of the St. Maries River Railroad pose in front of the road's headquarters at St. Maries, Idaho.

ST. MARYS RAILROAD

The St. Marys Railroad was incorporated in 1924 as successor to the Atlantic, Waycross & Northern — which had succeeded the St. Marys & Kingsland Railroad, incorporated in 1906. The railroad runs from a junction with Seaboard System (the former Seaboard Air Line main line) to the town of St. Marys, Georgia, at the mouth of the St. Marys River, which forms the Georgia-Florida boundary there. The railroad is owned by Gilman Paper Co.

Address of general offices: P. O. Box 520, St. Marys, GA 31558

Miles of road operated: 11
Reporting marks: SM
Number of locomotives: 3
Number of freight cars: 1192
Principal commodities carried: Pulpwood, paper products
Junctions with other railroads: Seaboard System: Kingsland, Ga.
Radio frequencies: 160.620
Date: May 1983

St. Marys Railroad SW1500 No. 503 hauls a long string of boxcars west toward the Seaboard interchange at Kingsland, Ga.

William J. Husa Jr.

SAN DIEGO & ARIZONA EASTERN TRANSPORTATION CO.

In 1907 John D. Spreckels broke ground at San Diego, California, to start construction of a railroad that would give the city a direct route east. Financial backing for the San Diego & Arizona came from Spreckels and from E. H. Harriman of the Southern Pacific. The new railroad would bring SP into San Diego and break Santa Fe's monopoly there — a reversal of the usual situation in California in those days. The route of the railroad was south across the Mexican border to Tijuana, east to Tecate, back into the U. S. and north through awesome Carriso Gorge, and east to a connection with SP at El Centro, the principal town in California's Imperial Valley. The last spike was driven in 1919.

In 1951 the San Diego & Arizona Eastern Railway, as it was then called, operated its last passenger train. The slow trip east to a connection with the secondary trains of SP's Golden State Route — and El Centro was not on the main line — was no match for Santa Fe's frequent *San Diegans* to Los Angeles and the best of Santa Fe, Union Pacific, and Southern Pacific from there. In 1970 SP sold the Mexican portion of the line, the Tijuana & Tecate Railway, to the Mexican government; it has become an isolated part of the Sonora-Baja California Railway. (SP retained trackage rights for through traffic.) A hurricane in September 1976 damaged a 40-mile stretch of the line, and Southern Pacific petitioned for abandonment of all but a few miles from El Centro to Plaster City.

In 1979 San Diego's Metropolitan Transit Development Board purchased three portions of the SD&AE: from Plaster City to the border, from San Diego south to the border between San Ysidro, Calif., and Tijuana, Baja California, and from San Diego east to El Cajon. MTDB began construction of a 16-mile transit line from the Amtrak (ex-Santa Fe) station in San Diego to the border. The trolley line, which was constructed without federal funds, shares track with the freight trains of the SD&AE. The trolleys began operating in July 1981.

MTDB contracted with Kyle Railways to operate freight service on the line. Kyle set up the San Diego & Arizona Eastern Transportation Co. for that purpose. SD&AE also operates the Mexican segment of the line, not only to connect the two U. S. portions of its line but also to do local work for Sonora-Baja California.

Address of general offices: 861 Sixth Avenue, San Diego, CA 92101
Miles of road operated: 60
Reporting marks: SDAE
Number of locomotives: 9
Principal commodities carried: Grain, copper concentrates
Shops: San Diego, Calif., San Ysidro, Calif.
Junctions with other railroads:
Atchison, Topeka & Santa Fe: San Diego, Calif.
Southern Pacific: Plaster City, Calif.
Radio frequencies: 160.530
Passenger routes: San Diego Metropolitan Transit Board — San Diego-San Ysidro (*Tijuana Trolley*)
Date: June 1983

William T. Morgan.

A pair of GP9s and a GP20 lead a San Diego & Arizona Eastern freight across Campo Creek at Campo, Calif.

A train of three German-built articulated trolleys rolls north toward downtown San Diego on track shared with SD&AE freight trains.

J. W. Swanberg.

SEABOARD SYSTEM RAILROAD

The Seaboard System Railroad is the product of a long series of mergers. The two principal railroads involved are the Seaboard Coast Line, which was formed in 1967 by the merger of the Atlantic Coast Line and the Seaboard Air Line, and the Louisville & Nashville, which was controlled by Atlantic Coast Line. Other components of Seaboard System are the Clinchfield Railroad and the Georgia Railroad (both in the ACL-L&N family — details of the relationships are explained below) and the Atlanta & West Point and the Western Railway of Alabama. For several years before the formation of the Seaboard System the SCL-L&N group called itself The Family Lines, and indeed the organization resembles a large family, much complicated by second cousins and half-sisters.

Atlantic Coast Line dates from the organization in 1830 of the Petersburg Railroad, which opened in 1833 from its namesake city in Virginia to the bank of the Roanoke River at Weldon, North Carolina. The Richmond & Petersburg Railroad was organized in 1836 and formed a connection with the Petersburg Railroad in 1838. In 1898 the name was changed to Atlantic Coast Line Railroad of Virginia. In 1900 it became simply Atlantic Coast Line and absorbed the Norfolk & Carolina, the Wilmington & Weldon, the Southeastern, and the ACL of South Carolina, creating a railroad from Richmond, Va., to Charleston, S. C.

In 1902 ACL took over the Plant System, a railroad, steamship, and hotel system assembled during the preceding two decades by Henry B. Plant. The railroad portion extended from Charleston, S. C., through Waycross, Georgia, to Tampa, Florida, with branches from Waycross to Montgomery, Alabama, and Jacksonville, Fla. At the same time ACL acquired control of Louisville & Nashville. Later ACL and L&N jointly leased the Clinchfield Railroad and the Georgia Railroad. On December 31, 1945, ACL merged with the Atlanta, Birmingham & Coast (Atlanta and Birmingham to Waycross) and in 1959 merged with the Charleston & Western Carolina (Port Royal, S. C., to Anderson, Greenville, and

Continued on next page.

Seaboard System's new image relies on the colors used by Family Lines and a logo that is a stylized double S.

Two Seaboard Coast Line C30-7's and an SD45 lead a freight through Greystone, N. C. The first car in the train is a well-hole flat car; the third is a heavy-duty flat car carrying a large generator.

Spartanburg, S. C.). Both roads had been controlled by the ACL for years.

The Atlantic Coast Line's latter-day system comprised a main line from Richmond, Va., to Tampa, Fla., via Rocky Mount and Fayetteville, N. C., Florence and Charleston, S. C., Savannah, Ga., and Jacksonville and Orlando, Fla.; lines from Waycross, Ga., to Montgomery, Ala., Birmingham, Ala., and Atlanta, Ga.; a line from Rocky Mount to Norfolk, Va; several lines to Wilmington, N. C. (location for many years of ACL's headquarters); and a network of lines in the central and western parts of the Florida peninsula.

ACL participated in the lucrative New York-Florida passenger trade with such trains as the *Florida Special* and a fleet of streamlined *Champions*. In the early years of the diesel era ACL was unique in having purple diesels.

The Louisville & Nashville was incorporated in 1850, and the line between its title cities was opened in 1859. (One of L&N's later acquisitions was the Lexington & Ohio, chartered in 1830 and the first railroad west of the Alleghenies.) It expanded south to Montgomery, Ala., in 1871 with the acquisition of the Nashville & Decatur and the South & North Ala-

bama. A decade later it reached New Orleans by acquiring the Mobile & Montgomery and the New Orleans, Mobile & Texas, and it reached Cincinnati over the rails of the Louisville, Cincinnati & Lexington's "Short Line." By the turn of the century L&N's main line linked Cincinnati to New Orleans via Louisville, Kentucky, Nashville, Tennessee, and Birmingham and Montgomery, Ala., with a branch from Bowling Green, Ky., to Memphis, Tenn. A secondary main line ran south from Cincinnati through the coalfields of eastern Kentucky to Knoxville, Tenn., and Atlanta, Ga.

In 1957 the Nashville, Chattanooga & St. Louis was merged into the L&N, which had long controlled it. NC&StL's main line ran from Hickman, Ky., on the Mississippi River, through Nashville and Chattanooga to Atlanta; it leased a line from Paducah, Ky., to Memphis from parent L&N. L&N purchased Chicago & Eastern Illinois' line from Woodland, Ill., to Evansville, Indiana, from Missouri Pacific in 1969. That, plus trackage rights north from Woodland, gave L&N a line from the Ohio River to Chicago. In 1971 L&N merged with the Monon, gaining a second route into Chicago, this time from Louisville.

Louisville & Nashville is a coal road, and typical of L&N's operation is a lash-up of gray diesels on the point of a train of coal.

The Clinchfield was incorporated in 1905 as the South & Western Railway, and in 1908 it became the Carolina, Clinchfield & Ohio. In 1924 ACL and L&N jointly leased the CC&O and organized the Clinchfield Railroad to operate the line. Clinchfield's line from Elkhorn City, Ky., to Spartanburg, S. C., formed a bridge route between the Ohio River and the South and also tapped coalfields.

The Georgia Railroad was not a corporation but was the organization that represented ACL and L&N as lessees of the railroad property of the Georgia Railroad & Banking Co. That company was incorporated in 1833, and the bank became a separate entity in 1892. In 1881 the Georgia Railroad & Banking Co. leased its railroad to William Wadley, who assigned a half interest in the lease to the L&N. The other half was later vested in the L&N, which assigned half of that — a one-quarter inter-

Continued on next page.

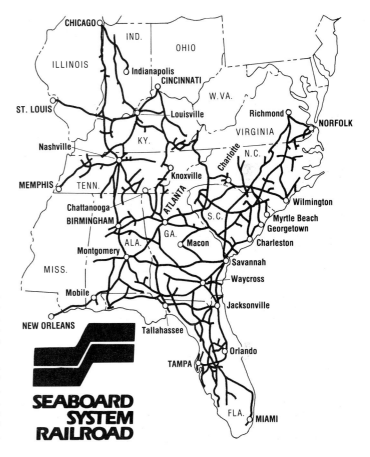

SEABOARD SYSTEM RAILROAD

Gary Dolzall.

The Clinchfield's route is across mountains away from large cities and through places like Fremont, Va., where four SD40s coax a coal train into motion.

est — to ACL. Georgia Railroad did not join Amtrak in 1971 and until recently ran a mixed train over its main line between Atlanta and Augusta, Ga., and on branches to Macon, Athens, and Washington, Ga.

Atlanta & West Point (Atlanta to West Point, Ga.) and **Western Railway of Alabama** (West Point through Montgomery to Selma, Ala.) were completed before the Civil War and formed a through route between Atlanta and Montgomery. They were long affiliated with the Georgia Railroad — Georgia Railroad & Banking Co. owned a half interest in the Western of Alabama and 38 percent of the Atlanta & West Point. Together the two roads were known as the West Point Route. For many years Southern Railway's premier *Crescent Limited* was routed between Atlanta and Montgomery on the rails of the West Point Route and on to New Orleans on the L&N rather than on Southern's own line.

Seaboard Air Line had its genesis in the Portsmouth & Roanoke Rail Road, which was formed in 1832 to build a railroad from Portsmouth, Va., to Weldon, N. C., on the Roanoke River, shortcutting a long, three-sided water route. The Seaboard Air Line Railway was organized in 1900, although the name had been used for some time to designate a group of railroads that formed a route from Portsmouth through Raleigh and Hamlet, N. C., to Atlanta. SAL soon took over the Florida Central & Peninsular Railroad, which had a line from Columbia, S. C., through Savannah, Ga., and Jacksonville to Tampa and a line west from Jacksonville to the Chattahoochee River in the Florida panhandle.

The Florida boom of the 1920s saw SAL extended southeast from Coleman, Fla., near Wildwood, to Miami. Concurrently SAL built a number of cutoffs and branches in Florida, including a line south to Fort Myers and Naples, formerly ACL territory.

The Florida boom collapsed and SAL, which for most of its length was between the lines of the Southern and the Atlantic Coast Line, both stronger and wealthier, went into receivership in 1930. The Naples extension was abandoned in 1942. The railroad emerged from receivership in 1945 and began an improvement program that included signaling, something SAL had been almost innocent of. SAL purchased two short lines, the Macon, Dublin & Savannah (Macon-Vidalia, Ga.) in 1958 and the Gainesville Midland (Athens-Gainesville, Ga.) in 1959.

The Seaboard Coast Line merger was proposed in 1958 and it took effect on July 1, 1967. The merger permitted the elimination of some duplicate trackage, such as SAL's line between Charleston and Savannah, parts of each road's route into the Norfolk-Portsmouth area, and much of the dense network of track in central Florida.

In 1969 SCL absorbed the Piedmont & Northern, a former interurban line owned by the Duke interests with separate divisions in North and South Carolina, and in 1976 SCL purchased the Durham & Southern, obtaining access to Durham, N. C. About 1974 SCL's advertising began to refer to SCL, L&N, Clinchfield, Georgia, and the West Point Route as the "Family Lines," but the title was simply that, not the name of a corporation. The reference usually included a list of the members of the family.

On November 1, 1980, Seaboard Coast Line and Chessie System were merged into the CSX Corporation. On December 29, 1982, Louisville & Nashville merged with Seaboard Coast Line, and on that same date the charter of SCL, the surviving corporation, was amended to change the company's name to Seaboard System Railroad.

Address of general offices: 500 Water Street, Jacksonville, FL 32202
Miles of road operated: 15,408
Reporting marks: ACL, AWP, CRR, GA, LN, MON, NC, SAL, SBD, SCL, WA
Number of locomotives: 2367

Number of freight cars: 116,511
Principal commodities carried: Coal, phosphate rock, chemicals, wood products
Major yards: Atlanta (Tilford); Birmingham (Boyles); DeCoursey, Ky.; Hamlet, N. C.; Nashville (Radnor); South Louisville, Ky. (Osborn); Waycross, Ga. (Rice)
Principal shops: Erwin, Tenn.; Jacksonville, Fla.; South Louisville, Ky.; Tampa, Fla.; Waycross, Ga.
Radio frequencies:
SCL: 160.590, 161.100, 161.400 (SAL yard), 160.290 (ACL yard)
L&N: 161.370 (road, dispatcher to train), 161.520 (train to dispatcher)
CRR: 160.860
GA, AWP, WRA: 161.310 (road), 161.430 (yard)
Passenger routes:
Amtrak: Richmond, Va.-Raleigh, N. C.-Savannah-Jacksonville (*Silver Star*); Richmond-Fayetteville, N. C.-Savannah-Jacksonville (*Silver Meteor, Palmetto*); Jacksonville-Wildwood-Miami (*Silver Star, Silver Meteor*); Jacksonville-Orlando-Tampa-St. Petersburg (*Silver Star, Silver Meteor*); Tampa-Auburndale-Miami (*Silver Palm*); Chicago-Crawfordsville, Ind. (*Hoosier State*)
Date: June 1983

SEATTLE & NORTH COAST RAILROAD

On March 1, 1980, the Milwaukee Road withdrew from the Pacific Northwest. One of the lines abandoned was the isolated line on Washington's Olympic Peninsula from Port Townsend to Port Angeles. The line had been established in 1915 as the Seattle, Port Angeles & Western Railroad, and within three years the Milwaukee Road had taken it over. It became one of the road's most profitable branches, bringing out lumber and wood products from the forests of the area. In recent years, though, the Milwaukee Road wanted to abandon the line.

North Coast Lines, a locomotive leasing company, was seeking a short line to purchase and operate. They negotiated with Milwaukee Road for the Port Townsend-Port Angeles line, closed the deal the day before Milwaukee shut down, and, delayed by union injunctions, began service on March 21, 1980. The Seattle & North Coast serves Crown Zellerbach newsprint and kraft paper plants and ITT Rayonier pulp and plywood plants at Port Angeles. Traffic consists largely of outbound products of those operations and inbound chemicals.

Seattle & North Coast's only connection with the rest of the North American rail system is via a 45-mile barge haul along Admiralty Inlet and Puget Sound to Pier 27 on Seattle's waterfront. At nearby Whatcom Yard the road interchanges with Burlington Northern and Union Pacific.
Address of general offices: 2150 N. 107th St., Seattle, WA 98133
Miles of road operated: 50

Continued on next page.

STRAIT OF JUAN DE FUCA

Port Angeles

Sequim

Port Townsend

Fairmont

WASHINGTON

ADMIRALTY INLET
PUGET SOUND

SEATTLE

Bill Parkins.

Reporting marks: SNCT
Number of locomotives: 7
Number of freight cars: 299 (all 50-foot wide-door boxcars)
Principal commodities carried: Paper, plywood, chemicals
Junctions with other railroads:
Burlington Northern: Seattle
Union Pacific: Seattle
Radio frequencies: 160.770

Two ex-Burlington Northern F7s idle on the siding at Port Townsend, Wash., while cars are unloaded from the barge just in from Seattle. Approximately half the cars are Seattle & North Coast's own, marked by V-striped double doors.

172

SIERRA RAILROAD

The Sierra Railway was incorporated in 1897 to build a line into the gold rush country east of Stockton, California. The line was opened from Oakdale to Tuolumne, 57 miles, in 1900, and a branch was built from Jamestown to Angels Camp in 1902. More important to the Sierra Railway than gold, however, were the forests of the region. The road's principal business was and is carrying lumber and wood products. The Sierra connected with a number of logging roads, among them the Sugar Pine Railway of the Pickering Lumber Co. and the railroad of the West Side Lumber Co. Dam construction also provided revenue for the Sierra. Two branches, long since abandoned, led to dam construction sites, as did the Hetch Hetchy Railroad, which was part of a construction project that built a dam and an aqueduct to carry water to San Francisco.

Another face of the Sierra is much better known to the general public. From the 1920s on Hollywood moviemakers have used the railroad as a setting for such westerns as *High Noon* and *Duel in the Sun*; the Sierra has also appeared in television series such as "Tales of Wells Fargo" and "Petticoat Junction." At various times in recent years the railroad has operated excursion trains and tourist railroad service.

Today's Sierra Railroad was incorporated in 1935 and acquired the property of the Sierra Railway at a foreclosure sale in 1937. The Angels Camp branch was abandoned in 1935, and the main line was cut back from Tuolumne to Standard, 7 miles, in 1981. The principal customers served by the Sierra Railroad are the lumber mills of Standard Lumber Co. at Standard and of Sequoia Pine Mills at Keystone.

Address of general offices: 13645 Tuolumne Road, Sonora, CA 95370
Miles of road operated: 50
Reporting marks: SERA
Number of locomotives: 3
Number of freight cars: 250 (all 50-foot boxcars)
Principal commodities carried: Wood products
Shops: Oakdale, Calif.
Junctions with other railroads:
Atchison, Topeka & Santa Fe: Oakdale
Southern Pacific: Oakdale
Radio frequencies: 160.590
Recommended reading: *Mother Lode Shortline*, by Ted Benson, published in 1970 by Chatham Publishing Co., P. O. Box 283, Burlingame, CA 94010

Ronald N. Johnson.

Two of Sierra's three Baldwin S12s bring a freight train across a stream in the meadows east of Oakdale, Calif.

SONORA-BAJA CALIFORNIA RAILWAY (Ferrocarril Sonora-Baja California)

The Sonora-Baja California had its beginning in 1923 when a 43-mile line was constructed under the aegis of the Ministry of Communications and Public Works (Secretaria de Comunicaciones y Obras Publicas) southeastward from Mexicali, the capital of Baja California. No further work was done on the railroad until 1936 when construction resumed across the Altar Desert. The line was opened as far east as Puerto Peñasco on the Gulf of California in 1940. Construction resumed again in 1946. In 1948 the line was completed to a connection with the Southern Pacific of Mexico (now Ferrocarril del Pacifico) at Benjamin Hill, Sonora. The S-BC furnishes an all-Mexican link between Baja California and the rest of the country. S-BC owns the former Tijuana & Tecate Railway, but San Diego & Arizona Eastern (page 166) operates it, both to connect the two U. S. segments of its line and also to perform local business in Mexico for S-BC. It is not included in the mileage figure below.

Address of general offices: Final Calle Ulises Irigoyen, P. O. Box 3-182, Mexicali, Baja California, Mexico

Miles of road operated: 379

Reporting marks: SBC
Number of locomotives: 20
Number of freight cars: 561
Number of passenger cars: 43
Principal commodities carried: Cotton, barley, asphalt, cement, beer
Major yards: Benjamin Hill, Son., Caborca, Son., Mexicali, B. C., Puerto Peñasco, Son., Pascualitos, Son.
Principal shops: Benjamin Hill, Son., Mexicali, B. C.
Junctions with other railroads:
Pacific Railroad (Ferrocarril del Pacifico): Benjamin Hill, Son.
San Diego & Arizona Eastern: San Ysidro, Calif.
Southern Pacific: Calexico, Calif.
Radio frequencies: 167.150, 167.625, 167.100
Passenger routes: Mexicali, B. C.-Benjamin Hill, Son.
Map: See National Railways of Mexico, page 132
Date: February 1983

Train 4, *El Mexicali*, is ready to leave Mexicali behind GP40-2 No. 2309. Ahead is Sonora's Altar Desert and a connection with the Pacific Railroad (Ferrocarril del Pacifico) for Guadalajara at Benjamin Hill, Son.

SBC.

SOO LINE RAILROAD

In the 1870s the flour millers of Minneapolis sought a new outlet for their products to avoid the high freight rates charged by existing railroads through Chicago. James J. Hill, who later built the Great Northern, tried to persuade the Canadian Pacific to construct its line to the west through Sault Ste. Marie and Minneapolis, but nationalistic feeling in Canada dictated CP's all-Canada route north of Lake Superior.

In 1883 a group of Minneapolis men incorporated the Minneapolis, Sault Ste. Marie & Atlantic to construct a line from the Twin Cities east to a connection with the Canadian Pacific at Sault Ste. Marie. A year later the Minneapolis & Pacific was incorporated by many of the same men to build northwestward into the wheat areas of Minnesota and North Dakota. In 1888 these two roads and two others were consolidated to form the Minneapolis, St. Paul & Sault Ste. Marie. Canadian Pacific acquired control of the MStP&SSM largely to block any attempt CP's rival Grand Trunk might make to build to western Canada via the U. S.

In 1893 the Soo Line, as it was nicknamed, built northwest to connect with CP at Portal, N. Dak., and in 1904 completed a line north from Glenwood, Minn., to a connection with CP at Noyes, Minn. In 1909 Soo Line leased the properties of the Wisconsin Central, gaining access to Chicago, the industrial Fox River Valley of Wisconsin, and the iron ore deposits of northern Wisconsin.

The Duluth, South Shore & Atlantic was a merger of several lines along the south shore of Lake Superior. Its traffic consisted largely of iron ore and forest products. Canadian Pacific obtained control of the DSS&A for the same reason as it did the Soo Line — blocking possible construction by Grand Trunk.

Continued on next page.

Stanley H. Mailer.

Two SD40-2s and an SD40 bring an eastbound freight through the far northwestern suburbs of Milwaukee, Wis. The long string of covered hoppers testifies to the importance of grain to the Soo Line.

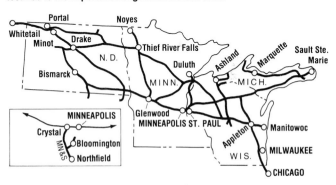

Today's Soo Line is the product of the 1961 merger of the Minneapolis, St. Paul & Sault Ste. Marie, its Wisconsin Central subsidiary, and the Duluth, South Shore & Atlantic. Soo Line's corporate structure actually dates from the 1949 reorganization of the DSS&A. Canadian Pacific Limited owns 55.7 percent of Soo's outstanding stock. In 1982 Soo Line acquired the 74-mile Minneapolis, Northfield & Southern Railway, which operates between Northfield, Minn., and the suburbs of Minneapolis.

Address of general offices: Soo Line Building, Box 530, Minneapolis, MN 55440

Miles of road operated: SOO, 4433; MNS, 74

Reporting marks: SOO, MNS

Number of locomotives: SOO, 237; MNS, 10

Number of freight cars: SOO, 11,677; MNS, 850

Principal commodities carried: Grain, paper, lumber, potash, sulfur, intermodal traffic, steel

Major yards: Fond du Lac, Wis., Minneapolis, Minn. (Shoreham), Neenah, Wis., Schiller Park, Ill., Stevens Point, Wis., Superior, Wis., Thief River Falls, Minn.

Principal shops: Fond du Lac, Wis., Minneapolis, Minn.

Radio frequencies: 161.085 (road, Stevens Point-Chicago), 161.370 (road, except Stevens Point-Chicago), 161.520 (road), 160.470 (MNS road), 160.980 (MNS switching)

Passenger routes: Neenah, Wis.-Sault Ste. Marie, Mich. (in caboose)

Historical and technical society: Soo Line Historical & Technical Society, 3410 Kasten Court, Middleton, WI 53562

Date: January 1983

SOUTH CENTRAL TENNESSEE RAILROAD

On July 1, 1978, Louisville & Nashville (now part of Seaboard System) abandoned service on its ex-Nashville, Chattanooga & St. Louis branch from Colesburg to Hohenwald, Tennessee. The South Central Tennessee Railroad, a subsidiary of Kyle Railways, took over service immediately. The major user of SCTR service is the Lewis Products Co. at Hohenwald, which receives carbon black by rail; a wood chip plant between Hohenwald and Centreville provides large amounts of outbound traffic for the railroad.

Address of general offices: P. O. Box 259, Centreville, TN 37033

Miles of road operated: 50

Reporting marks: SCTR

Number of locomotives: 3

Number of freight cars: 95

Timothy M. Baggett.

RS11 No. 29, a veteran of the Southern Pacific, returns from the Seaboard interchange at Colesburg, Tenn., having exchanged seven cars full of wood chips for seven empties.

Principal commodities carried: Wood chips, carbon black

Junctions with other railroads: Seaboard System: Colesburg, Tenn.

Radio frequencies: 161.355

Date: June 1983

SOUTHEASTERN MICHIGAN TRANSPORTATION AUTHORITY

Grand Trunk Western's commuter trains between Detroit and Pontiac, Michigan, were the last regularly scheduled steam-hauled standard-gauge passenger trains operated by a U. S. Class 1 railroad (they were dieselized in 1960). Like most commuter trains, they were a financial burden on their operator, and the Southeastern Michigan Transportation Authority was created in 1967 by the Michigan state legislature to deal with the problem. On November 1, 1974, SEMTA made its first purchase-of-service agreement with GTW for operation of the trains, and in 1977 SEMTA began purchasing the rolling stock used for the service. SEMTA now owns the locomotives, cars, and stations; GTW crews operate the trains for SEMTA. SEMTA also operates bus services in the Detroit area.

Address of general offices: 660 Woodward Avenue, 13th Floor, Detroit, MI 48226
Miles of road operated: 28
Number of locomotives: 5
Number of freight cars: 30
Shops: Pontiac, Mich.
Radio frequencies: 160.590, 160.530 (GTW frequencies)
Passenger routes: Detroit-Pontiac, Mich. (Grand Trunk Western)
Date: June 1983

In 1978 SEMTA repainted and refurbished its equipment. The first trainset to appear in the new colors was nicknamed "Silver Streak." This photo shows an ex-Grand Trunk Western GP18 and a train consisting of a former Union Pacific coach, three ex-Pennsylvania coaches rebuilt from 22-roomette sleepers, and a Grand Trunk Western office car passing through Royal Oak, Mich.

George C. Diebel.

SOUTHEASTERN PENNSYLVANIA TRANSPORTATION AUTHORITY

Southeastern Pennsylvania Transportation Authority was created by the legislature of the commonwealth of Pennsylvania in 1963 to plan, develop, and coordinate a regional transportation system for Philadelphia, Bucks, Chester, Delaware, and Montgomery counties. In 1968 SEPTA acquired Philadelphia Transportation Co., which operated streetcar, subway, elevated, and bus services in Philadelphia. In 1970 it purchased Philadelphia Suburban Transportation Co. (Red Arrow Lines), which operated 5'2¼" gauge trolley lines to Sharon Hill and Media, a standard gauge third-rail line (the former Philadelphia & Western) to Norristown, and numerous bus routes from a terminal shared with PTC's Market Street elevated at 69th Street in Upper Darby.

Cooperation between Philadelphia's two principal railroads, the Pennsylvania and the Reading, and governmental authorities for operation of commuter service began in 1958 with Operation Northwest, an experiment with increased service and reduced fares on the Chestnut Hill branches of the two railroads. Government's role in commuter service increased — by 1974, SEPTA was purchasing rolling stock for Penn Central (successor to the Pennsylvania) and Reading commuter trains.

The commuter rail system is now called the SEPTA Regional High Speed Lines. They operate from two terminals in Philadelphia, Reading Terminal (ex-Reading) and Penn Center Suburban Station (ex-Pennsyl-

Larry A. DeYoung.

A westbound Paoli local pauses at Strafford, Pa., deep in the "Main Line" suburbs of Philadelphia. The station building at the right was originally a pavilion at the Centennial Exposition in Philadelphia.

vania). All trains from Suburban Station stop at 30th Street Station, Amtrak's Philadelphia station, on the west bank of the Schuylkill River. SEPTA owns the ex-Pennsylvania lines to Chestnut Hill, Manayunk, and West Chester, and the ex-Reading lines to Chestnut Hill, Doylestown, Newtown, Norristown, Warminster, and West Trenton, New Jersey. Two major construction projects in Philadelphia are under way: a line to link 30th Street Station with Philadelphia International Airport, and a tunnel connecting Reading Terminal with Suburban Station, the former Pennsylvania station in downtown Philadelphia.

The transition from Conrail to SEPTA operation at the beginning of 1983 did not go smoothly. The system was closed by a strike by rail unions on March 15, 1983. The strike ended July 1, 1983, and service resumed shortly afterwards.

Address of general offices: 130 S. 9th Street, Philadelphia, PA 19107

Miles of road operated: 284
Number of locomotives: 3
Number of self-propelled passenger cars: 343 electric, 16 diesel
Number of passenger cars: 6
Shops: Paoli, Pa., Wayne Junction, Pa.
Radio frequencies: 160.350

Passenger routes:
(ex-Pennsylvania) Philadelphia to Trenton, N. J., and Chestnut Hill, Manayunk, Marcus Hook, Paoli, and West Chester, Pa.
(ex-Reading) Philadelphia to West Trenton, N. J. and Chestnut Hill, Doylestown, Newtown, Norristown, and Warminster, Pa.
Date: June 1983

SOUTHERN PACIFIC TRANSPORTATION CO.
ST. LOUIS SOUTHWESTERN RAILWAY

Three widely separated and apparently unrelated events in 1850 influenced construction of the Southern Pacific: the state of California was admitted to the union and two railroads were chartered, the New Orleans, Opelousas & Great Western and the Buffalo Bayou, Brazos, & Colorado. The new state would need a railroad to connect it to the rest of the country, and there was considerable debate about the route of that railroad — south toward the slave states or north toward the free states? The debate was settled a decade later by the outbreak of the Civil War.

Explanation of the Southern Pacific route by route, much as the passenger timetables were arranged, makes understanding SP's history easier than a strict chronological discussion.

Overland Route: In 1852 the Sacramento Valley Rail Road engaged Theodore D. Judah to lay out its line from Sacramento, Calif., east a few miles to Folsom and Placerville. The line was opened in 1856, but Judah had higher goals — a railroad over the Sierra Nevada to Virginia City, Nevada. He scouted the mountains for a route, incorporated the California Central Railroad, and got the backing of four Sacramento merchants: Collis P. Huntington, Mark Hopkins, Charles Crocker, and Leland Stanford. In 1862 Congress passed the Pacific Railroad Bill, which called for two companies, one to build west from the Missouri River at Omaha, Nebraska — the Union Pacific — and the other to build east from California — the Central Pacific Railroad. The latter was incorporated with Leland Stanford as president. The four men were unable to get financial backing in San Francisco, which considered itself a seaport, not the terminal of a railroad, so they financed the project themselves.

The first train operated to what is now Roseville, 18 miles east of Sacramento, in 1863. By 1867 the Central Pacific had crossed the state line into Nevada, and on May 10, 1869, the Central Pacific and the Union Pacific met at Promontory, Utah, creating the first transcontinental railroad.

In 1900 Collis P. Huntington, the last of the four founders of the SP, died. Edward H. Harriman mortgaged his Union Pacific and bought out the Huntington estate. Under Harriman the road built the Lucin Cutoff across the Great Salt Lake, shortening the route by 44 miles (and bypassing Promontory, site of the Golden Spike ceremony in 1869), and double-tracked the line over the Sierra, in many places building a new line with easier grades.

Much of the line across the Sierra was covered by snowsheds. Not until recent years has snowplow technology been a match for the weather of the Sierra Nevada, and even then not always. The snowsheds and tunnels of the route were the reason for SP's cab-forward articulateds.

Continued on next page.

179

California Lines: After meeting the UP at Promontory, Central Pacific extended itself west to San Francisco Bay, first by construction of the Western Pacific Railroad to Oakland over Altamont Pass (don't confuse this Western Pacific with the modern railroad of the same name, page 205), and then by acquisition in 1876 of the California Pacific Railroad from Sacramento to Vallejo. In 1879 a line was completed from Port Costa, across the Carquinez Strait from Vallejo, along the shore of San Francisco Bay to Oakland. Train ferries made the connection between Port Costa and Benicia (just east of Vallejo) until the construction of the Carquinez Straits bridge in 1929.

The San Francisco & San Jose Railroad was opened along the San Francisco peninsula in 1864. It merged with the Southern Pacific Railroad, which was intent on building a line south along the Pacific coast to San Diego and then east to connect with a proposed railroad from the Mississippi River. The Central Pacific acquired the Southern Pacific by 1868. In 1870 Central Pacific acquired the California & Oregon, which had built 90 miles north from Roseville, and the San Joaquin Valley Rail Road, which had started building a line south from a point near Stockton. Central Pacific pushed the line down the San Joaquin Valley, reaching Bakersfield in 1874.

One of Harriman's improvements in California was the Bayshore Cutoff south of San Francisco, which replaced a steeply graded inland route with a water-level route along the shore of San Francisco Bay. The Coast Line between San Francisco and Los Angeles was opened in 1901.

In 1907 SP and Santa Fe formed the jointly owned Northwestern Pacific, which consolidated several lines north of San Francisco. NWP built north through the redwood country and down the canyon of the Eel River (unfortunately, a river prone to flood) to Eureka, Calif. SP bought out Santa Fe's share in 1929.

Sunset Route: The railroad continued to build south from Bakersfield, now working under Southern Pacific's charter. The line ascended the Tehachapi Mountains and then detoured southward through Los Angeles, reaching there in September 1876, before turning east. The line reached Yuma, Arizona, on the Colorado River in 1877. Further construction, this time as the Galveston, Harrisburg & San Antonio, put the line into El Paso, Texas, in 1881, and on the banks of the Pecos River in 1883

Jim Zwernemann.

The Tehachapi Mountains are a formidable barrier between the south end of the San Joaquin Valley and Los Angeles. Espee's steep, curving line between Bakersfield and Mojave, Calif., makes a complete loop — Tehachapi Loop — at one point. It is not uncommon for the head end of a freight train to cross its own tail.

it met the line being constructed from San Antonio. The line at that point has since been relocated, crossing the Pecos on the highest bridge on a U. S. common carrier (320 feet).

The SP lines east of El Paso grew from the Buffalo Bayou, Brazos & Colorado and the New Orleans, Opelousas & Great Western. The BBB&C

Continued on page 182.

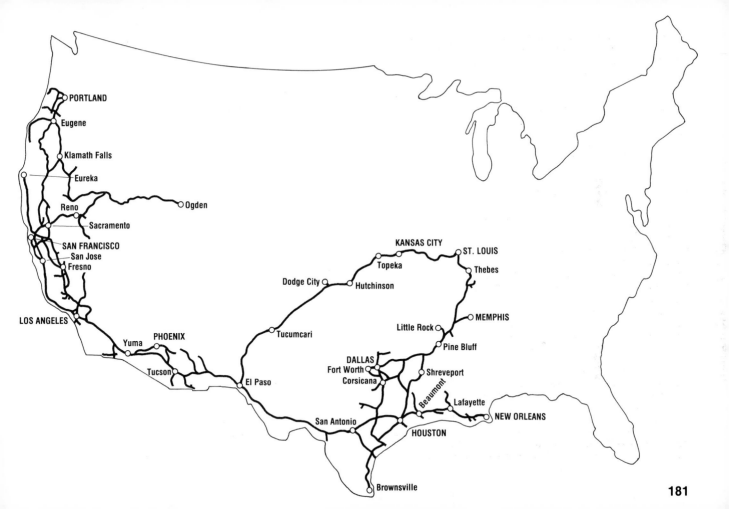

PORTLAND
Eugene
Klamath Falls
Eureka
Reno
Sacramento
Ogden
SAN FRANCISCO
San Jose
Fresno
LOS ANGELES
Yuma
PHOENIX
Tucson
El Paso
KANSAS CITY
ST. LOUIS
Topeka
Thebes
Dodge City
Hutchinson
Tucumcari
MEMPHIS
Little Rock
Pine Bluff
DALLAS
Fort Worth
Shreveport
Corsicana
Beaumont
Lafayette
San Antonio
NEW ORLEANS
HOUSTON
Brownsville

was reorganized as the Galveston, Harrisburg & San Antonio in 1870. It reached San Antonio in 1877, engaged in some machinations with and against Jay Gould's Missouri Pacific system, and continued building west. The Opelousas, sold in 1869 to steamship magnate Charles Morgan and later resold and reorganized as Morgan's Louisiana & Texas Railroad, built across the bayou country west of New Orleans to form a route between New Orleans and Houston in conjunction with the Louisiana Western and the Texas & New Orleans.

In 1934 all these railroads became the Texas & New Orleans. Even after the repeal in 1967 of the article in the Texas constitution requiring railroads operating in Texas to be headquartered there, the T&NO lines were operated as a separate entity. This division of Espee into Pacific Lines and Texas & Louisiana Lines had parallels, though, with many other large roads, among them the Santa Fe and the Pennsylvania.

SP constructed a line east from Mojave, Calif., to the Colorado River at Needles, arriving there on July 1, 1883, little more than a month before the Santa Fe, which was building west across Arizona. SP later traded this line to Santa Fe for the Sonora Railway that Santa Fe had constructed between Nogales and Guaymas, Sonora, Mexico. (See Atchison, Topeka & Santa Fe, page 17, and Pacific Railway, page 150.)

Golden State Route: In 1924 SP acquired the El Paso & Southwestern System, which had a line from Tucson, Ariz., through Douglas, Ariz., and El Paso to Tucumcari, New Mexico, where it connected with the Rock Island. This route, the Golden State Route, was opened in 1902; the former Rock Island line from Tucumcari east to Kansas City is now the property of SP subsidiary Cotton Belt.

Shasta Route: The California & Oregon Railroad was pushed north through Redding, Calif., up the Sacramento River canyon, and over the Siskiyou Range to connect with the Oregon & California at Ashland, Oreg., in 1887. SP acquired the O&C at that time, extending its system north to Portland, Oreg.

In 1926 SP opened the Natron Cutoff between Eugene, Oreg., and Black Butte, Calif., via Klamath Falls, Oreg. The portion of this line south of Klamath Falls was opened in 1909. The north end was a line into the mountains southeast of Eugene that was originally intended to meet a Union Pacific line to be constructed west from the Idaho-Oregon border.

That linkup never happened, but SP saw that extending this line over the Cascade Range and south along the plateau to Klamath Falls might head off the Great Northern, which had begun constructing a line south from the Columbia River to connect with a Western Pacific line being pushed north from Keddie, Calif. As it turned out, GN wound up on SP rails between Chemult, Oreg., and Klamath Falls. The Cascade Line, as the Natron Cutoff was renamed, had much easier grades and curves than the original route through Ashland, and it became SP's main route in Oregon. At about the same time SP opened a line between Klamath Falls and the Overland Route at Fernley, Nev. Some of this Modoc Line, as it is called, was new construction; other portions of it were the former 3-foot-gauge Nevada-California-Oregon, suitably widened.

Construction of Shasta Dam between 1938 and 1942 and the resulting lake required relocation of much of SP's line in the lower Sacramento River canyon. The Pit River bridge, which carries both railroad and highway traffic, was at the time of its construction the highest in the U. S. (433 feet). Subsequent flooding of Shasta Lake has brought the water level up to just below the girders; most of the height of the piers is under water.

The St. Louis Southwestern (usually called the Cotton Belt) is SP's principal subsidiary. It began as the 3-foot gauge Tyler Tap Railroad, chartered in 1871 and opened in 1877 between Tyler, Tex., and a junction with the Texas & Pacific at Big Sandy. Rechartered as the Texas & St. Louis Railway, the road was extended to Texarkana and a connection with the St. Louis, Iron Mountain & Southern in 1880. A year later the west end of the railroad was extended to Waco.

In 1881 Jay Gould purchased the Iron Mountain (he already had the T&P), returning the Texas & St. Louis to one-connection status. The T&StL decided to fulfill its name. In 1882 it reached Birds Point, Missouri, across the Mississippi River from Cairo, Illinois. There it connected by barge with the narrow gauge St. Louis & Cairo, and by 1885 a continuous line of 3-foot gauge railroads reached from Toledo, Ohio, to Houston, Tex., with intentions of heading for Laredo and eventually Mexico City.

In 1886 the T&StL was reorganized as the St. Louis, Arkansas & Texas Railway. It converted its lines to standard gauge, built branches to Shreveport, Louisiana, and Fort Worth in 1888, and entered bankruptcy

Tim Zukas.

Southern Pacific's main line between Eugene and Klamath Falls, Oreg., traverses the Cascade Mountains on a spectacular line. Here as on the line over the Sierra between Sacramento and Reno SP must battle snow.

in 1889. Jay Gould organized the St. Louis Southwestern Railway in 1891 and took over the StLA&T. The road gained access to Memphis, Tennessee; acquired trackage rights over Missouri Pacific from Thebes, Ill., to St. Louis in exchange for letting MP operate over SSW between Illmo, Mo., and Paragould, Ark.; and joined with MP in constructing a bridge over the Mississippi between Thebes and Illmo.

After World War One bridge traffic began to increase on the Cotton Belt. The Rock Island purchased a controlling interest in the road in 1925 and sold it almost immediately to Kansas City Southern. KCS proposed a

regional system to include KCS, SSW, and the Missouri-Kansas-Texas, but the ICC refused approval. KCS lost interest in the Cotton Belt about the time Southern Pacific was looking for a connection to St. Louis from its Texas lines. SP applied for control and in 1932 took over. Cotton Belt weathered receivership between 1935 and 1947; in recent years it has been essentially a division of the SP, though its equipment is still lettered "Cotton Belt." In 1980 SSW acquired the former Rock Island line from St. Louis through Kansas City to Santa Rosa, N. M. (RI owned the line between Santa Rosa and Tucumcari, N. M., but it had long been leased to SP.) Most of the St. Louis-Kansas City route is not being operated; from Kansas City west the road is a fast freight route in conjunction with parent SP from Tucumcari to El Paso.

Until the supermergers of recent years, SP was one of the largest railroads in the U. S., ranking third behind Pennsylvania and New York Central in operating revenue. SP was perhaps the most diverse of the major railroads. Its lines penetrated the dense forests of Oregon and the deserts of Nevada and New Mexico, and they extended from Portland, Oreg., south to Guadalajara, Mexico (until 1951), and east to New Orleans. SP had several subsidiary traction lines. The Portland, Eugene & Eastern served Oregon's Willamette Valley. The Interurban Electric Railway served the East Bay cities of Oakland, Berkeley, and Alameda and for a short period connected them with San Francisco via the Bay Bridge. Blanketing the Los Angeles Basin was the Pacific Electric, largest interurban line in the U. S. In addition, the Marin County suburban lines of subsidiary Northwestern Pacific were electrified until the Golden Gate Bridge opened and buses replaced the train-and-ferry service. SP's empire also included a narrow gauge line, the former Carson & Colorado, which connected western Nevada with some of the emptiest parts of eastern California. The Laws-Keeler, Calif., segment of the line lasted long enough to be dieselized. Another former SP subsidiary is the San Diego & Arizona Eastern (see page 166).

Address of general offices: 1 Market Plaza, San Francisco, CA 94105
Miles of road operated: 11,143
Reporting marks: SP, SPFE, SSW
Number of locomotives: 2389
Number of freight cars: 78,624

Continued on next page.

Principal commodities carried: Food products, chemicals, lumber
Major yards: Colton, Calif.; Eugene, Oreg.; Houston, Tex.; Kansas City, Kans. (Armourdale); Los Angeles, Calif. (Taylor); Roseville, Calif.
Principal shops: Sacramento, Calif.; Los Angeles, Calif.; Pine Bluff, Ark.
Radio frequencies: 161.550
Passenger routes:
Amtrak — New Orleans-Los Angeles (*Sunset Limited*), Los Angeles-San Jose-Sacramento-Klamath Falls, Oreg.-Portland (*Coast Starlight, Spirit of California*), Oakland-Reno, Nev.-Ogden, Utah (*California Zephyr*), Oakland-Port Chicago, Calif. (*San Joaquins*)
Caltrans — San Francisco-San Jose
Historical and technical society: Southern Pacific Historical & Technical Society, 218 Norton, No. 6, Long Beach CA 90805
Recommended reading: *Southern Pacific*, by Neill C. Wilson and Frank J. Taylor, published in 1952 by McGraw-Hill Book Co., New York, N. Y.
Date: June 1983

LOOK AHEAD-LOOK SOUTH

SOUTHERN RAILWAY SYSTEM

The South Carolina Canal & Rail Road Company was chartered in 1828 to build from Charleston, S. C., to Hamburg, S. C., on the north bank of the Savannah River, to bring trade to the port of Charleston from inland points and divert trade bound down the Savannah River to the port of Savannah, Georgia. When the 136-mile line was opened, it was the longest railroad in the world. By 1857 it was part of a line from Charleston to Memphis, Tennessee — at the time the longest connected system of railroads in the world. (Two of the railroads involved, the Georgia Railroad and the Western & Atlantic, are now part of Seaboard System.)

The Richmond & Danville Railroad was chartered in 1847 and completed in 1856 between the two Virginia cities of its name. At the same time the Orange & Alexandria Railroad was under construction from Alexandria, Va., across the Potomac River from Washington, D. C., southwest through Manassas and Gordonsville to Lynchburg, Va.

The American Civil War greatly affected the railroads that became the Southern Railway. The Civil War is considered the first modern war, and it was the first war in which railroads were strategically and tactically important. Junctions were captured: The First Battle of Bull Run centered on the junction of the Orange & Alexandria and the Manassas Gap railroads, and Chattanooga was fought over for more than a year because lines from Richmond to Memphis and from Nashville to Atlanta crossed there. Equipment was seized: The Confederates made two raids on the Baltimore & Ohio at Martinsburg, West Virginia, and took home locomotives and cars for use on railroads in the south, dragging them along dirt roads behind teams of horses. Railroads were destroyed to prevent their use: This was General William T. Sherman's specialty, and destruction was the purpose of James J. Andrews' capture of a Western & Atlantic train at Big Shanty, Ga. (it resulted mostly in a much-described chase of two locomotives, the *General* and the *Texas*). The railroads moved troops and, less than a week before Lee's surrender at Appomattox, the Richmond & Danville evacuated the Confederate government from Richmond to Danville on April 2, 1865.

At the end of the Civil War what little remained of the railroads in the south was controlled by the federal government. The difficulty and expense of rebuilding had the salutary effects of pruning weak and unnecessary lines and encouraging consolidation of small companies into large ones.

During the 1870s the Richmond & Danville obtained control of the North Carolina Railroad and built an extension to Atlanta, Ga. The Orange, Alexandria & Manassas, successor to the Orange & Alexandria, built an extension from Lynchburg to Danville, connecting with the Richmond & Danville and forming what is now the main line of the Southern Railway. All of these railroads came into the Richmond & Danville and Richmond Terminal family, forming an association of independent companies rather than a single railroad. The R&D foundered in the Panic of 1893.

In 1869 two railroads out of Knoxville, Tenn., the East Tennessee & Virginia and the East Tennessee & Georgia, were consolidated to form the East Tennessee, Virginia & Georgia Railroad, with a line from Bristol, Va., to Dalton, Ga. West of that line the Cincinnati Southern was under construction from Cincinnati, Ohio, to Chattanooga, Tenn. The railroad was owned by the city of Cincinnati and leased to the Cincinnati, New Orleans & Texas Pacific for operation. The CNO&TP was owned by British interests which had earlier gained control of a line from Chattanooga to Meridian, Mississippi, reorganized it as the Alabama Great Southern, and then completed the New Orleans & North Eastern between Meridian and New Orleans. The combined railroads were known as the Queen & Crescent Route, referring to the terminals, Cincinnati (the Queen City) and New Orleans (the Crescent City).

The Southern Railway was organized in 1894, acquired the Richmond & Danville and the East Tennessee, Virginia & Georgia, and began to build a railroad system under the direction of Samuel Spencer.

The Southern system now encompasses many subsidiaries acquired over the years. The major recent acquisition was the Central of Georgia in 1963; Southern purchased the Norfolk Southern (Norfolk, Va., to Charlotte, N. C.) in 1974 and in 1982 did some name-changing so the NS name could be used for the merged Southern and Norfolk & Western system (see Norfolk Southern, page 142). Three subsidiaries, the CNO&TP, the AGS, and the CofG, are Class 1 railroads in their own right. There are many short lines in the Southern system whose existence is still evidenced by initials on locomotives and reporting marks on cars: Geor-

Continued on next page.

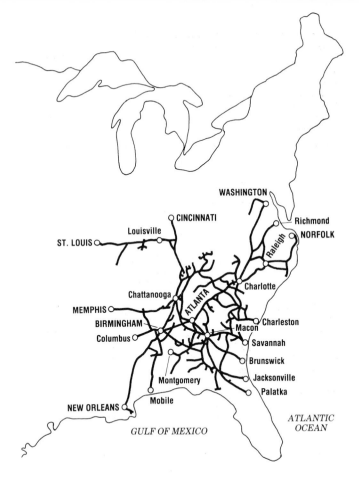

gia & Florida; Interstate; Savannah & Atlanta; and Tennessee, Alabama & Georgia, to list four.

Southern did not join Amtrak at first, continuing to run its remaining passenger trains and gradually trimming service to just the Washington-Atlanta-New Orleans *Southern Crescent*. Amtrak took over operation of that train on February 1, 1979. In the past two decades Southern, one of the first large railroads to dieselize, has operated a number of steam locomotives in conjunction with museums and enthusiast groups.

On March 25, 1982, the Interstate Commerce Commission approved the acquisition by Norfolk Southern Corporation, a newly organized holding company, of two railroads: the Southern Railway and the Norfolk & Western Railway. Actual merger took place on June 1, 1982.

Address of general offices: 99 Spring Street, S.W., Atlanta, GA 30303

Miles of road operated: 10,200

Reporting marks: CG, CRN, GF, INT, LSO, NS, SA, SOU, TAG

Number of locomotives: 1324

Number of freight cars: 72,977

Principal commodities carried: Coal, chemicals, pulp and paper products

Major yards: Atlanta, Ga. (Inman); Birmingham, Ala. (Norris); Chattanooga, Tenn.; Knoxville, Tenn. (Sevier); Linwood, N. C. (Spencer); Macon, Ga.; Sheffield, Ala.

Principal shops: Atlanta, Ga.; Chattanooga, Tenn.; Spartanburg, S. C.

Radio frequencies: 160.950 (road), 160.245 (dispatcher to train), 160.830 (train to dispatcher), 161.490 (yard)

Passenger routes: Amtrak — Washington-New Orleans (*Crescent*)

Historical and technical society: Southern Railway Historical Society, P. O. Box 4094, Martinez, GA 30907

Date: June 1983

Illustrating the flexibility of double track and centralized traffic control, a southbound piggyback train (left) overtakes and passes a southbound coal drag on Southern's main line at Shelton, N. C. Southern prefers high short hoods on its diesels and often as not runs them long hood forward.

Curt Tillotson Jr.

TERMINAL RAILROAD ASSOCIATION OF ST. LOUIS

There were difficulties when the Eads Bridge was completed across the Mississippi River in 1874. The bridge company could not operate a railroad, and the railroads chartered to operate in Missouri could not operate in Illinois and vice versa. Several railroad companies were chartered to resolve the situation.

In 1881 the bridge company, the terminal railroads on each side of the river in St. Louis, Mo., and East St. Louis, Ill., and the company that owned the tunnel at the west end of the Eads Bridge all came under the control of Jay Gould. To forestall any possibility of the St. Louis gateway being controlled by one railroad system, the major railroads serving St. Louis formed the Terminal Railroad Association in 1889. TRRA leased the Eads Bridge and the tunnel; built another bridge across the Mississippi, the Merchants Bridge; and built St. Louis Union Station, which was the largest in North America in terms of the number of tracks on one level.

By 1974 locomotives and cars had outgrown the century-old Eads Bridge. The last train rolled across it and the rails were removed (it still carries highway traffic). TRRA is owned by the ten railroads marked with an asterisk in the list of connecting railroads below.

Address of general offices: 2016 Madison Ave., Granite City, IL 62040

Miles of road operated: 100
Reporting marks: TRRA
Number of locomotives: 63
Major yards: Granite City, Ill.
Connects with:
Alton & Southern
Burlington Northern*
Chessie System*
Chicago & North Western
Conrail*
Illinois Central Gulf*
Manufacturers Railway
Missouri-Kansas-Texas*
Missouri Pacific*
Norfolk & Western*
St. Louis Southwestern*
Seaboard System*
Southern Railway*
all within the St. Louis-East St. Louis Switching Districts
Radio frequencies: 160.500 (road), 161.535 (Harlem Yard), 160.650 (Madison Yard)

J. David Ingles.

SW9 1210 and transfer caboose 596 exemplify TRRA's equipment, which is typical of most switching and terminal roads.

TEXAS MEXICAN RAILWAY

In 1875 the Corpus Christi, San Diego & Rio Grande Narrow Gauge Railroad was chartered to build from the Gulf of Mexico at Corpus Christi, Texas, west across the southern tip of Texas to the Mexican border at Laredo. The road received its present name in 1881. The road came under the control of National Railways of Mexico, but since 1902 NdeM's interest in the road has been held by the Manufacturers Hanover Trust Co. of New York. In 1982 NdeM sold the railroad to a private Mexican firm.

Most of Tex-Mex's traffic is freight interchanged with NdeM at Laredo; the road's line extends to the center of the Rio Grande bridge between Laredo, Tex., and Nuevo Laredo, Tamaulipas. TM dieselized in 1939 with unique Whitcomb rigid-frame 8-wheel diesels; in 1946 the road built four similar units with a 1-D wheel arrangement.

Address of general offices: P. O. Box 419, Laredo, TX 78040
Miles of road operated: 157
Reporting marks: TM
Number of locomotives: 16
Number of freight cars: 1121
Principal commodities carried: Grain, chemicals, machinery, scrap iron, gravel
Shops: Laredo, Tex.
Junctions with other railroads:
Missouri Pacific: Corpus Christi, Laredo, Robstown
National Railways of Mexico: Laredo
Southern Pacific: Alice, Corpus Christi
Radio frequencies: 161.130 (yard), 161.220 (road and dispatcher)
Date: June 1983

J. David Ingles.

Texas Mexican's diesel fleet once included such exotica as rigid-frame locomotives and a cut-down former Boston & Maine baggage-mail-power car. Now the road's power is of conventional cut, exemplified by these GP38-2s.

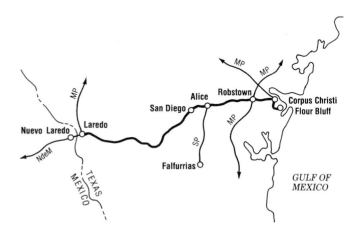

TEXAS, OKLAHOMA & EASTERN RAILROAD/DE QUEEN & EASTERN RAILROAD

The Texas, Oklahoma & Eastern was incorporated in 1910 and opened in 1911 between Valliant, Oklahoma, and the Oklahoma-Arkansas state line. It was originally the property of the Dierks Lumber & Coal Co.; it is now controlled by the Weyerhaeuser Corp., which owns more than 99 percent of the stock.

Sharing the same headquarters and offices is the De Queen & Eastern, which was incorporated in 1900. It is wholly owned by Weyerhaeuser.

Address of general offices: 421 E. Stilwell, De Queen, AR 71832
Miles of road operated: 40 (TOE), 46 (DQE)
Reporting marks: TOE, DQE
Number of locomotives: 9 (TOE), 3 (DQE)
Number of freight cars: 1269 (TOE), 15 (DQE)

Principal commodities carried: Forest products
Shops: De Queen, Ark.
Junctions with other railroads:
TOE
Burlington Northern: Valliant, Okla.
De Queen & Eastern: West Line, Ark.
DQE
Kansas City Southern: De Queen, Ark.
Missouri Pacific: Perkins, Ark.
Texas, Oklahoma & Eastern: West Line, Ark.
Radio frequencies: 160.230 (road), 160.650 (yard), 160.785 (yard)

James B. Holder: Collection of Louis A. Marre.

GP40 D-14 of the Texas, Oklahoma & Eastern sits outside the De Queen enginehouse. It is considerably larger and more powerful than the average short-line locomotive.

TOLEDO, PEORIA & WESTERN RAILROAD

The Toledo, Peoria & Western was chartered in 1863 as the Toledo, Peoria & Warsaw Railway. The line was opened in 1868 from the Indiana-Illinois state line at what is now Effner through Peoria to Warsaw, Ill., on the Mississippi River. In 1880 the road was reorganized as the Toledo, Peoria & Western Railroad and leased to the Wabash, St. Louis & Pacific for a term of 49½ years — the lease lasted until 1884. The TP&W Railway was chartered in 1887 to take over the railroad. In 1893 the Pennsylvania and a predecessor of the Burlington each acquired a large stock interest in the TP&W, which by then had been extended across the Mississippi to Keokuk, Iowa. In 1927 the TP&W made a connection with the Santa Fe at Lomax, Ill., over a 10-mile line from La Harpe, Ill.

In 1927 George P. McNear Jr. purchased the road at foreclosure. He saw the road's potential as a bridge route bypassing the congestion of Chicago and St. Louis, and he began to improve the physical plant. In 1941 McNear refused to go along with an industry-wide pay increase, proposing instead hourly wages and the elimination of inefficient practices. A bitter strike ensued, followed by government operation of the road during World War Two and the 1947 murder of McNear. That year new management took over and the railroad resumed operation after a 19-month work stoppage.

The present Toledo, Peoria & Western was incorporated in 1952, succeeding at least three previous Toledo, Peoria & Westerns. In 1960 the

Roger A. Holmes.

Toledo, Peoria & Western freights meet at El Paso, Illinois.

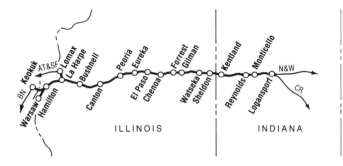

Santa Fe purchased the railroad and sold half to the Pennsylvania Railroad. The TP&W formed a Chicago bypass for traffic moving between the Pennsylvania and the Santa Fe. The formation of Conrail changed traffic patterns, and TP&W didn't fit into Conrail's plans. In 1976 TP&W bought the former Pennsylvania line from Effner to Logansport, Ind., where it could interchange traffic with Conrail and Norfolk & Western. In 1979, the Pennsylvania Company, a subsidiary of the Penn Central, sold its half interest in the TP&W back to the Santa Fe. Merger with Santa Fe is expected in the near future.

Address of general offices: 2000 E. Washington Street, East Peoria, IL 61611

Miles of road operated: 301

Reporting marks: TPW

Number of locomotives: 29

Number of freight cars: 382

Principal commodities carried: Coal, grain

Major yards: East Peoria, Ill.

Shops: East Peoria, Ill.

Junctions with other railroads:

Atchison, Topeka & Santa Fe:
 Fort Madison, Iowa
 Lomax, Ill.

Burlington Northern:
 Bushnell, Ill.
 Canton, Ill.
 Keokuk, Iowa
 Peoria, Ill.

Chicago & North Western: Sommer, Ill.

Chicago, Milwaukee, St. Paul & Pacific: Kentland, Ind.

Conrail: Kentland, Ind., Logansport, Ind., Sheldon, Ill.

Illinois Central Gulf: Chenoa, Ill., Gilman, Ill.

Kankakee, Beaverville & Southern: Sheldon, Ill., Webster, Ill.

Keokuk Junction: Keokuk, Iowa

Louisville & Nashville: Reynolds, Ind., Watseka, Ill.

Missouri Pacific: Watseka, Ill.

Norfolk & Western:
 Fairbury, Ill.
 Farmdale, Ill.
 Forrest, Ill.

Peoria & Pekin Union: Peoria, Ill.

Radio frequencies: 161.400 (road), 161.310 (yard)

Historical and technical society: TP&W Historical Society, RR1, Box 174B, Morocco, IN 47963

Date: June 1983

TORONTO, HAMILTON & BUFFALO RAILWAY

The Toronto, Hamilton & Buffalo was incorporated in 1884 to build a railroad directly from Hamilton, Ontario, to Fort Erie, across the Niagara River from Buffalo, New York. Existing routes were circuitous and Hamilton was a one-railroad city. Before construction began, the road modified its goal and aimed the line at Welland, Ont., on the main line of the Michigan Central. In 1895 four railroads agreed to buy and own the TH&B: Canadian Pacific, 27 percent; New York Central, 37 percent; Michigan Central, 18 percent; and Canada Southern, 18 percent. The latter two were part of the New York Central System, so ownership was essentially one-fourth CP and three-fourths NYC.

The railroad was opened in December 1895. Michigan Central operated the road for two years, but in 1897 TH&B took over its own operation. The road formed the middle third of a Buffalo-Toronto route for its two principal owners and provided Canadian Pacific with access to the industries of Hamilton.

In 1977 CP purchased the Penn Central (ex-New York Central and Michigan Central) and Canada Southern interests in the road and assumed sole ownership. The last passenger service, a Toronto-Buffalo RDC run operated in conjunction with CP and Conrail, was discontinued April 25, 1981.

Continued on next page.

Address of general offices: 36 Hunter Street East, Hamilton, ON L8N 1M1, Canada

Miles of road operated: 111

Reporting marks: THB

Number of locomotives: 17

Number of freight cars: 1121

Principal commodities carried: Fertilizer, chemicals, iron and steel products

Major yards: Welland, Ont., Hamilton, Ont.

Principal shops: Hamilton, Ont.

Junctions with other railroads:

Canadian National: Brantford, Ont.; Hamilton, Ont.

Canadian Pacific: Hamilton, Ont.

Conrail: Waterford, Ont.; Welland, Ont.

Lake Erie & Northern (Canadian Pacific): Brantford, Ont.

Radio frequencies: 161.265 (yard), 161.505 (road)

Recommended reading: *In The Shadow of Giants,* by Norman Helm, published in 1978 by Boston Mills Press, RR 1, Cheltenham, Ont. L0P 1C0 (ISBN 0-919822-22-3)

John Uckley.

Maroon-and-cream SW9 58 pulls a freight out of the Hunter Street tunnel in Hamilton, Ont., on its way to switch the industrial area in the eastern portion of the city.

TUSCOLA & SAGINAW BAY RAILWAY

On October 1, 1977, the Tuscola & Saginaw Bay began operation on former Conrail track southeast of Saginaw, Michigan — track that had once been part of New York Central's line from Detroit to Bay City, Mich. In 1982 the railroad became the operator of part of the Ann Arbor, which had been purchased by the state of Michigan. Tuscola & Saginaw Bay received the middle portion of the AA, from Ann Arbor to Alma, with trackage rights over Grand Trunk Western from Durand to Ashley, and from Owosso, former operating headquarters of the AA, northeast 27 miles to Swan Creek.

Address of general offices: 538 E. Huron Avenue, Vassar, MI 48768
Miles of road operated: 208
Reporting marks: TSBY

Number of locomotives: 6
Number of freight cars: 159
Principal commodities carried: Grain, auto parts, molasses, coal
Shops: Owosso
Junctions with other railroads:
Chessie System: Alma, Ann Pere (Howell), Vassar
Grand Trunk Western: Durand, Harger
Michigan Interstate: Ann Arbor
Michigan Northern: Alma
Radio frequencies: 160.575
Date: May 1983

U. S. Leasing.

Tuscola & Saginaw Bay's name is carried across the country on freight cars such as this Center Flow covered hopper car.

UNION PACIFIC RAILROAD

The Union Pacific was chartered by an act of Congress in 1862. Several routes to the Pacific had been surveyed, but not until the South seceded was there majority support for any one of them. The chartering act provided subsidy and land grants to UP and to Central Pacific, which was to build east from Sacramento, California, to meet the UP. Construction began in 1865, and the two roads met at Promontory, Utah, on May 10, 1869. Ceremonies and a golden spike celebrated the completion of the first railroad across North America.

The ensuing three decades were difficult for Union Pacific because of bad management, overextension, the effect of the Credit Mobilier scandal, and the debt owed the federal government. During that period affiliated or subsidiary lines were extended north from Ogden, Utah, to Butte, Montana (Utah & Northern), and northwest from Granger, Wyoming, to Portland, Oregon (Oregon Short Line). UP gained control of the Colorado & Southern, briefly extending its system into Texas.

In 1897 E. H. Harriman gained control of UP and built a system that also included Southern Pacific, Illinois Central, and Chicago & Alton. Harriman improved the UP considerably, double-tracking the main line from Omaha west to Granger and building a second line over Sherman Hill between Cheyenne and Laramie. In 1907 the Los Angeles & Salt Lake was completed between its namesake cities, but severe floods in several successive years in Nevada and western Utah destroyed much of the line in the Meadow Valley Canyon. The line was rebuilt and placed in service in 1912. In 1913 UP was required to divest itself of its SP stock, but close affiliation continued between the two railroads, aided by a 1924 agreement that permitted SP to control Central Pacific and required SP to solicit traffic to move via Ogden and the UP.

Union Pacific Railroad is wholly owned by Union Pacific Corporation, which also has extensive land and energy holdings. Several UP subsidiaries still have a corporate existence: Oregon Short Line, Oregon-Washington Railroad & Navigation Co., Los Angeles & Salt Lake, St. Joseph & Grand Island, Spokane International (which operates a line from Spokane north to the Canadian border), and Yakima Valley Transportation Co. (a short traction line at Yakima, Wash.).

Continued on page 196.

John C. Lucas.

Union Pacific has the longest average freight haul in the U. S., and UP's double-track main line between Omaha and Ogden is one of the busiest stretches of freight railroad in North America. The major barrier on this route is Sherman Hill, between Cheyenne and Laramie, Wyo. UP usually assigns sufficient power, though, that freights sail up and over the hill at speeds many flatland railroads would envy. Here a UP SD45 and five assorted Western Pacific units lead an eastbound freight through Dale, Wyo., high on Sherman Hill.

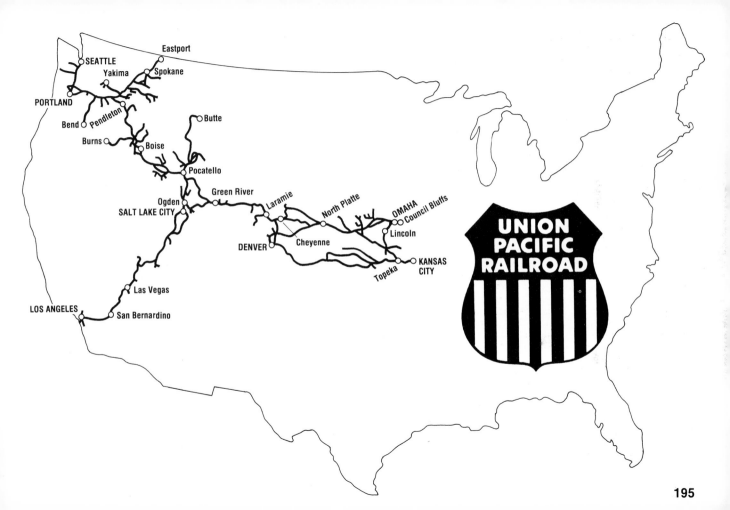

Union Pacific's desire to run fast trains through mountainous territory has resulted in such massive motive power as the 4000-class Big Boy (4-8-8-4), three series of gas-turbine-electrics, and several classes of eight-axle diesel locomotives. The 6900-series DDA40X, dubbed Centennial, because they were delivered in 1969, the centennial of the Golden Spike, were the last such units UP received. Two of them are shown here trailing and dwarfing an SD40-2 on Santa Fe rails at Cajon, Calif. UP uses Santa Fe track from Daggett, Calif., over Cajon Pass to San Bernardino.

Bob Gottier.

On December 22, 1981, the Union Pacific, Missouri Pacific, and Western Pacific merged. UP and MP will retain their identities; Western Pacific has become the Fourth Operating District of the UP. The name Pacific Rail Systems is used to describe the combined railroads, but it is simply a name, not a company or corporation.

Address of general offices: 1416 Dodge Street, Omaha, NE 68179
Miles of road operated: 9460 (excluding Western Pacific)
Reporting marks: UP, UPFE
Number of locomotives: 1413
Number of freight cars: 57,948
Principal commodities carried: Farm products, soda ash and chemicals, forest products, foodstuffs, coal
Major yards: Kansas City; North Platte, Nebr.; Omaha; Pocatello, Idaho; Hinkle, Oreg.; Yermo, Calif.
Principal shops:

Locomotive: Omaha, Nebr.; Salt Lake City, Utah
Car: Portland, Oreg.
Radio frequencies: 160.740, others
Passenger routes: Amtrak: Salt Lake City-Ogden, Utah (*California Zephyr*); Salt Lake City-Barstow, Calif. (*Desert Wind*); Ogden-Portland, Oreg. (*Pioneer*)
In addition, UP operates excursion trains several times a year, often with steam locomotives 8444 (4-8-4) and 3985 (4-6-6-4)
Recommended reading:
Union Pacific Country, by Robert G. Athearn, published in 1971 by Rand McNally & Co., Chicago, Ill.
Union Pacific Motive Power Review 1968-77, edited by F. Hol Wagner Jr., published in 1978 by Motive Power Service, P. O. Box 17111, Denver, CO 80217
Date: January 1983

UNION RAILROAD

The Union Railroad was incorporated in 1894 and opened in 1896. In 1937 it merged with two railroads that were subsidiaries of Carnegie-Illinois Steel Corp., the Monongahela Southern Railroad and the St. Clair Terminal Railroad. The Union Railroad serves a number of U. S. Steel mills and other customers in the Monongahela River Valley south of Pittsburgh, Pennsylvania. Two-thirds of Union's freight cars are gondolas for carrying steel in its various forms between plants and from plant to customer, and four SD9s are its only locomotives that are not switchers. The railroad is owned by U. S. Steel, as is the Bessemer & Lake Erie, with which it connects at North Bessemer, Pa.

Address of general offices: 135 Jamison Lane, Monroeville, PA 15146
Miles of road operated: 31
Reporting marks: URR
Number of locomotives: 115
Number of freight cars: 1776
Principal commodities carried: Steel products, iron ore, coal, coke
Major yards: North Bessemer, Monongahela Jct.
Principal shops: Hall (Monroeville), Monogahela Jct.
Junctions with other railroads:
Bessemer & Lake Erie: North Bessemer
Chessie System: Bessemer, Rankin
Conrail:
　Clairton

Scott Hartley.

Union Railroad SW1200 586 switches a pair of hot-metal cars at U. S. Steel's plant at Rankin, Pa. The locomotive is a boomer from the Florida East Coast via the Newburgh & South Shore, a former U. S. Steel road at Cleveland, Ohio, now owned by Chessie System.

　Hays
　Kenny Yard
　Munhall
　South Duquesne
　Thomson
McKeesport Connecting: Riverton
Norfolk & Western: Clairton, Mifflin Jct.
Pittsburgh & Lake Erie:
　Bessemer
　Howard Jct.
Radio frequencies: 160.260 (road), 160.500 (yard), 160.620 (yard)
Date: June 1983

UNITED SOUTH EASTERN RAILWAYS
(Ferrocarriles Unidos del Sureste)

The first railroad in Mexico's state of Yucatan was the standard-gauge Ferrocarril Progreso a Merida (Progreso to Merida Railway), authorized in 1874 and opened in 1881 between the city of Merida and the port at Progreso, 24 miles away. Most of the railroad's business was in hauling sisal, a fiber from which rope is made. Two other railroads were begun about the same time, the Ferrocarril Merida a Valladolid (Merida to Valladolid Railway), and the Ferrocarril Peninsular, which completed a line to Campeche in the state of the same name in 1898. Both these lines were 3-foot gauge. These three railroads were combined in 1902 as the United Railways of Yucatan, and a fourth railroad, the 3-foot-gauge Ferrocarril de Merida a Peto, was added in 1909. A third rail for narrow-gauge trains was added to the Merida-Progreso line between 1958 and 1960.

The trackage of the United Railways of Yucatan was isolated until 1950, when the Southeastern Railway (Ferrocarril del Sureste) was completed from Allende, Veracruz, on the Rio Coatzacoalcos, to Campeche. The line from Campeche to Merida was standard gauged between 1953 and 1957, and the Rio Coatzacoalcos was bridged in 1962, finally giving Yucatan a rail connection with the rest of Mexico. The Southeastern Railway was constructed by the Ministry of Communications and Public Works (Secretaria de Comunicaciones y Obras Publicas, abbreviated SCOP), which also built the Sonora-Baja California Railway.

In 1969 the Southeastern and the United of Yucatan were merged to form the United South Eastern Railways (Ferrocarriles Unidos del Sureste). The railroad is owned by the Mexican government. Some of the former UdeY lines south and east of Merida are still narrow gauge.

Address of general offices: Apartado Postal 117, Merida, Yucatan, Mexico

Miles of road operated: 555 standard gauge, 266 3-foot gauge, 22 dual gauge

Reporting marks: FUS

Number of locomotives: 31

Number of freight cars: 834 standard gauge

Robert Redden.

The Sureste's terminal at Merida, capital of the state of Yucatan, is this Italianate building. In the train shed behind it are both standard-gauge and narrow-gauge trains.

Number of passenger cars: 59

Principal shops: Merida, Yuc.

Junctions with other railroads: National Railways of Mexico: Coatzacoalcos, Ver.

Passenger routes: Coatzacoalcos-Merida, Merida-Tizimin, Merida-Valladolid, Merida-Sotuta, Merida-Peto

Recommended reading: *Mexican Narrow Gauge*, by Gerald M. Best, published in 1968 by Howell-North, P. O. Box 3051, La Jolla, CA 92038

Map: See National Railways of Mexico, page 132

UTAH RAILWAY

The Utah Railway was incorporated in 1912. It was opened in 1914 and was operated for three years by the Denver & Rio Grande; the Utah Railway took over its own operation in 1917. It carries coal from mines in the mountains of central Utah north to Provo. Much of the haul is on Denver & Rio Grande Western rails — trackage rights from Utah Railway Junction to Thistle and paired track with D&RGW between Thistle and Provo. The road shares terminal facilities in Provo with Union Pacific. Sharon Steel Corp. controls the Utah Railway.

Address of general offices: 136 E. South Temple Street, Salt Lake City, UT 84111

Miles of road operated: 95
Reporting marks: UTAH
Number of locomotives: 12
Principal commodities carried: Coal
Shops: Martin, Utah
Junctions with other railroads:
Denver & Rio Grande Western: Provo, Utah; Utah Railway Jct., Utah
Union Pacific: Provo, Utah
Radio frequencies: 160.560, 161.145
Date: January 1983

Utah Railway dieselized with Alco RSD4s that were white, hardly the norm for a coal road. Nearly 30 years later a quartet of the six-motor units still looks reasonably clean as they head a string of empty hoppers at Jacobs.

Bob Gottier.

VERMONT RAILWAY

First chartered in 1843, the Rutland Railroad had all the characteristics that railroad enthusiasts appreciate: a picturesque setting; a past that included control by other railroads (Central Vermont and New York Central), bankruptcy, and receivership; and a series of adversities, each worse than the previous one — floods, labor troubles, loss of a connecting Great Lakes boat line, and various stockholder and bondholder proposals for salvation. The Rutland's lines extended from Bellows Falls, Vermont, and Chatham, New York, to Ogdensburg, N. Y., via Rutland and Burlington, Vt., and Rouses Point, N. Y.

A strike shut down the Rutland in September 1961, and the railroad was officially abandoned two years later. Much of Vermont was left without rail service. There was still a need for it, so the state of Vermont purchased the railroad in 1963 and engaged Jay Wulfson to operate the portion between White Creek, N. Y., west of Bennington, Vt., and Burlington. The Vermont Railway was incorporated in 1963 and began operation in January 1964. Freed of the Rutland's worst problems, such as labor difficulties and the long tentacle across the Lake Champlain islands and the top of New York to Ogdensburg, VTR regained lost business and attracted new. The road bought many of the Rutland's box cars and acquired a large fleet of piggyback trailers. Soon more shippers were shipping and receiving tonnage on the VTR than had used the entire Rutland before the 1961 strike. In 1972 VTR purchased the Clarendon & Pittsford from Vermont Marble Co.

Other portions of the Rutland that were revived are Bellows Falls-Rutland (Green Mountain Railroad, page 91) and Norwood-Ogdensburg, N. Y. (St. Lawrence Railroad, page 163).

Address of general offices: 267 Battery Street, Burlington, VT 05401
Miles of road operated: 131
Reporting marks: VTR
Number of locomotives: 7
Number of freight cars: 1263
Principal commodities carried: Grain, petroleum products, limestone, rock salt
Junctions with other railroads:

Jack Armstrong.

Bright red SW1500 501, the first new locomotive that Vermont Railway purchased, heads a southbound freight in 1972.

VERMONT RAILWAY

Boston & Maine: White Creek, N. Y.
Central Vermont: Burlington, Vt.
Clarendon & Pittsford: Center Rutland, Vt.; Florence, Vt.
Delaware & Hudson: Rutland, Vt.
Green Mountain: Rutland, Vt.

Radio frequencies: 161.010 (dispatcher), 160.710 (road and yard)
Recommended reading: *The Rutland Road* (second edition), by Jim Shaughnessy, published in 1981 by Howell-North, P. O. Box 3051, La Jolla, CA 92038
Date: January 1983

VIA RAIL CANADA

VIA Rail Canada was created on January 12, 1977, as a subsidiary of Canadian National Railways. On June 1 of that year it assumed responsibility for marketing rail passenger service in Canada. On March 31, 1978, VIA acquired Canadian National's passenger equipment and took over management of CN rail passenger service. The next day, April 1, 1978, VIA became a separate crown corporation. On September 29 of that same year VIA took over CP Rail (Canadian Pacific) passenger service, acquired CP's passenger equipment, and assumed the employment of all CN and CP unionized and ground passenger-service employees.

VIA's first major change, in October 1978, was to combine the *Canadian* and the *Super Continental*, former transcontinental flagships of CP and CN, respectively, east of Winnipeg, thereby eliminating the duplication of services from Montreal and Toronto to Sudbury and Capreol, Ontario, and combining both trains to operate over the CP between Sudbury, Ont., and Winnipeg, 971 miles. In the summer of 1979 the two trains swapped eastern terminals and both operated through to Vancouver, exchanging cars at Winnipeg. In the Maritimes, VIA discontinued CN's Montreal-Halifax *Scotian*, added a Montreal-Mont Joli local, *Le Saint-Laurent*, and extended CP's Montreal-Saint John, New Brunswick, *Atlantic Limited* east to Halifax — all in October 1979. The *Atlantic*,

John D. Thompson.

VIA purchased LRC (Light, Rapid, Comfortable — except in Quebec, where the initials mean Leger, Rapid, Confortable) trainsets to upgrade its services in the Quebec-Montreal-Toronto-Windsor corridor. The trains were VIA's first new rolling stock and introduced a new color scheme of light gray, yellow, and blue.

which cut across the middle of Maine, provided a much faster ride to the Maritimes than the *Ocean* on CN's all-Canada route, business on the train increased dramatically, and the four-car CP train quickly tripled in size. Indeed, between 1977 and 1980 ridership system-wide had increased 41 percent.

On November 15, 1981, Canadian transport minister Jean-Luc Pepin ordered the discontinuance or reduction of service on more than one-fifth of VIA's routes. The two principal trains discontinued were the *Atlantic* and the *Super Continental*, leaving such cities as Saint John, N. B., Sas-

Continued on next page.

katoon, Saskatchewan, and Edmonton, Alberta, without through train service. Local trains were inaugurated to maintain service on a few portions of the discontinued routes, and the *Canadian* was extended from Toronto east to Montreal by the expedient of adding its cars to a Toronto-Montreal local train. Elsewhere in Canada branchline services were reduced from daily to triweekly or discontinued altogether. Pepin announced that the cuts would permit the purchase of LRC trainsets for service in the Maritimes and in the West. In the spring of 1983 VIA was concentrating its marketing efforts and its new equipment in the Quebec-Montreal-Toronto-Windsor corridor where the bulk of Canada's population lives.

Address of general offices: Suite 1300, 1801 McGill College Avenue, Montreal, PQ, Canada H3A 2N4

Route-miles: 13,271

Number of locomotives: 148

Number of passenger cars: 1,032

Passenger routes: (train names in italics, operating railroads and junctions in parentheses)

Sydney-Truro-Halifax, Nova Scotia (CN)

Halifax-Yarmouth, N. S. (CP)

Halifax-Truro-Moncton, New Brunswick-Mont Joli, Que.-Montreal: *Ocean* (CN)

Moncton-Fredericton, N. B. (CN-Saint John-CP)

Mont Joli, Que.-Montreal: *Le Saint-Laurent* (CN)

Matapedia-Gaspe, Que. (CN)

Quebec-Montreal: *Frontenac*, *Citadelle*, and *Champlain Rapidos* (CN via Drummondville, Que.); unnamed trains (CP via Trois Rivieres)

Montreal-Hervey, Que.-Senneterre, Que.-Cochrane, Ont. (CN)

Montreal-Hervey-Chicoutimi, Que. (CN)

Montreal-Ottawa: *Ville Marie*, *Rideau*, and *Laurier Rapidos* (CN)

Ottawa-Sudbury, Ont. (CP)

Ottawa-Toronto: *Exec Rapido*, *Capital*, *Cavalier* (CN-Smiths Falls-CP-Brockville-CN)

Montreal-Toronto: *York*, *LaSalle*, *Renaissance*, *Meridian*, and *Simcoe Rapidos*; *Cavalier*, *Lakeshore*, *Bonaventure*, *Ontarian* (CN)

Toronto-Stratford-London (CN)

Ronald N. Johnson.

Typical of VIA's long-distance trains is the Montreal-Halifax *Atlantic*, since discontinued, shown arriving Saint John, N. B., behind a Montreal-built FPA4/FPB4 set.

VIA uses Budd Rail Diesel Cars extensively for local services. Here three RDCs running in multiple as Toronto-London train 661 approach Stratford, Ont.

Brian C. Nickle.

Toronto-Brantford-London-Sarnia, Ont.: *St. Clair Rapido, International* (CN)

Toronto-Brantford-London-Windsor, Ont.: *Great Laker, Trillium, Ambassador, Erie,* and *Mohawk Rapidos* (CN)

Toronto-Hamilton-Niagara Falls, Ont.: *Maple Leaf* (CN)

Toronto-Kapuskasing, Ont.: *Northland* (CN-North Bay-ONR-Cochrane-CN) (the Toronto-Timmins, Ont., *Northlander* is an Ontario Northland train which operates CN-North Bay-ONR)

Montreal-Toronto-Vancouver: *Canadian* (CN-Parry Sound, Ont.-CP-Winnipeg-CN-Portage-la-Prairie, Man.-CP)

Capreol, Ont.-Winnipeg (CN)

Hearst-Nakina, Ont. (CN)

Thunder Bay-Sioux Lookout, Ont.: mixed train (CN)

Winnipeg-Thompson-Churchill, Man.: *Hudson Bay* (CN)

The Pas-Lynn Lake, Man.: mixed train (CN)

Winnipeg-Saskatoon, Sask. (CN-Portage-la-Prairie-CP-Regina-CN)

Saskatoon-Edmonton (CN)

Edmonton-Jasper-Prince Rupert, B. C.: *Skeena* (CN)

Calgary-South Edmonton, Alta. (CP)

Victoria-Courtenay, B. C. (CP)

Recommended reading: *VIA Rail Canada: The First Five Years,* by Tom Nelligan, published in 1982 by PTJ Publishing, Inc., P. O. Box 397, Park Forest, IL 60466 (ISBN 0-937658-08-1)

WASHINGTON TERMINAL CO.

The Washington Terminal Co. was incorporated in 1901 by an act of Congress to build a Union Station in Washington, D. C. The combination stub and through station opened in 1907.

In recent years the station has been partially converted to a visitor center; passengers have had to walk long distances through the largely unused visitor center to a small station behind the main building. Restoration of the building to its original function is now in progress.

Chessie System (Baltimore & Ohio) and Amtrak each own half of Washington Terminal Co. The station is used by Amtrak and Maryland Department of Transportation trains.

Address of general offices: Union Station, Washington, DC 20002
Miles of track operated: 32
Reporting marks: WATC
Number of locomotives: 7
Junctions with other railroads:
Baltimore & Ohio and Amtrak: Washington, D. C.
Radio frequencies: 160.290

Alex M. Mayes.

Washington Terminal 44, an RS-1 built by Alco in 1945, shuffles an Amcafe 30 years its junior in the Ivy City coach yard in the northeast section of the District of Columbia.

This view of Washington Union Station dates from before World War Two. Note that the five platforms at the near (east) end of the concourse are lower than the others. Tracks serving these platforms lead to the tunnel under Capitol Hill for trains to and from the south.

Association of American Railroads.

WESTERN PACIFIC RAILROAD

While this book was in preparation the Western Pacific became the Fourth Operating District of the Union Pacific. WP was the newest of the transcontinental railroads, and it was better known than might be expected for a road its size, particularly a road surrounded by such giants as Southern Pacific, Union Pacific, and Santa Fe. There are several reasons: an active public relations and advertising campaign in the 1940s and 1950s, a passenger train — the *California Zephyr* — that many considered the best Chicago-to-the-West Coast cruise train, and, of course, the propensity of enthusiasts to root for the underdog.

In 1900 the Gould railroads (Western Maryland, Wabash, Missouri Pacific, and Denver & Rio Grande chief among them) stretched from Baltimore to Ogden, Utah, with only a short gap in Pennsylvania. The Southern Pacific connection at Ogden furnished considerable traffic to the system, but that traffic vanished when E. H. Harriman obtained control of Union Pacific and Southern Pacific, effectively shutting Denver & Rio Grande out of the Ogden Gateway. At the same time California shippers and merchants considered themselves at the mercy of Southern Pacific, which had a virtual monopoly in the area.

From time to time railroads had been proposed and surveyed through the Sierra Nevada, the mountain range along much of the eastern boundary of California, via the Feather River canyon and Beckwourth Pass on a route 2,000 feet lower than the route the Central Pacific (later Southern Pacific) had taken over Donner Pass. One such survey had been made by W. H. Kennedy, assistant to the chief engineer of the Union Pacific at the time when Jay Gould controlled UP. Arthur Keddie used the Kennedy survey to obtain a franchise for a railroad on that route. Keddie's partner signed an agreement with George Gould, Jay Gould's eldest son and successor, to take over the various surveys, franchises, and incorporations.

The Western Pacific (the name chosen was also that of the railroad that originally extended the Central Pacific from Sacramento to Oakland) was incorporated in 1903 to build a railroad between Salt Lake City and San Francisco. Gould's Denver & Rio Grande underwrote $50 million in bonds for construction. The last spike was driven in 1909 on the trestle at Keddie, Calif.

The new road had no branches to feed it, and as a result revenue didn't cover operating expenses and construction costs. WP entered bankruptcy and pulled the Rio Grande in with it. At the same time the eastern end of Gould's empire collapsed as the cost of building the Wabash Pittsburgh Terminal (later Pittsburgh & West Virginia) bankrupted the Wabash. The Western Pacific was sold in 1916.

In 1917 the WP purchased control of the Tidewater Southern, an interurban that ran south from Stockton, Calif., and took over the south end of the narrow-gauge Nevada-California-Oregon to gain entry to Reno,

Continued on next page.

Nevada. Operation of WP by the United States Railroad Administration introduced paired track operation with Southern Pacific between Winnemucca and Wells, Nev., 182 miles. The arrangement was discontinued after the USRA relinquished control, but resumed in 1924. With the payment it received from the government for damages — chiefly the result of lack of maintenance — WP purchased control of Sacramento Northern, an electric line from Sacramento to Chico, Calif.

In 1926 Arthur Curtiss James acquired control of WP; he already had large holdings in Great Northern, Northern Pacific, and Burlington. WP purchased the San Francisco-Sacramento Railroad, an interurban between the two cities of its title, in 1927 and merged it with Sacramento Northern. Construction to link the railroad with the Great Northern at Bieber, Calif., was completed in 1931, creating the Inside Gateway and making the WP a north-south carrier in conjunction with GN and the Santa Fe line in the San Joaquin Valley. Western Pacific underwent voluntary reorganization in 1935.

After World War Two WP teamed up with Rio Grande and Burlington to operate the *California Zephyr* between Chicago and Oakland, Calif. Plans for the train had been laid in 1937, but the war postponed their realization. The postwar period brought the Vista-Dome, and the *CZ* was the first long-distance train to carry Vista-Domes — five per train. Because of the routing, the train could not compete on the basis of speed against the Union Pacific-Southern Pacific-Chicago & North Western *City of San Francisco*, but the *CZ*'s schedule was planned to take full advantage of the Vista-Domes for viewing the scenery. The train was an immediate success.

In 1962 Southern Pacific and Santa Fe sparred for control of Western Pacific; neither won. Western Pacific became part of Union Pacific in 1982, giving UP the extension to San Francisco that it surveyed so long ago.

WP owns two switching roads on the east shore of San Francisco Bay jointly with Santa Fe: the Oakland Terminal Railway and the Alameda Belt Line. WP, Santa Fe, and Southern Pacific jointly own the Central California Traction Co. (see page 48), which runs between Stockton and Sacramento, Calif.

Address of general offices: 526 Mission St., San Francisco, CA 94105

Bill Rettberg.

A Western Pacific freight skirts the shore of the Great Salt Lake near Magna, Utah, in 1977. The train is only a few miles out of Salt Lake City on its trip to California.

Miles of road operated: 1,436
Reporting marks: WP
Number of locomotives: 163
Number of freight cars: 5,498
Principal commodities carried: Foodstuffs, pulp and paper, automobiles and parts
Major yards: Oakland, Calif.; Oroville, Calif., Stockton, Calif.
Principal shops: Sacramento, Calif.; Stockton, Calif.
Radio frequencies: 160.260 (train to dispatcher), 160.380 (dispatcher to train)
Recommended reading: *Western Pacific's Diesel Years*, by Joseph A. Strapac, published in 1980 by Overland Models, RR 12, Box 445, Muncie, IN 47302 (ISBN 0-916160-08-4)

Lawrence Treiman.

WHITE PASS & YUKON CORPORATION LTD.

The White Pass & Yukon was born in the Yukon gold rush of 1898. A railroad was necessary to carry machinery and supplies from tidewater at Skagway, Alaska, over the Coast Mountains to the Yukon River in Canada's Yukon Territory. Construction of the 3-foot-gauge railroad began in 1898, and crews working from Skagway and from Whitehorse, Y. T., met at Carcross, Y. T., on July 29, 1900.

Continued on next page.

White Pass & Yukon carries much of its freight in containers on flat cars. This daily mixed train, shown at Bennett, B. C., has both open and closed containers on the cars behind a pair of GE-built six-motor diesels.

WP&Y's corporate structure encompassed three railroads — the Pacific & Arctic Railway & Navigation Co. (Alaska, 20.4 miles), the British Columbia-Yukon Railway (British Columbia, 32.2 miles), and the British Yukon Railway (Yukon Territory, 58.1 miles) — all operated by the White Pass & Yukon.

The WP&Y prospered for a few years; then gold mining slackened and the company entered reorganization. The approach of World War Two roused the economy of the Yukon. The railroad's business increased and in 1937 it even inaugurated air services (WP&Y had operated steamboats on the Yukon River for many years). The bombing of Pearl Harbor in 1941 triggered the construction of the Alaska Highway. One of the jumping-off places for construction crews was Whitehorse, the northern terminal of the railroad.

The WP&Y found itself with too big a job to do, and the U. S. Army's Military Railway Service moved in to operate the line. The Army purchased locomotives from several narrow-gauge lines in the U. S. to handle the increased traffic — in 1943 the road handled the equivalent of 10 years' worth of prewar tonnage.

After the war the WP&Y returned to its primary business of bringing the necessities of life into the Yukon and carrying out silver, lead, and zinc. In addition, the railroad developed a tourist business, connecting with cruise ships calling at Skagway.

To reduce the cost of transferring cargo between ship or truck and train, the White Pass developed a container that would fit on the narrow-gauge cars and on flatbed trucks. In 1954 WP&Y designed and bought a ship, the *Clifford J. Rogers*, to carry the containers between Vancouver, B. C., and Skagway. WP&Y also owns an oil pipeline paralleling the railroad between Skagway and Whitehorse.

Much of the railroad's traffic in recent years has been for the Yukon mining industry, but a slump has shut down the mines. As this book went to press, WP&Y had suspended operation temporarily for lack of ore traffic and because of competition in the form of a new highway from Skagway to Whitehorse.

Address of general offices: P. O. Box 4070, Whitehorse, YT, Canada Y1A 3T1
Miles of road operated: 111
Reporting marks: WPY
Number of locomotives: 19
Number of freight cars: 420
Number of passenger cars: 30
Principal commodities carried: Ore concentrates
Shops: Skagway, Alaska
Junctions with other railroads: None
Radio frequencies: 160.305 (road), 160.425 (yard)
Passenger routes: Skagway, Alaska-Whitehorse, Y. T.
Recommended reading:
MORE RAILROADS YOU CAN MODEL, by Mike Schafer, published in 1978 by Kalmbach Publishing Co., 1027 North Seventh Street, Milwaukee, WI 53233 (ISBN 0-89024-534-6)
The White Pass and Yukon Route, by Stan Cohen, published in 1980 by Pictorial Histories Publishing Co., 713 South Third West, Missoula, MT 59801 (ISBN 0-933126-08-5)

WISCONSIN & SOUTHERN RAILROAD

In 1978 the Milwaukee Road was considering abandonment of several branches of its former Northern Division. These branches served the territory northwest of Milwaukee, Wisconsin. The FSC Corporation of Pittsburgh, Pennsylvania (which also operates the Upper Merion & Plymouth Railroad, a switching road at Conshohocken, Pa.), won the bidding to operate the lines, purchased them with state and federal aid, and organized the Wisconsin & Southern Railroad. The road began operation on July 1, 1980, but the official celebration was delayed a few weeks to coincide with Marsh Days in Horicon, the line's headquarters. (Horicon Marsh is a wildlife refuge area which hosts migrating Canadian geese — hence the goose in the road's herald.) Soo Line trains to Milwaukee operate over W&S between Rugby Jct., south of Slinger, Wis., and North Milwaukee.

Stanley H. Mailer.

Wisconsin & Southern GP9 4491 leads a short freight between Atwater and Burnett, Wis., past the stubble of the previous year's corn crop.

Address of general offices: P. O. Box A, Horicon, WI 53032
Miles of road operated: 147
Reporting marks: WSOR
Number of locomotives: 3
Number of freight cars: 1,303
Principal commodities carried: Canned goods, grain, agricultural lime, coal, light machinery, appliances
Junctions with other railroads:
Chicago & North Western: Minnesota Jct., Wis.
Chicago, Milwaukee, St. Paul & Pacific: North Milwaukee, Wis.
Soo Line: Rugby Jct., Wis.
Radio frequencies: 160.575
Date: June 1983

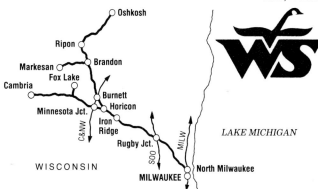

NORTH AMERICAN RAIL TRANSIT SYSTEMS

The field of fixed-guideway transportation systems encompasses things that are railroads and things that are not. The continuum stretches from the Burlington Northern — definitely a railroad — through roller coasters — which are not railroads. The dividing line lies somewhere below the commuter authorities and above airport people movers. Straddling the line is rail transit. Rail transit operations have several characteristics: passenger-only traffic in self-propelled electric-powered cars; rolling stock built to other than standard AAR dimensions; track not connected to the regular railroad network (not counting a single connection used only for delivery of new rolling stock); track in, over, and under public streets; fare payment by cash, token, or magnetic card; and operation every so many minutes rather than according to published timetables (or so the riders perceive). Each of these characteristics can be found on one or more railroads in this book, but the combination constitutes "rail transit." For the purpose of inclusion in this book the touchstone, the test question, is "Does it interchange carload freight with other railroads?" The commuter authorities, which took over a portion of the railroads' business, can be included by changing "does" to "could." But a number of the commuter authorities are also in the transit business, and moreover rail transit is for the most part steel wheel on steel rail. This brief listing of North American rail transit systems may prove useful.

A few terms require explanation. Transit cars draw their power from either an overhead wire through a trolley pole or a pantograph or from a third rail through a shoe. Many transit systems are built with station platforms at the level of the car floor for quick loading and unloading. "Heavy rail" operations are characterized by separate rights of way and high platforms; "light rail" is characterized by station platforms at rail level and street or center-strip right of way (though several light-rail routes are in subways for part of their length). "Light Rail Vehicle" or "LRV" means "new streetcar."

Much of the information presented here has been drawn from the most recent directory of transit systems, an annual feature of *Modern Railroads*, a monthly trade magazine published by Enright/Reilly Publishing Company, Park Ridge, Illinois.

Atlanta, Georgia: The first 16 miles of Metropolitan Atlanta Rapid Transit Authority's heavy rail subway system has been in operation since 1979, and another 9 miles is under construction.
Route miles: 16   Stations: 20   Cars: 120

Baltimore, Maryland: The first section of Baltimore's heavy rail Metro from Charles Center to Reisterstown Plaza, opened November 21, 1983. The line is operated by the Mass Transit Administration, an agency of the Maryland Department of Transportation.
Route miles: 8   Stations: 9   Cars: 58

Boston, Massachusetts: In addition to its railroad commuter services, Massachusetts Bay Transportation Authority operates the Boston subway system. Four separate lines intersect in downtown Boston. Three lines use high-platform third-rail equipment; the fourth, which runs through the oldest subway in the U. S., uses PCC streetcars and LRVs. Several lines occupy former railroad rights of way; extensions of two heavy-rail lines are under construction.
Route miles: 42   Stations: 56   Cars: 411 (HR)
Route miles: 35   Stations: 27   Cars: 290 (LR)

Buffalo, New York: Niagara Frontier Transit Metro System is constructing a 6-mile light-rail line which is expected to open in 1984.

Calgary, Alberta: The first line of Calgary's light-rail system was opened in 1981 by the City of Calgary Transportation Department. It is operated with German LRVs on the streets downtown and on private right of way parallel to a Canadian Pacific line south of downtown.
Route miles: 8   Stations: 16   Cars: 27

Chicago, Illinois: The Chicago Transit Authority, an agency of the city of Chicago, operates the elevated and subway lines in Chicago. A notable part of the system is the elevated loop that defines downtown Chicago. The heavy-rail cars draw current from a third rail, except on the Skokie

CTA.

These Chicago Transit Authority cars draw power from a third rail and require floor-level station platforms — both typical of heavy-rail transit.

Swift line, which uses catenary. Almost all of a new extension to O'Hare airport was in operation by the end of 1983.

Route miles: 89 Stations: 140 Cars: 1,200

Cleveland, Ohio: Greater Cleveland Regional Transit Authority operates two lines: a heavy-rail line that uses overhead wire, not third rail, between 155th Street in the eastern part of the city and the airport on the west, and a light-rail line, the former Shaker Heights Rapid Transit line, from downtown Cleveland (the station is the former Cleveland Union Terminal) to Shaker Heights. The dissimilar cars of the two routes share track and stations east of downtown.

Route miles: 19 Stations: 18 Cars: 90 (HR)
Route miles: 13 Stations: 29 Cars: 102 (LR)

Edmonton, Alberta: Edmonton Transit has a single light-rail line running east and west through the city operated with German light rail vehicles. A short extension is under construction.

Route miles: 6 Stations: 6 Cars: 21

Mexico City, Mexico: Mexico City's expanding subway system, operated by the Sistema de Transporte Colectivo, uses rubber-tired trains. The same agency also operates a two-pronged PCC streetcar line to Xochimilco and Tlalpan from the Taxqueña Metro terminal.

Route miles: 45 Stations: 74 Cars: 900 (Metro)
(no information available on the streetcar line)

Miami, Florida: Dade County Transportation Administration is building a heavy-rail system. The first 10 miles are scheduled to open in December 1983. The cars under construction are identical to those being built for the Baltimore Metro.

Montreal, Quebec: In addition to the former Canadian Pacific and Canadian National commuter services, Montreal Urban Community Transit Commission operates the Montreal Metro. The system has several routes, entirely underground, operated with rubber-tired equipment.

Route miles: 29 Stations: 51 Cars: 759

Newark, New Jersey: NJ Transit operates a single subway route with PCC cars from the basement of the Amtrak-NJ Transit station in Newark out along the bed of an old canal. From the upper level of the station Port Authority Trans-Hudson Corporation operates heavy-rail trains to two terminals in New York: the World Trade Center and (via the former Erie Lackawanna station at Hoboken, N. J.) West 33rd Street and Sixth Avenue. The line is the former Hudson & Manhattan Railroad.

NJT
Route miles: 5 Stations: 10 Cars: 26
PATH
Route miles: 14 Stations: 13 Cars: 290

New Orleans, Louisiana: New Orleans Public Service Inc. operates

Continued on next page.

211

the last conventional streetcars in regular revenue service in North America on a single route along St. Charles Street.

Route miles: 7   Cars: 35

New York, New York: New York City Transit Authority, a division of Metropolitan Transportation Authority, operates the New York subway system, by far the most extensive in the country. Another MTA division, the Staten Island Rapid Transit Operating Authority, runs heavy-rail trains on Staten Island on a line that was once part of the Baltimore & Ohio. Port Authority Trans-Hudson subway trains run between two Manhattan terminals and Hoboken, Jersey City, and Newark, N. J. — see the listing for Newark, above.

NYCTA

Route miles: 230   Stations: 465   Cars: 6,295

SIRTOA

Route miles: 14   Stations: 22   Cars: 52

Philadelphia, Pennsylvania: Southeastern Pennsylvania Transportation Authority operates two heavy-rail routes, the north-south Broad Street subway (standard gauge) and the east-west Market-Frankford subway and elevated (5′2¼″ gauge), and many streetcar routes, several of which operate through part of the Market Street subway. The Market-Frankford line connects at its west end, 69th Street Terminal in Upper Darby, with the 5′2¼″-gauge streetcar routes and the standard-gauge Norristown line of the former Philadelphia Suburban Transportation Co. (Red Arrow), now also operated by SEPTA. In addition, SEPTA provides rail commuter service in the Philadelphia area. In 1969 the Port Authority Transit Corp. of Pennsylvania and New Jersey, PATCO, opened a line from a subway terminal in Philadelphia across the Delaware River via the Benjamin Franklin Bridge and Camden, N. J., to Lindenwold, N. J., on former Pennsylvania-Reading Seashore Lines right of way.

SEPTA

Route miles: 83   Stations: 72   Cars: 378 (HR)

Route miles: 217   Stations: 48   Cars: 308 (LR)

PATCO

Route miles: 15   Stations: 13   Cars: 121

Pittsburgh, Pennsylvania: The Port Authority of Allegheny County operates several streetcar lines that share a common loop around downtown, cross the Monongahela River, pass through the South Hills Tunnel (on a paved right of way shared with buses), and diverge to Library, Dormont, and Castle Shannon. A downtown subway for the streetcar line is under construction.

Route miles: 24   Cars: 92

Portland, Oregon: Tri-County Metropolitan Transit District is building a light-rail line from downtown Portland east to Gresham. Service is expected to begin in 1986.

San Diego, California: In 1981 San Diego Trolley, an agency of the city of San Diego, began operation between the Amtrak station in San Diego and the Mexican border at San Ysidro, a mile from downtown Tijuana, Baja California, Mexico. The light-rail line was built by the Metropolitan Transit Development Board along the former San Diego & Arizona Eastern right of way. Passenger counts on the bright red German-built cars quickly outstripped projections, and double-tracking of the single-track part of the line is under way.

Route miles: 16   Stations: 18   Cars: 24

San Francisco, California: The San Francisco Municipal Railway (Muni) is best known for its cable cars, currently out of service for system renovation. The Muni has five streetcar lines which come together in the upper level of the subway under Market Street. The lower level of the subway is occupied by the 5′6″-gauge heavy-rail trains of the Bay Area Rapid Transit District. They operate south to Daly City and east under San Francisco Bay to Oakland, where lines diverge to Hayward, Walnut Creek, and Richmond. The BART and Amtrak stations in Richmond are adjacent.

Muni

Route miles: 21   Stations: 9   Cars: 150 (LR)

Route miles: 9   Cars: 41 (CC)

BART

Route miles: 71   Stations: 34   Cars: 440

Massachusetts Bay Transportation Authority's Riverside Line was built in 1959 by predecessor Metropolitan Transit Authority along the right of way of Boston & Albany's Highland Branch. PCC car 3298 discharges passengers at Newton Highlands in the first summer of the line's operation.

Seattle, Washington: In May 1982 Seattle Metro completed and put into service a short trolley line along the waterfront using 1927-vintage streetcars from Melbourne, Australia.

Route miles:	2	Stations:	2	Cars:	4

Toronto, Ontario: Toronto Transit Commission operates a number of surface lines with PCC cars and two subway lines, one east-west and the other a north-south U-shaped route, with conventional high-platform, third-rail cars.

Boeing's first light rail vehicle is shown here being loaded on a flatcar at its builder's plant near Philadelphia in 1975. Cars of this type are now used in Boston and San Francisco.

Route miles:	36	Stations:	58	Cars:	635 (HR)
Route miles:	46			Cars:	369 (LR)

Washington, D. C.: Washington Metropolitan Area Transit Authority opened its first subway in March 1976. Its heavy-rail lines now extend into nearby Maryland and across the Potomac River to Arlington, Virginia, and Washington National Airport. Connection is made with Amtrak trains at Union Station and New Carrollton, Md.

Route miles:	39	Stations:	44	Cars:	298

GLOSSARY

Affiliate: a company effectively controlled by another or associated with others under common ownership or control.

Association of American Railroads (AAR): the coordinating and research agency of the American railroad industry. It is not a government agency but rather an organization to which railroads belong, much as local businesses belong to a chamber of commerce.

Bankrupt: declared legally insolvent (unable to pay debts as they fall due) and with assets taken over by judicial process to be distributed among creditors.

Centralized Traffic Control (CTC): a traffic control system whereby train movements are directed through remote control of switches and signals from a central control panel. The trains operate on the authority of signal indications instead of the authority of a timetable and train orders.

Class 1 Railroad: a railroad with average annual gross revenue of $50 million or more.

Class 2 Railroad: a railroad with average annual gross revenue between $10 and $50 million.

COFC: Container on Flat Car — see Piggyback.

Common carrier: a transportation company that offers — indeed, must offer — its services to all customers, as differentiated from a contract carrier, which carries goods for one shipper. The difference is like that between two buses, one signed "Main Street;" the other, "Charter."

Commuter service: passenger service that takes people to and from work. Characteristics include morning and evening peak periods, fares with multiple-ride discounts, the same riders Monday through Friday, and luggage consisting mostly of briefcases.

Company-owned railroad: a railroad whose stock is held by a company, not by individuals.

Consolidation: the unification of two or more corporations by dissolution of existing ones and creation of a single new corporation.

Controlling interest: sufficient stock ownership in a corporation to exert control over policy.

Continuous welded rail (CWR): rail laid in lengths of 1500 feet or so, rather than 39-foot pieces bolted together. It doesn't buckle, because the track structure resists thermal expansion and contraction, and the elasticity of the steel forces dimensional changes to occur in the cross section of the rail rather than in its length.

CTC: see Centralized Traffic Control.

Degree: a measure of the sharpness of a curve. It is the angle through which the track turns in 100 feet of track. The number of degrees is equal to 5729 divided by the radius of the curve in feet.

Embargo: an order issued by a common carrier or public regulatory agency that prohibits the acceptance of some or all kinds of freight for transportation on the carrier's lines or between specified points or areas because of traffic congestion, labor difficulties, or other reasons.

Federal Railroad Administration (FRA): the agency of the U. S. Department of Transportation that deals with transportation policy as it affects railroads.

Grade: the inclination or slope of the track. It is usually measured as a percent — for example, a rise of 2 feet in 100 feet of track is 2 percent. Occasionally it is expressed as "1 in n," where n is the number of feet in which the track rises 1 foot. Both measures are ratios — 1 in 50 is the same as 2 percent. The steepest mainline grade in North America is 4.7 percent on a Southern Railway line near Saluda, North Carolina. The usual maximum for a main line in mountainous territory is about 2 percent.

Industrial railroad: a railroad owned and operated by an industry to move cars within a factory, plant, or mill and to and from a common-carrier interchange. Industrial railroads are usually not common carriers.

Interchange: a junction of two railroads where cars are transferred from one road to another.

Intercity passenger service: as distinguished from commuter service, the passengers don't make the trip every day, tickets are for single trips, and the luggage contains clothing, not the newspaper and work to do at home. Intercity passenger trains usually include such amenities as sleeping cars and food service.

Interstate Commerce Commission (ICC): the agency of the federal government that carries out the provisions of the Interstate Commerce

Act and other federal laws regulating interstate transportation.

Interurban: an electric railroad running between cities, often of lighter construction than "steam" railroads and often operating in the streets of cities and towns instead of on private right of way. Interurbans had their rise and fall during the first four decades of the twentieth century.

Line-haul railroad: a railroad that performs point-to-point service, as distinguished from a switching or terminal railroad. For line-haul railroads, interline revenue is usually some portion of the through rate.

Merger: absorption by a corporation of one or more others.

Mixed train: a train carrying both freight and passengers, the latter either in passenger cars or in the caboose.

Percent: see Grade.

Per diem: the daily rental paid by one railroad for the use of the cars of another.

Piggyback service: the transportation of highway truck trailers and containers on flatcars.

Push-pull: a mode of operation, usually of commuter trains. In one direction the train operates conventionally, but in the other direction the train backs up with the locomotive pushing. The car at the opposite end from the locomotive has a control cab for the engineer.

Rebuilt locomotive: a locomotive that has had some major components replaced with new or renovated ones. The basic reason for rebuilding a locomotive is that it is cheaper to replace worn-out parts, possibly upgrading the locomotive at the same time, than to buy a whole new locomotive.

Receiver: a person appointed by a court to manage a corporation during a period of reorganization in an effort to avoid bankruptcy.

Receivership: management by a receiver.

Reorganization: the rehabilitation of the finances of a business concern under procedures prescribed by federal bankruptcy legislation.

Route mile: a mile of railroad line without regard to the number of tracks on that line. For example, the Milwaukee Road line from Chicago to Milwaukee is 85 route miles. The line is double track, so it includes 170 track miles for main track alone, not counting sidings and spurs.

Short line: a railroad with less than 100 miles of mainline track. There is no official or legal definition of the term; this is the criterion used by the railroad industry and the American Short Line Railroad Association.

Subsidiary: a company wholly controlled by another that owns more than half its voting stock.

Switching district: an area within which a shipper located on one railroad has equal access to other railroads, either through a terminal or switching railroad or through reciprocal switching agreements among the line-haul railroads.

Switching railroad or

Terminal railroad: a railroad whose business is not point-to-point transportation but rather pickup and delivery service for a connecting line-haul road. Switching and terminal companies usually receive a flat per-car amount for their services.

TOFC: Trailer on Flat Car — see Piggyback.

Trackage rights: rights granted by a railroad to another to operate on the tracks of the first, usually for a rental fee or a toll and usually without rights to service customers along that line.

Track mile: a mile of track — see Route mile.

Transit: short-distance, high-density passenger service usually characterized by electric propulsion, fare payment by token, magnetic card, or cash, and operation under, above, and on streets.

Unit train: a train carrying a single bulk commodity, usually coal or grain, from shipper to consignee without any switching or classification en route.

INDEX

UPDATE

The railroad scene, never static, continued to change after the research for this first edition of THE TRAIN-WATCHER'S GUIDE was completed. Among the important changes that occurred before this book went to press in January 1984 are:

Amtrak: The *California Zephyr* now operates between Salt Lake City and Wells, Nevada, on Union Pacific's former Western Pacific line. The *Pioneer* connects with the *California Zephyr* at Salt Lake City. The Philadelphia-Pittsburgh *Pennsylvanian* was extended east to New York. The *Illini* was discontinued on July 11, 1983, and the overnight Sacramento-Los Angeles *Spirit of California* made its last run on October 1, 1983. Amtrak's Auto Train began operation between Lorton, Virginia, and Sanford, Florida, on October 30, 1983.

Atchison, Topeka & Santa Fe: In September 1983 Santa Fe and Southern Pacific agreed to merge. Santa Fe completed its merger with Toledo, Peoria & Western on December 31, 1983.

Burlington Northern: On August 13, 1983, BN closed the ex-Northern Pacific line over Stampede Pass east of Auburn, Washington.

Chicago & North Western: C&NW acquired the former Rock Island route between Minneapolis/St. Paul and Kansas City.

Grand Trunk Western: The merger of Detroit, Toledo & Ironton into GTW was completed on December 31, 1983.

Maine Central: Operation on MEC's track through Crawford Notch in New Hampshire's White Mountains has ceased. Boston & Maine handles local business between Whitefield, N. H., and St. Johnsbury, Vermont.

Ontario Central/Ontario Midland: The affiliated Ontario Eastern has been abandoned.

Pittsburgh & Lake Erie obtained trackage rights over Norfolk & Western (ex-Nickel Plate) from Ashtabula, Ohio, to Buffalo for coal trains.

San Diego & Arizona Eastern has petitioned to abandon its line because of trestle fires in Carriso Gorge.

Southeastern Michigan Transportation Authority passenger trains ceased operation October 17, 1983.

Southern Pacific: In September 1983 Southern Pacific and Santa Fe agreed to merge. SP's petition to abandon subsidiary Northwestern Pacific was given added impetus by a tunnel fire just north of Willits, California. Subsidiary St. Louis Southwestern was granted trackage rights between Kansas City and St. Louis over Missouri Pacific.

Toledo, Peoria & Western: Merger with Santa Fe was completed December 31, 1983.

Vermont Railway purchased Delaware & Hudson's line between Whitehall, New York, and Rutland, Vermont, through VTR's subsidiary Clarendon & Pittsford.

You'll find locomotive facts in these eigh

Steam's Finest Hour — This huge 11″ x 16″ book features 98 notable steam locomotives from NYC's Hudson to C&O's Alleghany to UP's Big Boy. Builder and action photos accompany a description of each locomotive. **$30**

The Mohawk That Refused to Abdicate and other tales — Writer David P. Morgan and photographer Philip R. Hastings record the farewell performance of steam. Return to the mid-fifties in this 304-page classic. **$25**

Our GM Scrapbook — The marvelous motive power of Electro-Motive, in 150 pages. Builder and action photos complement a fact-filled text. Includes HO scale drawings of 12 diesel types. Soft-cover. **$10.95**

The Second Diesel Spotter's Guide — The definitive source for diesel identification, with 460 pages and 548 photos. Includes spotting features, specifications, and production figures for each locomotive model. Soft-cover. **$12.75**

Diesel Spotter's Guide <u>Update</u> — A sequel to The Second Diesel Spotter's Guide, this book includes all diesel models constructed for use in North America since 1965, plus electrics and turbo power cars. Soft-cover. **$7.95**